*The* Spiritual Design

## Books by Christine Kromm Henrie and David Henrie
*Published by Access Soul Knowledge*

---

The Spiritual Design, Channeled Teachings, Wave 1

The Spiritual Design, Channeled Teachings, Wave 2

Notes from the Second Dimension, Volume 1

Helig Design; Kanaliserade Budskap, Första Vågen
(*Svenska Derivat*)

Helig Design; Kanaliserade Budskap, Andra Vågen
(*Svenska Derivat*)

Notes from the Second Dimension, Volume 2

## Books Scheduled for Publication in 2022

---

The Spiritual Design, Channeled Teachings, Wave 3

Notes from the Second Dimension, Volume 3

# The Spiritual Design

*Channeled Teachings,*

**WAVE 1**

---

Christine Kromm Henrie

&

David Henrie, Sp.D.

Access Soul Knowledge
Stockholm, Sweden
2021

*Copyright © 2017, 2021 by Christine Kromm Henrie, David Henrie.*

*All rights reserved. No part of this book may be reproduced, stored in or introduced into an information storage or retrieval system, or transmitted in any form, or in any manner, including electronic, photographic, mechanical, recording, or otherwise, without prior written permission of the copyright owner. For information, please contact the author.*

**The Library of Congress has cataloged the hardcover edition as follows**
Names: Henrie, Christine Kromm | Henrie, David
Title: The spiritual design: channeled teachings, wave 1 /
    By Christine Kromm Henrie and David Henrie
Description: 341 pages ; 23 cm. | Access Soul Knowledge, 2017
Identifiers: LCCN 2017943706 | ISBN 9780998987019
Subjects: 1. Spirituality. 2. Channeling (Spiritualism). 3. Reincarnation.
LC record available at https://lccn.loc.gov/2017943706
Classification: •BF1275.D2 H-- 2021 | DDC 133.9'01'35—dc22

Other Formats Available
    ISBN 9780998987002 (Paperback Edition)
    ISBN 9780998987026 (E-book Edition)
    ISBN 978-1-951879-00-6 (Swedish Language Paperback)
    ISBN 978-1-951879-01-3 (Swedish Language E-book)

*Cover Art © Michael Pelin | Dreamstime.com*

**Printed in the United States of America**
*First Edition Published 2017*
*Revised Format December 2021*

**Access Soul Knowledge**
Stockholm, Sweden & Williamstown, WV, USA

*Publisher information at* www.AccesSoulKnowledge.com

# Contents

| Page | Section |
|---|---|
| 1 | Introduction |
| 12 | Our Spirit Team |
| 21 | The Basic of the Soul |
| 28 | Introduction to Dimensions |
| 39 | The Life Review |
| 48 | The Mental Realm |
| 79 | You, the Spirit |
| 99 | You, the Soul in a Human |
| 146 | Earth, 2nd and 3rd Dimensions |
| 215 | Dimensions in Detail |
| 248 | The Art of Living |
| 286 | About the Authors |

# *Introduction*

This book is a compilation of channeled teachings given to us by a group of spiritual beings. Their stated goal is to educate and awaken us to our place and purpose as co-creators both here on Earth, and in the spirit world when this life is over. They have provided an entire framework for how the spirit world is organized and how it functions, revealing a magnificence only glimpsed in near-death experiences or between-lives hypnotic regressions. We always have been, and always will be, spiritual beings with a home and a creative role within this great organization. An unfortunate part of incarnating as a human is that your conscious mind is required to forget who you are. Because so few remember, humanity has become trapped within ideologies of half-truths and untruths promoted by most religious and scientific organizations. The spirits who watch over our planet decided it is time to give more knowledge to our species, and begin the process of liberating people from these chains. These masters have been delivering remarkable teachings through an extraordinary trance channel, the co-author of this book, Christine. Because of her abilities, they are able to speak directly, clearly, and in exquisite detail, just as if they were sitting beside us, about things previously hidden from man. Our spiritual friends leave no room for misinterpretations or confusion about what they mean. The primary focus in this set of dialogues relates to how all life forms come into being, how each of us were created, why we are on Earth, and how we can make better use of our remaining time. Their intention, by giving us the entire process of creation, is to change the way we perceive and treat the other creatures that share the planet with us. Some cultures, in the very distant past, had a greater comprehension of the spiritual forces that create visible substances and life forms. Since that time many thousands of years ago, humans have fallen into a deep state of spiritual ignorance, and our civilizations are teetering on the brink of descending into yet another dark age. Scientists can explain a tree, but the way that dirt, water, air and sunlight become a tree is beyond human understanding. Our spirit team has stepped forward to share the details of processes that go on behind the scene before manifestations occur. Maybe, when we realize how everything is interconnected, we will grow to appreciate the power our choices have on ourselves and the world.

We are born into cultures and conditioned by society to look outside ourselves for guidance, wisdom, and meaning in our lives. But what if you could have the truth about everything you wanted to know regarding your soul, your purpose here on Earth, or what happens after your body dies? Or, about how the spirit world is structured and how it functions? And furthermore, what if you knew your spirit is as pure as the Creator? Would it change the way you live or think, if you knew to look inside yourself for answers? Or that no religious institutions or ideologies can stand between you and your Creator, and none have the right to judge your soul? Our spirit team has talked about these concepts, and many more, during frequent channeling sessions with Christine. It has been a privilege and an honor to be part of this project, and when they began giving these lectures, they made it clear it was to be shared, so every session is recorded and then painstakingly transcribed. They instructed us to compile certain core ideas from this collection into a book, so a large part of this manuscript was dictated to us, by them. In addition to bringing an awareness of the spiritual realities that are the source of life on this planet, the spirits want to make known the rules we live under as visitors here, which we call karma, so our time on Earth may be used wisely. By teaching people about the treasure and value of their life, the spirits hope to steer humanity in a more positive direction.

For centuries, religious organizations were able to control the flow of ideas, effectively keeping everyone ignorant of the true nature of the soul. Although, to be fair, there is no evidence religions have any secret insights about spirituality. Outside the church walls, there have always been healers, shamans, mystics, and others more aware of their spirit, who follow a solitary path, as we all must do, eventually. Religious institutions require loyalty and conformity from their subjects, where critical thinking is replaced by groupthink. For that reason, the supposed keepers of sacred knowledge have always been quick to find heretics among the flock and punish them, inciting fear among any who might question their authority. Faith, as it turns out, is nothing more than blind obedience to the mandates issued by the current church leaders. While it has sort of fallen out of fashion to light bonfires with people in them, many religions, especially those with origins between the Mediterranean and Arabian Seas, are still very narrow-minded about what their people are permitted to believe. One of their biggest problems, lately, has been the availability of ideas and experiences shared on the internet. The amount of heretical information must be overwhelming to those in charge of maintaining empires build on equal parts obedience and deception. The accounts of near-death experiences, and of people who remember past lives from either regression hypnosis or spontaneous recall, number in the hundreds of thousands, if not millions. To remain ill-informed today must be a herculean effort for those who refuse to open their eyes and ears. As more and more people turn away from traditional religions, it is all too common they find themselves somewhat adrift, as there are few guideposts to show the direction to take. It can be an uncomfortable feeling for individuals who have spent their whole life accepting outside instructions, to begin deciding how to act and think for themselves.

The scientific community is not immune to the same general criticism of being self-righteous. When science finally broke free of suppressive religious control, it went completely in the other direction. Now it seems the only proper attitude is one that rejects any notion of a divine origin for creation, choosing instead to pretend the beautiful Earth and surrounding cosmos was somehow organized into its complex mathematical precision by a random solar wind. In many respects, the scientific view begins with the assumption there is no Creator, and deliberately ignores any evidence pointing in that direction. The scientific disciplines operate much like religions, because they also require a blind obedience to groupthink, as dictated by various Universities and technical journals, all controlled by peer review. Most research is funded by governments or large corporations, who are aligned with one another, so the mischief they create can be immense in magnitude, as they regularly use technology in unspiritual, destructive ways. The comforting side to this story is that there are many scientists who privately believe in a higher power, and I count myself among them.

As a free and independent spiritual being, you are perfectly within your rights to do your own research and follow your own instincts on what may be true or not. Once you cross the threshold of accepting there is a soul that exists beyond the body, beyond death, then the door to all kinds of other truths and principles opens up. Step through and you can become what you have always been, a master of your own fate, unencumbered by the opinions of others. So, we invite you on a journey of self-discovery, if you are willing to take that step.

Because of this need to elevate humanity, a small group of spiritual beings agreed to participate in a project to re-introduce a basic understanding of how the life on this planet is created and maintained, and how each of us should interact with this reality. Hopefully, their teachings will lay a foundation upon which future generations of spiritual seekers can build a better world. This book represents the first wave of knowledge delivered primarily from three very advanced beings within the spiritual realms, each having unique knowledge about their specialty. Throughout all their discourses, they remain very loving, caring, joyful, and non-judgmental towards the human race, even as we wantonly destroy each other and many of their creations.

Christine and I were involved in the planning of this project before we were born into our current lives, and agreed to take on physical bodies to do our part in bringing certain knowledge into existence at this time. Don't think this is unique, because every incoming soul has a mission with specific goals they want to accomplish. In Earth years, it has taken quite a while to break ground on our project, as both of us had to prepare in our own way. For her part, she had to awaken the spiritual forces within herself and develop the ability to recognize and communicate with her higher self and other advanced spirits. She has since developed into a remarkably gifted trance channel, and many portions of this book are word-for-word messages from this spirit team, who are able to speak eloquently through her. While my career has been in the material world as a petroleum engineer, my true interests have followed a more spiritual path. Since Christine and I only recently found each other, the rest of our group remained waiting in the spirit realm for everything to come together, at which time they could begin transmitting their messages. They said this is a ten-year project, and we should view it as knowledge coming into the Earth, like waves on an ocean rolling towards the shore.

Christine was born and lived in Sweden, leading a typical life until 2009, when she began having visionary encounters that introduced her to an unknown world, a world beyond the physical that radiates love and deep compassion, that we have come to know as the pure spirit realm. After these unplanned encounters, she began to study and practice how to deliberately communicate with this reality. She entered workshops and training programs focusing on psychic development and spirit communication, where she met and became friends with a few like-minded people. For several years, she and her friends met weekly in Stockholm to practice and develop the skills necessary to shift awareness away from the physical plane into the higher vibrational state where the spirits could connect with her. During this time, she also undertook training at the Arthur Findley College in London, mainly focusing on trance mediumship. After several years of intense work, Christine became familiar with several of her personal guides. She operates much like Jane Roberts, who channeled Seth, or J.Z. Knight, who transmitted messages from Ramtha. There exists one significant difference, Christine is able to connect with many individual entities from the higher realms. Some of the beings who come through have never incarnated on this plane, while others have had many lives here and advanced to the point where incarnating does not contribute to their growth. Both types of spirits can and do work as guides to people here on Earth. Just as physical people are all different, in the world beyond, each spirit has its own personality and energetic signature, and this allows for easy identification once a relationship is established. The way they talk, the word choices and knowledge of different topics, are just as distinct and varied as you will find among any of your friends. During most of our sessions at least two spirits from our group step forward to deliver information. While some of the ideas are very complicated and hard to understand, such as the energy flow through the universes, how time and space interact, gravity waves, and other life forms, they have mostly focused on concepts that are more personal and relevant to us humans. Beginning in 2016, our spirit team began to transmit portions of this book, which they have called the first wave of knowledge. In addition to the work we do together with our spirit group, Christine also is a certified past life and between lives soul regression therapist, with offices in both Denver, Colorado, and Stockholm, Sweden. She has been living in the States since 2014, but spends several months each year in Stockholm.

 I was fortunate to have grown up in a rural area of West Virginia, where many people live close to nature and in relative solitude. Being alone in nature almost forces one to be reflective.

Over the years, I have probably owned or read at least 2000 books on spiritualism, Tibetan Buddhism, Native American religious traditions, channeling, past-life and between-life soul regressions, and perhaps most importantly, near-death experiences. One thing I have learned is to be selective about what to accept as a personal truth, meaning, what rings true to you. That's your higher self speaking, you know. A lot of books contain some very valid ideas, but are often mixed in with concepts that are misleading or inaccurate. You must learn to trust your inner voice, that immediate sensation that says "yes," or "no" almost constantly as you go about your day. You are given a mind with reasoning abilities, which should be used to weed out what your inner self does not agree with. I was raised as a Christian and, as a child, felt an affiliation with their ideas. However, as I grew up the incongruities compelled me to find my own way. My views and beliefs have changed somewhat over the years, but I have never felt connected to any specific ideology. In some way this is fortunate, because as I conduct the trance sessions with Christine, I am able to get explanations about things that have long confused me, since previously available research on the spirit world has left many questions unanswered. Even the wonderful books by Michael Newton only gave a few clues about how creation works. Our spirit team has been very open and granted us an amazing amount of information about what goes on "over there." Our teachers have described in vivid detail the processes by which our Universe is constructed, painting a complete picture of creation, and what it means to be a soul on Earth.

    Christine and I hold regular trance sessions, normally twice a week, lasting for about an hour. The main one is on Sunday around 10 in the morning. The second is on Wednesday or Thursday and, weather permitting, usually held somewhere in the mountains west of Denver, Colorado. No matter where we sit, the space is energetically cleaned and we always begin with a prayer for protection and guidance, requesting only those spirits from the higher realms be allowed to communicate or come near to us. Establishing a routine and setting the intention is very important for both us and the spirit team. On their side, our intention is heard as a call to come and join with us. I then lead Christine into a light hypnotic state using the same format each time. Through repetition, the ease and speed at which she is able to move into her higher self has been reduced from a ten-minute lead-in, to about one minute. Over the years, Christine has always gone to the same non-physical location to meet with her guides, which she sees as a small temple on a high cliff overlooking the sea. This is where her higher self meets with three personal spirit guides, Ophelia, Zachariah, and Bob, who form the core of our spirit team. Occasionally, they are joined by our main spirit guides, who come to offer encouragement or advice. Mine is known to us as Jeshua, and hers, Isaac. All these guides serve in different capacities and come from different areas of the spiritual world. We use the masculine and feminine to describe them, but that is only a reference to the type of energy they most strongly project. There are no genders beyond Earth, only patterns within each soul that are a function of where that spirit comes from. Its home frequency can be either more logical (masculine) or more emotional (feminine). Ophelia is in charge of this project, always present and observing, while Zachariah and Bob delivered much of the information in this first book. Christine and I are the main actors, so to speak, as we are the two spirits who incarnated to make the project a physical reality. Ophelia has told us she is managing this project for a higher group of beings. She controls both the content and who is granted access to our circle. They operate as one mind when they join us, and the constant interplay between them is evident to me during the sessions.

The process whereby Christine is able to connect with the spirits requires a lot of natural ability and advanced training. She raises her inner vibration upwards into what is called the seventh layer within the mental realm, which is detailed in a later section. When her awareness is shifted to this vibration, she has very little sense of her body and surroundings. It's like when you drift off to sleep, except her mind remains clear and focused within this inner reality. It is in this space where one of the guides approaches and, assuming the entity is familiar, she internally steps to the side, allowing the higher spiritual being to access her mind and speak. While this is going on, Christine is aware of the words, but is not able to recall them after she returns from this state. She sometimes sees images, but is unaware of discussions I hold with the guide. I believe Stuart White, an early 20th century spiritualist, wrote that it is like laying on the bottom of a stream, your senses muffled, hearing the words float by above, one by one, but lacking the ability to grasp them. Because it takes quite a bit of energy for Christine to hold this level of mental control, we try to limit the sessions to no more than about an hour and fifteen minutes. It requires more energy to make a bridge with spirits coming in from the highest dimensions, whereas Bob, who is closer to our vibration, can be very easy for her to connect with. In fact, he often will just say something to her during the day, which she hears clairaudiently, as clearly as someone speaking right beside her. Because she does not want any influence from her own mind to seep into what is being channeled, she has avoided reading spiritual books, and, since I transcribe the recordings, Christine is also unfamiliar with the bulk of the transcriptions. She does, however, listen to some of Bob's delightfully amusing discourses when the subject matter is outside of the *Spiritual Design* topics.

    The question of where to begin can be challenging, since everyone has their own understanding, based on their personal history, and it is not our intention to undermine anyone's belief system. However, some of their ideas may seem foreign to you and cause a bit of mental anxiety—especially those regarding reincarnation and methods of communicating with the energetic world beyond Earth. We offer these words of assurance should you be disposed to reject the ideas. While both Christine and I accept reincarnation as a normal part of soul progression, it is not necessary you agree. You may miss out on the fullness of the teachings, but the guidance on how to live in your current life is ultimately the most important aspect of any spiritual learnings. Regarding this method of conversing with the spirit world, it is said that one should always judge the tree by the fruit. They have offered us knowledge, guidance, comfort, and humor, for months, never once being judgmental or negative. The spirits truly want people to feel hope, joy, and optimism about their lives, and to realize no one is ever alone, and everyone has a purpose for being here. Christine does not have any recollection of what is said while in trance, but does feel their energy and intentions when they blend with her. As for me, I get to weekly sit and talk with the most brilliant, patient, and caring teachers, whose wisdom extends far beyond anything humans can comprehend. There have been times when the tenderness and concern they expressed made my eyes water from a sense of humility. And on more than one occasion they surprised me by describing incidents I had long forgotten and never mentioned to anyone, including Christine. This, I think, is done to validate they have been following us all our lives, watching over and encouraging us when we face difficulties. If only I had known how much help and guidance is always given from the spirit world, struggles would have been so much easier to endure, and life would have seemed less lonely.

You will read later about the difference between the pure spirit realm, the mental realm, and the physical plane of Earth. The spirits we communicate with are from the higher dimensions within the pure spirit realm, but Christine meets them mid-way, in the vibrational field around Earth known as the "mental realm." It is important to understand there are a variety of entities that can be found within the mental realm, which is a transitional reality between the physical Earth and the true spirit world. When people on Earth die, or more precisely, their body dies, the soul detaches and their awareness enters fully into this mental state. All souls must journey through this vibrational field, and detach from the memories and emotions of the life they left. There are levels within this reality, and the darker, slower vibrations can be found closer to Earth, in an area that has little light or love. These can even be hellish, although they are not real, in the spiritual sense, because they are created by human thought. Just as fluid of different densities segregate, like oil and water, there is a continuum of separation in the mental realm. The lower half holds all the karma and memories of Earth, and is where souls will sometimes get stuck for a while after death. The upper half is closer to the true spiritual dimensions, and is where spirit guides and other higher entities can be found. They lower their vibration down into this frequency in order to connect with individuals like Christine. Since many people can develop the ability to communicate with soul personalities on the mental plane, it should only be undertaken with caution, as not all energies within this realm are looking out for our best interests. However, the spirits that exist on the pure spirit realms are in harmony with the Creator, and these are the individuals and council members that Christine communicates with and are the source of the material in this book.

The spirit group has given us an outline of the entire process by which the soul is created and developed, the structure and function of different dimensions in the spirit realm, and how creation operates under the unifying direction of the Master Mind. I have noticed, over the months, they have never contradicted themselves on any idea or topic. In fact, they will correct me if I say something that does not match their messages, as they seem to have a perfect memory of every word they have spoken. During a typical session, they deliver anywhere from 5000 to 9000 words, speaking clearly and without pause on different subjects of their choosing. When they merge into Christine's energy field, they are able to access her mental database, so to speak. They can talk in either Swedish or English, but prefer English, and are limited by the words she knows. However, each spirit has its own personality and they talk differently and construct sentences in their own way. They have been very specific about what is to be included in this book, this first wave of knowledge. Subsequent waves of knowledge will be increasingly technical, covering such concepts as how waves of light and sound frequencies are combined with other properties such as gravity and vacuums to form celestial bodies and solar systems. We are as eager as anyone to learn more, and are committed to pass on any information they permit us to discuss.

The responsibility rests with each person to seek answers for themselves, and we strongly encourage you to continue reading and researching any of these topics you find interesting. Many books have been written containing the most remarkable experiences and encounters, especially by people whose souls have left their body during a brush with death. Remain open-minded and inquisitive, trusting your inner guidance, as you find and travel your own path of discovery. There exists a vast body of documentation from thousands of people who have experienced non-physical reality over the past century. Our spirit team has presented a comprehensive spiritual design that combines many of the better religious and scientific ideas under the same umbrella. In addition to providing all the channeled material, Christine is also a licensed past-life and between-lives soul regression therapist. She has collected accounts from many people regarding other lives and the pure spirit realm. There is a river of truth that runs through these diverse sources. We are souls with a divine origin, having a temporary experience as a human, whose awareness can never cease, on a continuous journey to acquire knowledge and experience.

The gift from the Creator is your personal identity. Without a personal identity, you would not have independent thoughts, but would receive and respond to signals sent to you from the Master Mind. You would be in complete harmony, but only react like a little robot. Your gift is your ability to generate thoughts, any kind of thoughts you want. Souls discover, through direct experience of being human, that thoughts, or the intention and the will behind the thoughts, are the only creative force that exist. There are ways to live that make the best use of the gifts we have been given. The path we all follow is to learn how to control and direct our thinking mind, and by doing so, become worthy co-Creators with the Master Mind. It is for this purpose that we and our spirit team humbly offer this knowledge to you, as an aid to understanding the beauty of life, the mystery of creation, and how to honor the true spirit within yourself.

# *Our Spirit Team*

Christine and I are publishing this book of teachings because we are certain these spiritual beings are who they claim to be. To date, over 300,000 words have been delivered, words meant to uplift and educate each of us about our true spiritual potential and purpose. Through all their talks, they remain free of judgment or negative messages of any kind. They do not claim supremacy over other spirits or pretend to understand what the Creator is thinking. Each spiritual being represents a different dimension, where they are experts in a particular role. Bob does not really comprehend everything that goes on in other dimensions, and Ophelia does not know all the specifics of what Bob does. During sessions, whomever has the most knowledge about a subject is the one who delivers the message.

Ophelia is one of the organizers, and the main control who is present during all the sessions. She is from the seventh dimension, which is considered somewhat of an angelic realm. We will discuss the dimensions in more detail, but the seventh is full of light. It is a reality where frequencies of spiritual light and sound are used to create the foundation for all living entities, like suns, planets, trees, butterflies, or human bodies. When Christine sees Ophelia, she has the appearance of what some describe as an angel, with a long white gown or robe, floating almost, somewhat ethereal. She has a motherly energy about her, which can also be gentle or quite firm, but yet loving. The seventh dimension is considered a feminine polarity, as it is more of an emotional realm. The sixth dimension, where the spiritual selves of both Christine and I reside, is more aligned with logic and form, making it somewhat male in polarity. Ophelia has told us there are other spirits from higher dimensions, the ninth and tenth, that are also participating in this project, but she is acting as their representative. She is the one who decides what information is to be let through to Earth, and which spirits are allowed to come near to Christine during the sessions. Ophelia occasionally gives talks on subjects which she has either the most knowledge or the deepest interest. I should mention that she is one of my primary guides, and I have often felt her around me during certain times in my life. Throughout this book, my questions are labeled as "D." Ophelia, as "O", talks about the project and her role in our sessions in the following exchange.

D. Are you in charge of this project?

O. I observe it. In some way, yes, I am in charge. Yet, we are several. Silent masters, if you like, that are also in charge. This group extends beyond those you are familiar with, as it actually reaches higher. Those who also observe may appear mute, as they do not necessarily communicate directly. But it is carefully designed for the current times and future times to come, which the two of you, on this level, do not know about. You will be guided in the way that you write and communicate, so it creates that ripple effect into the future generation and the way they will speak and the way they will receive and communicate information. Trust that you will receive the way the word will be written and said. Know that it is something that will give an echo into the future.

Zachariah is the main presenter of technical information, and shows himself (to Christine) as a scholar, wearing a purple robe with a face similar to those seen on statues of Aristotle. Christine's voice becomes quite deep, which seems a little odd coming from her tiny body, and the words are precisely delivered, as his ideas are very concise. Bob, the third spirit in our group, once called him the Ambassador of Knowledge, as he works in the Library and is responsible for teaching and documenting on many different levels of creation. His spirit body is between two and three meters high, similar to Ophelia's. Zachariah belongs within the ninth dimension, which functions as a council overseeing a lot of form-related creation. During our sessions, he usually comes in first and, after saying hello, will just start talking about his chosen topic for the day. The spirit team has an agenda for teaching, and they maintain control of the discussions. When there is an opportunity to ask questions, I usually keep to the subject at hand, although when I do go off-topic, the responses are always spontaneously brilliant and thought provoking. Zachariah has made casual comments about gravity, space, and time, that are a little mind-bending. Those ideas will be included in other waves of knowledge, since they want this first book to be about the spirit, and the structure of the spirit world. I should also add that many of the concepts he discusses in very specific detail, are topics Christine has no knowledge of, or interest in. From my perspective, as the conductor of these sessions, these personalities establish their credibility every time they speak.

Bob is a master designer from the second dimension, and has been the most entertaining of our spiritual friends. He requested the stage name, Bob, pointing out that each time we get a new body, we get to use a new name. Since the spirits on the second dimension do not incarnate, he thought it only fair that he gets to pick out another, more humorous name. We call him by his spiritual name in our sessions, but in our books, we will honor his request to call him Bob. Ophelia and Zachariah can be amusing as well, but they tend to be a bit more serious. After first being introduced by Zachariah, in early October 2016, Bob has come through and talked in almost every session. When he first began speaking, he struggled a little bit while he was figuring out how to communicate. Just as Christine had to learn how to shift her consciousness out of the way, the spirits also have a little learning curve as they practice merging into her energy field to access information in her brain, and then present their ideas using her vocal cords. Bob's skills have improved dramatically, and he can now deliver long speeches quite rapidly. And I do mean rapidly. He talks at nearly twice the speed of the other spirits Christine channels, and it can be a challenge to transcribe the sheer volume of words he delivers. Bob usually comes in after Ophelia or Zachariah have delivered their messages. The first few months, Christine could feel him pacing back and forth on her left side, waiting for his turn to speak. Once he became familiar with how and when to merge, he stopped moving around and now waits, almost patiently, for his turn. He has quite a joyful personality and will sing, hum, or make some odd noises when he first merges his energy with her. Bob has a strong desire to share his own views and ideas, and his discussions reveal a lot about his life and what he does in the spirit world. As far as we know, Bob is the first entity from the second dimension to ever channel messages through a human. The second dimension, as we will describe later, is the spiritual reality that is sort of the final step in generating all life on Earth. Because of Bob's contributions, we have been given an incredible amount of information on very diverse and fascinating subjects. The way he talks is quite endearing, rising and falling in almost a childish way, and his laughter is spontaneous and contagious. Whenever Christine does public seances, Bob always makes an appearance, and everyone just loves his personality.

Far from being random strangers, Zachariah, Ophelia, and Bob are some of our closest friends. We all work together and know one another as spiritual beings, even if our human mind can't recall the details. One aspect of the spiritual world everyone can appreciate is the opportunity to learn and expand your knowledge. All spirits are created with the desire to progress and move forward, following their own specific destiny. Bob was born into the second dimension and has mastered a lot of basic knowledge on that plane. He is now investigating how light and sound are combined to make different forms, which involves the sixth and seventh dimensions. Both Christine and I, our spiritual beings, that is, work on the sixth dimension, and Bob has been coming to our lab to study, where I mentor him. He also studies in a lab on the seventh dimension, where Ophelia teaches him about the ways light and sound energies are used in that reality. In return, my spiritual self goes to visit him on the second dimension to learn a little bit about the finer aspects of creating plants, trees, and animals, since he is a master designer of those types of things. Because Bob is working on a plane close to Earth, he has a physical body that is similar to a human, although smaller in stature. Christine sees him wearing sandals and a brownish robe, having sort of a roundish physique, which causes him to rock side to side as he walks. His eyes and nose are proportionally bigger than ours, his hair somewhat in disarray, but he has an endearing smile and personality. All the other spirits refer to him as either "the little one," or "your little friend," as he is about half their height, but they all seem to care about him very much.

In addition to his incredible knowledge about plants and animals, Bob is also a healer, which is easy to understand since his group designs the inner and outer workings of the human body. We do a huge disservice to the spirits on his plane with our definition of "evolution," because genetic changes are intentional and planned, to achieve specific goals. The second dimension works tirelessly to improve and adjust the energy patterns of plant and animal life on Earth. Bob refers to these modifications as upgrades, which are needed as the environmental conditions change. He quite frequently 'reads' the energetic structure of my body, as well as others, and gives very specific advice on how to correct certain conditions he observes. I have learned to deeply respect his abilities, as his insights have always proven to be accurate. He has a great interest in the engine, as he calls the digestive system, the liver, and the feet. Because he is always generous with advice, we will include some of his universal recommendations within the book.

Jeshua is another spirit from the upper parts of the ninth dimension. He is a member of the Elahim Council and the Council of Nine, which are introduced in *Wave 2*. Jeshua is my primary mentor. He comes through occasionally with specific messages, mostly about the long-term objectives of their teachings. In his often loud, booming voice, he has told both Christine and I we have to really clean up our bodies before the next group of spiritual beings arrive to deliver the second wave of knowledge. Among other instructions, we are told to eliminate all alcohol and sugar from our diet, as the high energy, or vibration, of these beings will damage the vehicle if it is not properly attuned. Jeshua will be more involved in later waves of knowledge, as this book is considered merely a stepping stone to what he wants to discuss.

Isaac is Christine's main guide, and works within the eighth dimension. According to Bob, he is very friendly and works closely with Ophelia on certain projects. Isaac is present at each session as a guardian for Christine when she begins to go into her trance state. Because of his advanced technical knowledge on certain subjects, he, too, will be presenting information in later books.

What is most fascinating, to me, is the close connection Christine and I have with these spirits. Based on the information they have given us, we have known and worked with each other for a long time, although "time", in the spiritual world, is measured in cycles of experience. This project, to bring certain knowledge to this plane, was planned before either of our bodies were conceived. These spirits agreed to help because they are our closest friends on the other side. Jeshua, Bob, Ophelia, and Zachariah have followed me in every lifetime, in different capacities. Zachariah, for instance, was in charge of my education, or should I say, my *real* education. As a young man, I moved frequently, following jobs to different cities. Being without friends or family nearby, one of my passions was looking for treasures in used bookstores, spiritual books that, in many cases, were long out-of-print. During those times, I sensed there was often someone with me, watching, nudging me to choose a certain book. So, it was not a surprise when Zachariah mentioned that it was he who had been guiding me during those decades of searching for truth, making sure I followed the pre-planned agenda. And Bob, my precious little friend, has also been observing me since birth. During our sessions, he will occasionally remind me of a long-forgotten incident from my childhood, or later as an adult, where he was beside me, trying to uplift my spirits when life was difficult. It almost makes me ashamed, knowing how devoted and loyal he has been, while I was completely unaware of his presence. Ophelia, too, has circled protectively like a second, watchful mother, directing events in my life towards specific goals, including jobs and places I have lived. But you should know the attention and guidance I received are not unique, as each person on Earth has at least one guide that follows and helps them throughout life. It is one of the Creators gifts, that we are never left alone.

At one point, I asked Zachariah who was responsible for bringing us all together for this project.

D. Within our little soul group here; you, Ophelia, Jeshua, Isaac, and Bob, when we came down, who was really the organizer who wanted this to happen?

Z. Ophelia initiated the project and asked for assistance. Two were selected, for specific reasons, to operate on the Earth plane. It was almost an audition to select which spirit guides would communicate; when, where, and at what time. For progress to begin, it had to begin in a slow, yet organized fashion. Ophelia combined with Jeshua, Isaac, and another party that has not yet been presented, this was the group of four who created the mission. All are from different dimensions; seven, eight, nine, and ten. The tenth has not been presented.

D. Very good. Have you been one of my guides in other lifetimes?

Z. Yes. When you chose lives that were essentially for education, yes. You have several lives where you have been writing. You like the words; she (*Christine*) likes the visual. You were picked on those criteria, to be as wide as you could possibly be in the way you deliver a message. You have different abilities to best reach out. Neither is better than the other, you need to work hand in hand. That is one reason why you were picked. Nothing is done by chance. No experiences you have had up to this point are by chance. Know that this is not the final destination on this journey.

These spirits are individual personalities, perhaps not in the way we conceive from our human awareness, but rather as beings who are like ourselves when we are not incarnated. They work within the spiritual world of form, helping the Creator. Everyone has a role to play in the grand drama of Earth. The important thing to remember is that we all have guides watching over us, always. Even when you feel most alone, you are not. You are never alone.

## The Writing Begins

(This section added in December 2021) In early 2016, the spirits began encouraging us to share the information they were giving. As the months passed and the transcripts piled up, we were left wondering how to fulfill their request. Their initial advice was for me to take their explanations and combine it with other information I had read or studied during the past 40 years. They kept urging me to find the truths within, and write it down. This session, from October 31, 2016, is an example of how they wanted *Wave 1* to be presented. I was unsure how to even begin, so Bob's recommendations were very helpful. As he points out, it is important to clear the mind and let words bubble up from the soul particle. The next day, I started using simple rituals, like lighting a candle and burning sage, to help establish a proper atmosphere. I also pay more attention to my state of mind. When I feel receptive, I write. If my mind is too cluttered, time is better spent transcribing recordings or tending to other business. Repetition is one key to improve psychic abilities. So now, when I write, there is always a candle burning right beside the computer, as a reminder to empty the mind and focus on the quiet voice inside.

D. Since I have to access information directly, what is the best way for me activate my connection?

B. Oh, it's when you sit in your room by yourself. You need to be more grounded. You can be with the feet on the ground like you always do and scrubble (*to rub the bare feet back and forth on carpet, building heat and energy*). And there's actually a way to activate the whole energy flow up into your center chakra, where you will receive information. But you need to be patient. You do not need to compare with someone else or what you think that you should accomplish because that only puts a block or a little bit of a barrier for you. But take your own time and do it in small steps. The pendulum, you don't need that anymore. You can put that down. You can channel with your pen and you can listen! Listen! You have ears! We talk to you all the time! Listen! You don't have to have to have visual proof like you use with your pendulum. The proof lies in your own knowledge and the knowing of the information that comes. You do not have to see it. That's just being lazy. SO, you have the ability to hear us, but you need to be quiet and patient and sit in your own space and create your own little ritual if you want to.

D. Alright, I will do that. What other information would be helpful for the book?

B. It's better if you constantly think of how you want to describe the topics that are presented to you, because what we present to you in these sessions you can just put in. And you can choose where you want to put it in. But in order for this to be from a human standpoint, you have to do the work with your pen and you have to activate your own wisdom that comes from within. So, you are much wiser than you give yourself credit for, and that is where you need to work more putting the theories together as unit in the bowl. So, if you have a lot of different theories, then you put it in the bowl and you mix them around, then you get a picture of how you want to present the whole thing. We want you to be creative. We want you to be inspired, because this is your work, this is not necessarily ours. We will help you, and in that regard, we are involved with the scripture, –but it is not just our writing. Because, you know, we could use some magic and just make the book. And then it could just appear in a library, if that was the idea, if you know what I mean. Things can manifest from a spiritual plane to a physical plane. SO, if that was the idea, it would have just been done. But this is YOUR project.

D. I really appreciate the advice.

B. You're gonna write now. Because you've been sloppy with your own ideas, just waiting for us to give you everything. Sloppy. So, this is where you come in and put in your own effort and your own wisdom. And you make it blossom into what you wanted it to be. This is your creation, the two of you. We simply assist with bringing forward what we discussed before coming.

It was with this guidance that we began writing *Wave 1*. As we all became more skilled in our various roles, our spirit friends delivered longer and longer talks on specific subjects. In *Wave 1*, they wanted us to build the platform to support the next waves of knowledge they bring forward. I felt the best way to do that was to include some of the evidence gleaned from NDEs, past life memories, and angelic encounters in the first few chapters. There are millions of people who have had extrasensory experiences. Our spirit team has unscrambled all the isolated and disconnected encounters with the divine, giving us a coherent spiritual design that explains the mysteries that have confounded humans for eons.

# *The Basics of Your Soul*

**How do we know there is a soul hiding in our body?** That may be the easiest question to answer, because there are innumerable accounts from people whose awareness left their body and went traveling somewhere else. They were able, in many cases, to accurately provide descriptions of other people's activities and thoughts, or identify objects that were nowhere near their body. To the individual who is out-of-body, the sense of self remains intact as a part of their awareness. Once their soul pops out of the body, their focus shifts and they no longer perceive with physical senses. They enter into the world of a spirit and can "see" in all directions at once, and "hear" peoples' thoughts. Objects no longer look solid, and the intention to travel somewhere results in instantaneous movement. This state of existence feels more real than living in a body, and many do not want to come back. Most of those people who have experienced themselves outside of the body know without a doubt their awareness is not dependent upon or derived from the brain. For someone on the path of self-realization, knowing the soul is a completely autonomous entity is the first step away from a materialistic view of the world.

**What is the physical body?** Human bodies were built specifically to serve as a host to soul energy that is sent to Earth as part of its education. It is constructed of the same material as everything else on the planet, but the body is still an experimental vehicle. Bob says humans are the highest mammal, and there have been several alterations over the millennia. In the distant past, the Creator was the sole occupant of the human form, but it was modified to permit individual souls to blend and experience Earth life. Experts in the spiritual dimensions are the entities who design the bodies. That process is described later in this book. There is currently a new model of human being designed with a bigger brain. The larger brain will allow for more soul energy to come in, so they will be less aggressive and have more self-control. The design is still ongoing, so the new human is not going to appear in our lifetime. Data is still being collected to properly adjust the energy patterns for the new body.

**How are the elements and solid objects made?** The human body is made of trillions of cells working together within an established pattern, but each cell is made up of trillions of many smaller parts, such as atoms and molecules, working together in harmony. Modern science, in many ways, has been on a pursuit of self-deception. Even though there is a constant stream of evidence showing a higher form of design within all living organisms, the scientific communities have built their cities in the land of materialism. Using their lingo, there are non-living things, such as atoms, which are made of elementary particles, such as quarks, leptons, gluons and photons. These elementary particles are made of something smaller, which flicker in and out of existence (in our reality) within a probability cloud. Endless speculation and theories will never explain how matter comes into existence, without organizational designs from an external, unknowable source. According to our spirits, the fundamental building blocks of matter are cosmic light, cosmic sound, gravity and vacuum. Cosmic light energy flows freely through the Universe, until it becomes locked in a pattern with the other fundamental building blocks. Cosmic light and sound are aspects of conscious energy, emanating from a source (the Creator) which is external to the Universe. Atoms and molecules, therefore, also have a foundation of awareness. All the material in our Universe is within a band of spiritual vibration, but other vibrations exist. Fundamental elements are created from patterns. The elements are used to construct other patterns. Human bodies, planets and stars exist because they were planned and designed. Our team explained how a multitude of spirits are involved in taking cosmic light and sound, and bundling it into patterns that create all the material and living things in our world. We live within a grid of energy we cannot see or detect. Our eyes cannot see, but many people who have had a near-death experience (NDE), or an out-of-body experience (OBE), describe seeing the world through spiritual senses. To them the physical world appears to be light filaments and particles in the shape of objects, and all the objects are intertwined with one another, bound together within a common field of energy. The light itself is a life force. From this perspective, there is no separation. Everything arises from a sea of energy. The individual cells within your liver, for example, are aware they are performing a certain task, and the collective intelligence of the liver understands it has a supporting role within the body. Everything is organized based on patterns of intent. Think about it, when you break a bone, how would the cells know how to mend the damage, if it wasn't working from an energetic blueprint? The body does the best it can to repair damage, even if you are unaware of how it is working.

**What type of creatures have souls?** Every living plant and animal that carries DNA or RNA is constructed from the intelligent elements of the Earth. Carbon, water, iron and different minerals all have an awareness of their surroundings, but are resonating at the slowest vibration of spiritual energy. These can be brought together to form complex organisms by creating a pattern, which we call DNA. To make this organism "living," as we think of it, there must be a spiritual energy that has a higher vibration put into the organism as it is developing. This spiritual energy is either from the universal cloud, or in the case of humans, from a soul. Without this energy, the DNA pattern will not be able to maintain its structure, and will disintegrate back into the elements. There is a cloud of spirit that exists throughout the Universe, which is identified as the "Master Mind". This cloud is connected to the Creator, and it is from this cloud that all living organisms get a little bit of universal spirit. From a flower in the forest to a whale in the ocean, everything has a little bit of this spirit within. As the flower or whale dies, this spirit is drawn back into the cloud. Humans are the exception, as our bodies are infused with the spiritual energy of our soul. When our bodies die, our soul is withdrawn back into the higher vibrations of the spiritual dimensions.

**If the soul exists independent of a body, where does it go after death?** Based on personal accounts from many people, we know death occurs when the soul fully detaches from the body. In the case of NDEs, astral projections, and other experiences when the consciousness is out of the body, there remains an energetic tether between the body and the soul, called by some the "silver cord." When the cord disconnects, the soul cannot return, and the body dies. Upon death, the soul first moves into the mental realm, which is described later in more detail, where thought forms, attachments, beliefs, and mental creations relating to the Earth are encountered. Some souls are reluctant to let go of their body, material possessions, or relationships with other people. In those cases, the soul will remain within the mental realm until it is ready to let go of those attachments. If the soul can accept its new condition and release any hold the Earth has on the mind, then the soul will move vibrationally upwards into the spirit dimensions, its true home. Upon returning home, it meets with its spirit guides and other mentors to review the life experiences, analyzing how well it worked on the goals and objectives established prior to the lifetime. And finally, this piece of the soul that journeyed to Earth is reunited with the other part of its spirit energy, the higher self, which had remained in the pure spirit realm.

**What is a soul?** What we call our spirit is a small bundle of spiritual energy, made entirely from and always part of the Creator. We will use the words "spirit" and "soul" somewhat interchangeably, but your soul is a piece of your spirit, which was temporarily split off in order to occupy a body on Earth, or some other planet. It could represent anywhere from just a few percent to a fairly high percentage of your total spiritual energy. When your body dies, your soul will return home and merge back with the rest of your spirit. As a spirit progresses, acquiring more knowledge and experience, their bundle of energy increases in luminosity by becoming larger and brighter. Therefore, younger souls normally bring a higher percentage of their spirit energy into the human body, whereas more advanced souls often bring in much less. Your spirit will never be destroyed, and the soul will not cease to exist upon death of the body. The Creator gave each spirit a unique configuration and specific role within the divine order of the spirit world. Your purpose is programmed into your energy pattern, so there is no way that you can become lost or disoriented about who you are. Most souls that occupy bodies on Earth come here as part of their education. Eventually, after your spirit has completed its pre-programmed destiny, or cycle of learning, it will return to the Creator, in what Zachariah described as the final ascension.

**Does hell exist?** It exists only within the transitional mental realm around the Earth, and within people's minds. It has no reality within the spiritual dimensions, as the vibrational frequencies such as fear, guilt, anger, and sadness are only found on Earth, or within the mental realm around Earth. Those vibrations cannot exist within the pure spiritual realms. Some people who have near-death experiences report frightening encounters in dark, loveless locations, but those are not places made by the Creator. They exist as karmic debris from human activities—the energetic mental and emotional residue. Over the centuries, many religions have concocted horrific images of torment where non-believers and sinners will be sent by their vindictive gods. Medieval and Renaissance painters joyfully helped out the Holy Roman Church by pouring their talents into making disturbing artwork, intended to generate fear in people. Over time, these ideas can manifest as creations within the vibrational field where human thoughts resonate. If someone has a belief and fear about such a place, they may be temporarily drawn to it as they leave the body. Souls are not sent here for being naughty, and certainly not condemned to spend eternity in such a location. As the soul is indestructible, the only harm is a temporary mental torment. The ideas promoted by many religions, that people must believe or do certain things to be "saved", are completely false doctrines. Spiritual guides are always around and can be called on for help, if you get stuck in such an environment while traveling back. Praying is a way to communicate with your guides.

**Why would a soul come to Earth if its true home is so perfect?** The Creator give assignments to souls in their blueprint. Some are destined to undergo a series of incarnations on this planet. Not as a punishment, but to develop and educate them in particular types of knowledge and experience. There are many different worlds where souls can incarnate in bodies, and each has a unique curriculum. The density of Earth and configuration of the human makes it difficult for the soul to be heard. While a soul is not forced to come to Earth, once a spirit begins the cycle, it is guided to continue incarnating. Only the soul can clean up karma it made during previous sojourns in different lifetimes. Each soul is responsible for what it has created. Every spirit is part of a small group that have similar energy patterns, and they help and assist each other to develop. When a soul has learned the lessons available on this plane, it can continue to come for other reasons, like to introduce certain knowledge, or help another incarnated soul. The schoolhouse of Earth gives spirits a deep understanding about the extremes of emotions and the struggles a soul has when immersed in dense matter. Gaining direct knowledge through experiences is one path of learning within the spiritual world.

**What becomes of the personality when the soul returns home?** Your spiritual being has a unique personality. Each body also comes programmed with certain dispositions. When a soul joins with the body, traits are activated that best fit the soul's mission for that lifetime. Sometimes the human personality is similar to the soul personality, and other times it is not. The soul (and guide) decides how much the human will mirror the soul's personality. Sometimes the spiritual personality is suppressed in favor of a dissimilar human personality, much like an actor at a masquerade ball. A soul has many lives, and some personalities are not that lovable. If someone is a real curmudgeon in life, that is a human attribute, and that will not remain with the soul after death. Spirits have an essence that is loving, compassionate, and joyful, and they also have a sense of humor and a willingness to be helpful. The experiences and knowledge gained while incarnated become part of the spirit's history, and can be recalled at will. Your spiritual being is always more magnificent and majestic than your earthly personality, so feel no sadness for the parts left behind.

**Does death separate those who love one another?** No, but, as we have mentioned, the departing soul loses all attachment to the Earth and the body, Sometimes, a difficult life will require a period of rest and solitude for the departed soul. However, a bond of love is never broken. You are always watched over and assisted by your guides, and the deceased may very well become another guide who helps you, when needed. Because time is not a reality on the other side, those who have returned home know their loved ones will soon join them.

**Why don't more people accept this information if it is so well documented?** People allow themselves to be imprisoned emotionally and logically, because of fear or indifference. No one, however, can control what is in your mind unless you give up the right to think for yourself. Mindlessly accepting others' opinions is the easy path in life, and is incompatible with free will. It is all too common for groupthink to become the only acceptable narrative. That is when topics that should be discussed are ridiculed or ignored. A relevant example would be the idea of eternal damnation, which is broadly accepted in some religious organizations. To believe that concept indirectly binds the person to those who promise to save them from this fabricated fate. The statistics on people who have had glimpses of the spiritual reality beyond death, show that many turn away from organized religion and its rhetoric, choosing instead to focus on the spirit within themselves. That is the location of the only true temple, the only place where divinity can be found. Spiritual energy comes into the human body from the soul, and then flows outward into the world. No one else can give you what you already possess.

**Do spirit guides exist?** We are never alone during our sojourn on Earth. Each soul is assigned one primary mentor. During an incarnation, there may be several other guides who offer guidance and intervene to make, or prevent, things from happening. These guides know you well, and some have incarnated with you in other lives. The spirits of family members and friends may also watch over and try to assist when they can. Millions of people have had experiences where a spiritual being temporarily materialized to comfort or protect someone in a time of need. Divine intervention is an ongoing process in everyone's life. Even if you are unaware, the spirit world is constantly working on your behalf to provide the best learning environment for your soul to develop. The primary way guides give you guidance is by popping thought bubbles into your consciousness, which happens with great frequency during the day. Never forget that your soul is an extension of the Creator. When you ask for guidance and help, know that you are not alone. As Bob once said, "First you believe, then we show you."

# *Introduction to Dimensions*

If you are going on a trip, the wise thing to do is study a map ahead of time and figure out the places you want to see, and what roads to follow to get there. Because we are going on a trip into what some might feel is an unknown territory, it may be a good idea to lay out some basic ideas for you to become familiar with. This section could have just as easily been titled, "Introduction to Creation," because they are one and the same. Nothing could come into existence without the dimensions, and the dimensions would be unnecessary if not for creation.

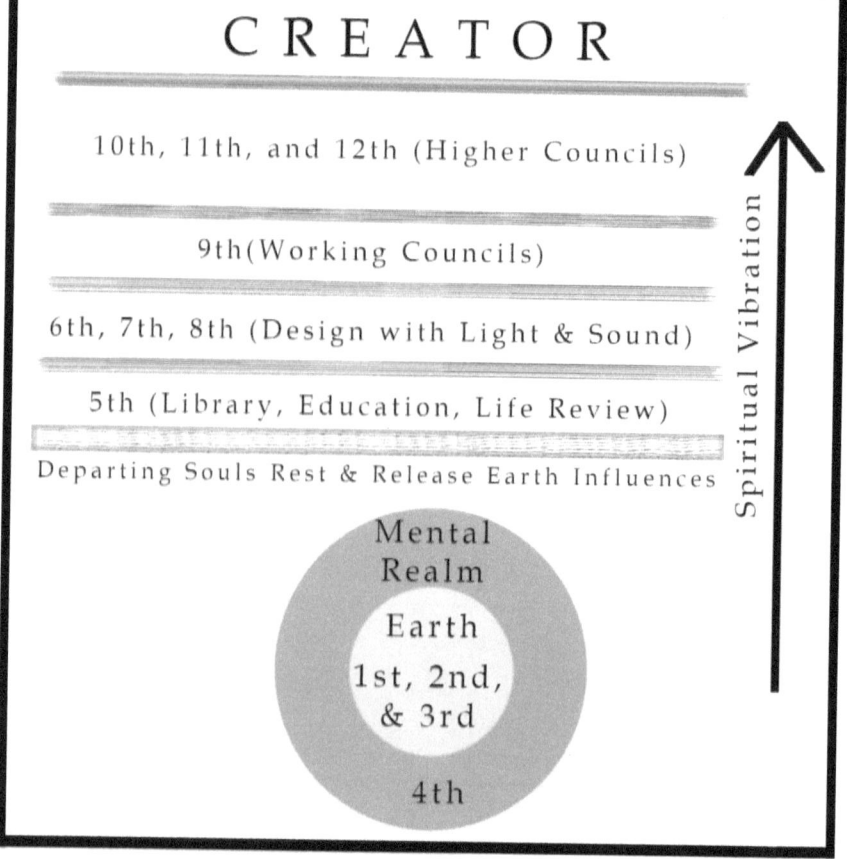

It is unquestionable that nature is an organized, intricately designed system that is continually being modified, but the question is, by whom? Our spirit team presents a loving, complex, and compassionate reality that controls life on Earth, facts which are also confirmed by NDEs and other sources. Through social conditioning, people often picture the Creator as an old man in a chair, scowling at us from way out in space somewhere. We have learned the opposite to be true. One aspect of the Creator, the Master Mind, is not remote and unreachable, but is present everywhere as the life force in animals, plants, trees, insects, microbes, and other things we ignore and exploit. And we humans are also spiritual beings, who have projected our soul to Earth and are inhabiting a body to learn certain lessons. The brain does not produce consciousness, but rather, our awareness is an extension of our spiritual self while we are incarnated. All living things on this planet have a soul energy that comes from somewhere else. This implies the Earth and everything on it are here by design, and exists within a greater purpose. To those of us who are incarnated, our home lies in the world beyond, and we are only here attending school. When we die, we are not hauled before a divine court of justice and potentially sent to prison for eternity. We are here to learn, and are assisted throughout life by spiritual beings who watch over and guide us, but do not sit in judgement of our failures. Many beliefs that are common in society are completely at odds with spiritual truth. Our spirit team has given us a new perspective that connects spirituality and science together within a theory of everything, with no mathematical proofs required.

As a youngster, I used to lay on my back and stare into the vastness of the night sky. There is no better way to feel tiny than to measure how insignificant the size of the Earth seems against this background. Those of us who have gone to church are told as children how the souls of the deceased go to heaven, assuming they were nice, and then spend eternity sitting on a cloud, playing a harp or singing. Even in my young mind, that never seemed very productive or necessary. As it turns out, spirits are actually quite busy on the other side. A great many are engaged in creating the very things seen in the canopy of the night sky. These aspects of creation are divided into what the spirits call dimensions, each carrying certain vibrations, colors, tones, and functions.

What is a dimension? Since most of us cannot relate to something that is invisible, it becomes a bit challenging to describe some of the upper dimensions. We will begin with our Universe, what the spirits call a fish tank. Our fish tank contains the first four dimensions, one through four. If we start with what is closest to us, our body, we have a chance to explain the visible manifestation of the lower ones. Everything we can see or detect is being manifested on the third dimension, but has different source vibrations, which are the dimensions. Looking in a mirror, we see a living third dimensional being, which is a combination of the first dimensional elements (carbon, nitrogen, hydrogen, etc.). Patterns of DNA have organized those first dimensional elements into a second dimensional form, the body. The body is transformed into a living entity by our soul energy, which is in resonance with the fourth dimension (the mental realm is the fourth dimension) while you are alive. Upon death, the soul leaves, and the body then becomes only an object carrying the vibrations of the first and second dimensions. Over time, the body will break down into the unorganized elements, leaving only the vibration of the first dimension. While the dimensions are actually different frequencies within a continuum of spiritual energy, human eyes can only see the manifested end result within the vibration of the third dimension, so this description is incomplete.

To add a little color to the fourth dimension, consider the difference between being awake and being asleep. While awake, your awareness is trapped within the vibration of the physical world, the third dimension. This trapped part of your awareness is termed consciousness, and is a product of the logical human mind. The soul mind is separate, and is located in your center point, between the heart and solar plexus. So there are two minds in a human. As you fall asleep, your human consciousness loses its grip and is more open to input from the soul mind. When people sleep, the soul usually detaches from the body and roams around in the fourth dimension. The mind picks up some of the soul input and tries to make sense of it, mingling it into dreams. After death, the soul will exit the fourth dimension and return to its home in one of the higher dimensions.

A final approach to visualizing the dimensions, perhaps the most understandable, is like a hierarchy of responsibilities, similar to what goes on in any manufacturing company. The spirit team has told us about twelve dimensions, and how the spiritual vibrations go from being quite dense on the first dimension, to a very high frequency without any form on the highest. The fifth and above are the spiritual realms, and the first through fourth are related to the material universes. You can think of the higher dimensions as being like the management, design, planning, record storage, engineering, and construction departments. What the spirit world constructs is everything you see. All things visible in the night sky, and everything in and on the Earth, have been created with an intention and a purpose. This following is not the best summary, but the suggests how the process works and will help with other topics.

> CREATOR – CEO. Ophelia once said that beyond the spiritual dimensions, there is an awareness of pure consciousness where no light, sound, or motion exists. It preceded creation and will reabsorb everything, if the creative cycle ends. The Creator is the source of all the cosmic light and sound energy that flows through the spiritual dimensions and the fish tanks. For our purposes, the Creator contains several aspects, including the Master Mind and the Mother energy. The Mother energy creates the souls who occupy the different dimensions. Souls are assembled as little bundles of awareness (from the Creator) and are each given a blueprint and purpose to fulfill within one of the dimensions. Design ideas originate from the Creator and are then sent down to these very same spirits in the different dimensions for execution. So one could say the Creator's creations are the ones who assist in creation. The Master Mind provides the soul energy that animates all living forms in our Universe. The Master Mind then experiences living as each entity.
> 10th to 12th Dimensions – Executive Groups. Very high spiritual councils. The twelfth dimension is involved with healing. Many of these spirits have been brought up from lower dimensions, if they were destined by their pattern to do so. The cloud of consciousness, or the spirit from the Master Mind that animates all life forms, is connected to these realms. Ideas for new creations originate here or in the Master Mind, and are sent into the 9th dimension for execution. The higher angelic beings, sometimes

identified with names like Gabriel, reside in this realm.

- 9th Dimension – Directors. The spirits on these levels decide how to implement the ideas that come to them from above. Bob once said the ideas are like raindrops that fall into the 9th, and are then filtered down, becoming formed as each dimension adds to it. Zachariah and Jeshua are council members on the 9th. These councils also solve problems within galaxies or solar systems.
- 8th Dimension – Design group who use light and sound energy to make color patterns for elements, gravity, and magnetic wave forms. This group adds gravity and magnetism to stars, planets and space. It works in conjunction with the sixth and seventh during the formation of celestial bodies and solar families. Isaac is one of those who work with gravity on this dimension.
- 7th Dimension – Predominantly uses light and sound energy to make suns and conditions on planets that carry living beings. Ophelia is a member of councils on this dimension. Humans would interpret spirits from the seventh as angels, since they radiate the highest form of love and compassion.
- 6th Dimension – Works with 7th and 8th dimensions, combining elements with light and sound to create the planets, setting the intention for what will be on the planet's surface, and establishing the gravity and vacuum needed to balance the solar family in orbits. The cores of all planets are living life forms, and contain color patterns that resonate with their purpose and location within solar groups. All celestial families are a combined work of the 6th, 7th and 8th dimensions.
- 5th Dimension – Center of learning that all dimensions can visit. The Library is found here. It is a central repository of knowledge from all universes and life forms, including the individual records of each spirit. There are beautiful gardens with plants and flowers that glow from an inner light, radiating colors unknown on Earth. The 5th dimension is

closely connected to Earth. The majority of humans are occupied by souls from the 5th. People occasionally glimpse this realm during a near-death experience. It is the first level of "heaven".

- 4th Dimension – The mental realm. A transitional vibration surrounding each 3rd dimension planet where life is found. It is not a true spiritual reality, but does hold the individual and collective memories of all beings who have incarnated on that planet. When your body dies, your awareness shifts into this reality, where you will have to face all of your creations made while incarnated. The mental realm holds the Coats of Karma. It is also where souls travel during dreams, NDEs, and OBEs.
- 3rd Dimension – the manifested, visible, tangible (to humans) reality. All the solid forms in our universe are contained in one "fish tank." The 3rd dimension is sort of the stage upon which other dimensions project energetic forms. All 2nd dimension patterns (trees, plants, animals, etc.) have some higher form of spiritual energy attached to be alive on the 3rd. Humans have a soul attached, and other living things have a little energy from "the cloud" of the Master Mind, which is directly connected to the Creator. All plant and animal life have an awareness bestowed by the Master Mind.
- 2nd Dimension – the vibration of all life forms, from water to the mammals. The 2nd is home to those spirits who nurture living organisms. They take on many forms, such as elementals, fairies, gardeners, or design engineers. The engineers take the patterns for life forms developed by the 5th through 8th dimensions and fine tune them. They do this by changing the energy configuration we "see" as DNA. They work closely with the water, atmosphere, plants, and animals on all living planets. Bob, in our spirit team, is a master designer from this dimension.
- 1st Dimension – the vibration associated with the elements, gravity and electromagnetism. It forms the core of all celestial bodies. It is the base from which

all manifestation is able to occur. You can think of it as a slow vibration of light and sound energy, sort of the polarity to the Creator. When the design patterns created in the 6th, 7th, and 8th dimension are sent into this slower vibration, they become structures like planets or stars. The elements are made from spiritual light and sound, and once manifested, these elements are used by the 2nd dimension to create vessels on the 3rd dimension for spiritual awareness to occupy.

Within the above dimensions, your spiritual self is currently involved with three of them simultaneously. Your body and sense perceptions are locked in the third, your soul is resonating within the fourth, and your higher self is somewhere in the fifth through the seventh. After you die, your soul will disconnect from the third, which has acted as an anchor, and after a brief pause in the fourth, will return to the dimension where your spirit is working. The two parts, your soul and higher spirit, will then blend back together. Even though you may feel complete as a human, a large part of who you are is still active in some other reality while your soul is on a mission to Earth. Once your soul reunites with your spirit, you will simply continue with normal spiritual activities. Both Christine and I will go back and join our spiritual beings who are now working in a lab on the sixth. You, and each person on Earth, have a spirit waiting somewhere for the incarnated soul to return. It should be pointed out that religious beliefs and ideas are irrelevant, as all souls return to "heaven" after death, even those who believe in nothing.

If you step back far enough, sometimes a picture may become clearer. Everything in existence has the same basic structure, and within all of creation, there are only three main pieces. First, there is the Creator, the source of energy and consciousness. One aspect of the Creator is the Master Mind, a cloud of awareness that is spread throughout the Universe. Second, there are the children, or spirits, who are made from the Creators consciousness, but have a separate sense of self and individuality. These children are the spirits who makes up the spiritual world, From the tiniest little sparkles to the most magnificent angels, we are all related as siblings. Each spirit is given a purpose and a function within one of the creative dimensions. The third piece of creation is a stream of conscious energy that radiates out from the Creator, and later returns back in a continuous cycle. This is the building material in all the dimensions. This energy is split into two streams, light and sound. The children of the Creator use this cosmic light and cosmic sound to build things. The objects in heaven and the rocks in a nearly field are made using the same source field, just vibrating on different frequencies.

We are the spirits who build things, which our Creator then takes for a ride, so to speak. The children of the Creator made everything that exists in our universe. Stars, planets, oceans, fish, animals, trees, grass, atmosphere, gravity; all was built by the untold numbers of spiritual beings who reside within different dimensions. If those things are alive, that is, if they have been organized by DNA, they are occupied by a tiny piece of the Master Mind. The Master Mind exists as a cloud of consciousness that is present throughout the universe. Anything that is alive has part of the Creator's awareness within. When a soul incarnates on Earth, 99.5 percent of the animating energy is from the soul, but there is a tiny fraction of Master Mind that accompanies the soul. (*When this book was first published, we did not know that. We have revised the manuscript to include the latest information.*) The Master Mind joins as an observer, but that tiny fraction provides a direct link to the Creator. Spirits incarnate to learn about creation by experiencing it first-hand. You are one of these spirits, sharing space on this planet with the many forms occupied by the Master Mind. So, there you have it, creation in a nutshell.

While incarnated on Earth, every soul has another part of themselves, which is sometimes referred to as the higher self, that remains within the spiritual dimensions. In simplistic terms, your spiritual being has a home on either the fifth, sixth, or seventh dimension. A spirit is able to divide and send a part of itself, the soul, down into the fourth dimension, where it blends with and is driving a third-dimension vehicle on Earth. Your spirit never leaves its home and serves as an anchor for your soul as it travels. One of the reasons we are forced to forget about our spiritual home is because our tiny little brains do not have the capacity to hold the memories. Bob frequently points out how small my computer is, meaning the brain, and once compared the amount of knowledge my mind can hold to a cheap computer from the early 1980s, whereas my spiritual being was more like a modern supercomputer. This limited access to spiritual knowledge is actually part of the design. We incarnate and learn through making mistakes within a world of linear thinking and polarity. If we came down here with the full understanding we have as a spirit, there would be no challenge to incarnating. The key to mastering the karmic web in which we are stuck is to learn how to detect and honor the impulses originating from your spirit. Otherwise, you are essentially running through an obstacle course while blindfolded. The only way to pass the test is to listen to and trust your own inner guidance system, your soul.

The fourth dimension, the mental realm, is a transitional reality that surrounds all third dimensional planets where life forms are found. Living beings contain a spirit or soul, and the interaction between the two, the thoughts and emotions, become an energy transmission into the mental realm. All humans, animals, trees, plants, fish and other creatures transmit thought waves into the mental realm, where it leaves a permanent energetic record. Within humans, the soul also records a second copy of everything that it experiences, thinks, and feels, and that copy goes with the departing soul upon death. The copy of your activities that stays in the fourth dimension has been called by our spirit team, the "Coat of Karma." It is a running record of everything you have done on Earth, memories from every lifetime. Because all spirits have a unique color pattern, every thought bubble gets tagged as your creation, so there is no escaping your Coat of Karma. The Coat also contains the blueprint, the reason a particular soul has for coming to Earth. From a human perspective, the blueprint defines the curriculum needed for graduation. (This important topic is explored in detail in our later books, *Wave 2* and *Notes from the Second Dimension*.)

The fourth dimension is not part of the spiritual world, in the sense that it contains all kinds of vibrations that do not have a corresponding reality in the spiritual dimensions. For example, hatred and fear are emotional vibrations that are unknown in the spirit world, but are definitely found within the mental realm of the Earth. This is where visions of hell are located, created by the ideas and emotions of humans while they were alive. These foreboding places exist as thought creations from the long history of man's involvement with the Earth. Many of the heavenly realms envisioned by the different religions are also found within this vibration, and can be as spiritually unreal as the hellish areas. What I mean is that people's expectations of heaven are unlikely to exist in the spiritual dimensions, but may exist within the mental realm. There is a segregation within the fourth dimension, however, where the lowest vibrations are lacking in light or love, but the higher are much lighter and closer to the spiritual dimensions. People who have near-death experiences often go through a tunnel, which is a passage for them to pass up through the mental realm. As they progress along the tunnel, many observe the increasing light and energy as they move away from Earth. Very few NDEs ever leave the fourth dimension, because the upper boundary of the fourth is perceived as a barrier they cannot cross.

When someone dies on Earth, their mind takes control and they will be drawn to a place that feels familiar. So, a Catholic, for example, could go hang out with the souls of some previously deceased Catholic friends and family within the fourth dimension. It can be a resting place, and from this vibration, it is pretty easy to observe activities back on Earth. If someone dies and their partner is grieving, the departing soul may choose to linger for a while and try to give comfort. The boundary between the fourth and fifth dimensions contains what some have called "Summerland," a space with incredibly beautiful flowers and gardens, similar to those found on the fifth, with friendly animals and beautiful nature settings. This vibration is a place where the soul may rest and reflect on the life just ended, and can visit with their spirit guide, deceased family members, or other friends. Some simply sleep to restore their energy, if the life was especially difficult or traumatic, while their guides patiently watch over them. Souls can be bathed in a shower of colored light to wash off any residue of Earth energies that may be stuck on their energetic soul body. Sadness, regrets, anger, and longings are all attachments that must be released before the soul can continue home. When they are ready, souls do eventually leave the fourth vibration, returning to their assigned place in the pure spiritual realm, somewhere in the fifth through the ninth dimensions. This is when they will be reunited with their higher self. As the soul merges into its spirit, the memory of who they are will be restored. The spirit benefits from the expedition, as it now has more travels and experiences on which to draw.

The fifth dimension is the closest spiritual frequency to our reality. There are quite a few people who have visited and described what this place really looks like. Some of the best descriptions are reported by people who have undergone between-life regression, but people who have had near-death experiences occasionally get a little tour before they are sent back. This is a place of bright light, radiant colors, and has an emotional vibration of immense love and acceptance. Spirits from all dimensions can study in the Library, as this is a realm of learning and teaching. (In this book and future books, when we are referring to the main library on the fifth dimension, it will be capitalized. Libraries exist throughout the spiritual dimensions, and also on certain planets.) The Library is often a focal point during between life activities, as all the records from creation, in all dimensions, are kept at this central repository of knowledge. Each spirit has its own book of life, or Akashic record, as some call it, stored at this location. The fifth also has vast gardens, where living examples of different flora and fauna are maintained. When your soul returns to the fifth dimension, the Library, gardens, and other features seem as real and as solid as objects do here. For a spirit to enter different realms, its own vibration has to match the frequency within that dimension. It is this complimentary resonance that brings certain realms into focus. As humans, we cannot see into other realities because our physical eyes are resonating on the vibration of the third dimension.

In all the spiritual dimensions, communication is done through telepathy, or passing thought bubbles back and forth. While you are in the body, your soul is on the fourth dimension, immersed in the thought bubbles being transmitted by all the other souls and spirits. The psychologists call this the sub-consciousness, but it's really your soul, the silent observer. On the soul level, you always know what others are thinking or feeling about you, and we will describe the implications of that in the section on the Mental Realm.

# *The Life Review*

Haphazard chance does not drive your fate in this world. Before the body you selected takes its first breath, you and your guides had carefully planned many of the struggles and joys in your life. And on that fateful day, when your heart takes its final beat, the empty shell will travel to the graveyard or crematorium, but the soul will joyfully head home. Passing first through the mental realm, all the memories of the life just ended will suddenly return with perfect clarity, along with a recollection of your mission from the pre-life planning. The mental realm, between the physical Earth and the spirit world, is where the departing soul will pause to reflect and do a little self-evaluation. If the soul feels it did well, it may barely slow down as it returns home to join its higher self. On the other hand, if it feels it drifted far off-course, spiritually, there may be considerable "time" spent going over the details of certain experiences. No one is ever left alone during this activity. Just as now, while you are incarnated, a guardian spirit will watch over and help during this process in the transitional zone after death.

After all emotional and mental attachments to the Earth have been released, you will once again return to the spirit realms to meet with your main guide and probably a council of higher beings, where an inventory of the last life occurs. This is a valuable step in the learning experience, because they show the newly liberated soul the purpose for certain experiences. The first question asked by the council conducting the life review is along the lines of, "What do you have to show for your life?" Can you imagine the feeling of being asked that question today? You were given the gift of expressing your soul through a body on Earth, so what have you done with that gift? We are usually aware of our many weaknesses and faults, but imagine how you will feel, standing with your spirit guide before a high council, when every thought and minute detail of your life is spread out for all to see. It may be a little unsettling. This life review will reveal the importance of what was in your heart, and all the thoughts and emotions held secret within. Your soul records everything you do, think, or feel, every second of your life, along with any effect these had on others. Even your dreams are stored away, in case they need to be referenced. A lot of it is chaff, of course. Not everything has some deep meaning. But patterns form by repetition, and beliefs influence your body, your experiences, other people, animals, plants, and even the Earth. The intent behind actions is frequently the measuring stick by which those actions are evaluated. The spirit guide and council are looking for evidence you learned how to think and act with love and empathy, working through problems by listening to your higher self and your spirit guide. While your life is on display and reviewed, no other souls or council members judge you. Your soul, now resonating on a spiritual frequency, evaluates each part of the life from this place of greater wisdom. There will be input from the other spirits assembled, but it is done in a loving and supportive way to help you interpret from their more advanced perspective. In this space of light and love, you will find none of the dangers convincingly yelled into the cameras each Sunday by red-faced televangelists. Your soul will not be judged and condemned upon arrival. There is no cloven-hoofed goat-man standing by, ready to carry your wretched soul down to some fiery lake where you will roast for all eternity. These are fables, repeated endlessly through the centuries, crafted only to scare people into obedience and submission.

I've had to do a bit of research when writing about certain unfamiliar topics, and the way religious organizations describe heaven to their devotees was one of those areas. I must admit to being a little surprised by what these groups promote. Some Muslims, it seems, will get wine, but no hangovers, very nice jewelry, luxurious robes, rivers of milk and honey, immense wealth, and sex with lots of virginal slaves who your spouse can't see. As best I could decipher, atheists and Jews can expect to have their awareness come to an abrupt end in nothingness. Christians don't really have much verbiage in their historical reference material about heaven, except in the last story in their Bible, Revelations. Someone named John conjured up a big gated community to keep out the riffraff, where the walls are made of jasper and have twelve pearly gates. Once the soul slips past the guards and makes it into the city they will find the streets are paved with solid gold and there are fruit trees growing on each side of a river. Seems like the Muslims are going to be having the most fun, eh? Well, before you go looking for a mosque so you can get in on their action, be advised those earthly pleasures are not available to you in the great beyond. The body stays on Earth, and the soul has no ability to drink, eat, and make babies. While it is possible that these places exist as temporary mental creations in the fourth dimension, it is definitely not part of the spiritual reality where your higher self is located.

The lesser emotional states of a human do not exist within the spiritual dimensions. What you will see, as a spirit looking back on Earth life, is that the primal struggle for survival of the body gives rise to fear and a sense of separation, which in turn generates non-spiritual emotions such as hate, greed, anger, arrogance, jealousy, cruelty, envy, and indifference. Even love, as often defined, is a watered-down version exchanged with contingencies and selfish motives. We have all been on the giving or receiving end of various physical, emotional, and mental interactions involving suffering, sorrow, abuse, loneliness, fear, anger, and loss. As we progress over many lifetimes, we learn to accept and deal with life's hardships, and do our best in these difficult circumstances to remain true to our spiritual self. Graduates from the Earth school have developed a level of emotional understanding and a strength of will and determination that most other realities do not provide. The most important lesson to learn, however, is empathy.

In a recent discussion, Zachariah opened the floor for me to get clarification on a few topics. So I asked how spirits see their past lives, and if any of the lesser emotions follow them home. His reference to a little chip will be covered in more detail, but it is essentially an energetic recording made within the soul during an incarnation, which is carried back home for analysis and inclusion within that spirit's personal journal.

- D. When a soul returns back home and rejoins its spirit, it doesn't bring back all the memories of its actions and everything it has done on Earth, does it?
- Z. It is stored in a little chip, if you like. The soul can absolutely have a look, but it is not colored, it doesn't color the soul. But it is available to look at and review. Research is done from the spirit realm. See it as your own journal, if you like. You are still allowed to look backwards in your journal, are you not? This is the same, but it is creating an objective standpoint to

your actions and thoughts, so in that regard it is not connected to you as a spirit.

D. The feelings that are Earth related, like guilt?

Z. They don't follow you.

D. When you look backwards on things that you have done, you don't feel the same sensations?

Z. You might, in a younger state of your evolution, have a problem understanding when you return and look at certain occurrences. Let's say your question was about fear. From a spiritual standpoint, from your soul's perspective, that doesn't exist. As you progress, you will remember and understand more of that bubble of fear, what that was. A younger soul needs assistance to understand that specific feeling, as it doesn't resonate with their soul. But it is true, it doesn't belong in the spiritual realm, and it doesn't follow the soul. It relates to this plane where that memory exists, or has been placed. Know that certain things, as fear and judgement, for instance, are in some way put in the Earth's atmosphere, its aura, if you like, in order for souls coming in to encounter them. If they didn't exist in a reality, they will not be experienced.

D. And the purpose of experiencing it, is what?

Z. To increase your knowledge. To have boundaries, struggles, challenges, put in front of you. In the spiritual reality, those do not exist.

D. Is it to strengthen the knowledge and willpower of souls?

Z. It is the power of creating thoughts and actions based on challenges that arise. Not all realities carry this experience. Due to certain actions that have happened priorly in Earth's existence, it is stored in the Earth's memory. Meaning, it is in its energetic atmosphere. Everything carries karma related to where it has occurred.

Soul development on this plane is a progression from selfish to selfless, from ignorance to understanding. We learn lessons about the physical body, our emotional and mental processes, and finally about the spiritual nature of being human. An example of some lessons about these concepts comes from a vivid dream Christine had recently, where she remembered a near-death experience she had in her last life as a woman named Alicia. Christine first recalled this lifetime during a past-life regression she had in 2011. We are including this to show how a soul experiences passing through the mental realm.

Alicia lived in Virginia and died in 1968 at the age of 56. Prior to her death, Alicia collapsed on the platform of a train station and had an NDE. Christine recounts that after Alicia left her body, she began having a life review, where the first part concerned the physical experiences. Alicia was shown actions, feelings and thoughts relating to the body. She saw herself as a child who fell over on her bike and scrapped her knee. Her mother came and comforted her and, after bandaging the knee, encouraged the little girl to get back on the bike and keep riding. The girl was quite afraid, but did finally summon the courage to overcome the fear of getting hurt. The next scene showed her as a young woman being pushed by someone, which was followed by a scene of her hugging a child. In each of the scenes, she felt the effects of those actions on both her physical body and the body of the other person. She realized the powerful healing and exchange of energy that can occur from hugging another person. During the second part of the NDE, Alicia was shown the emotional aspects of her entire life and their effects on other people. She saw her interactions and how her lack of self-love caused her to push others away emotionally. However, she also experienced the uplifting moments when she felt and expressed love and compassion for others. In the third part of the NDE, which was the most intense, she had to experience every thought she had during her life. She could objectively see how her thoughts had caused unnecessary suffering for herself and others. Throughout the three stages of the NDE, there were clear lessons relating to each aspect of being human. And so it is with each of us. Our lives present an ongoing opportunity to improve the way we think, feel and act towards ourselves, others, and the world around us. Through repeated incarnations the soul gradually learns the best way to avoid being hurt is to not hurt others, and develops the strength, the courage, and the will to stay true to the essence of its soul, which is in harmony with the Creator.

The conscious mind may not recognize the relationship between thoughts and what happens to the incarnated body, but the soul has the full understanding of this feedback loop. People who have NDEs, or do between-life regression therapy, can often see how thoughts and beliefs become the source of many situations in their life. From this perspective, it becomes clear the life we have is the life we planned and created. Our own soul designed many of the struggles before we incarnated, as a way to test ourselves. So, instead of seeing life as random events that happen to you from the outside, shift awareness inward and see these events as an obstacle course you set up yourself. The hand of fate may be offering a gift of knowledge, if looked at in this way. By accepting our experiences, it gives us permission to release negative responses and try to live moment to moment with more peace and love in our hearts. To use a simple example, if you have a stressful day at work, do you carry anger and sullenness with you on the drive home, to the grocery store, to dinner with the family, and finally to bed? We need to view every moment of the day as an opportunity to choose peace within ourselves, and to offer that peace to other people. As Zachariah pointed out in one of our readings, life is a treasure, a gift to you.

D. What other topics should we discuss in the book?

Z. The treasure of life. That life can be a treasure. It can sparkle and it can be joyful. Make people want to seek more. Make people dive into their own history. Why do they feel certain ways, why do they act in another? Where do they come from and where do the lessons they stumble upon come from? Make them understand that when coming into physical, they go through a process of wanting to learn a specific aspect, emotion or event. If they are judgmental, or even irresponsible, they have picked events to trigger that. It is not life that is punishing them. Together with their spiritual guidance and beings and helpers, they choose their path and events. Nothing is done by coincidence.

Morality, from a spiritual sense, is a personal pursuit. Religions often use their definition of morality as a cover for controlling, judging, and attacking others. True morality is, at its core, compassion for all creatures, not just other humans. It is to be kind and patient with other people, to uplift and encourage them to honor their soul. If you have a bad day at work, that should not be an excuse to drive aggressively to the grocery store, where you snarl at the cashier, before going home to ignore the children and yell at your husband or wife over some trivial issue. Those are all pebbles thrown in the lake of your life, so what sort of ripples and waves do you want to be remembered for? This is something to take seriously, because those who have a life review during NDEs see how their behavior and intentions created both good and bad experiences in the lives of others. Your contribution to what someone else experiences becomes your responsibility. I will point out, although it should be obvious, that this discussion is about interacting with others in normal situations. You also have a right to protect your body, which was a gift to you, from being injured or killed by some random act of violence. There is no spiritual mandate for you, or those who rely on you for protection, to be someone else's victim.

What we call the conscience is really your soul or your spirit guides trying to encourage you towards a path that will cause less suffering. After every life, the soul returns home and sees with great clarity how its thoughts and patterns of belief created much of what it experienced during the lifetime. After a period of study, rest, and reflection, the spirit vows to not repeat the same mistakes, and sends part of itself to Earth again, taking on a new body, hoping to prove it mastered the lessons. As the soul overcomes difficulties, its knowledge increases, and the inner voice becomes stronger and easier to follow. When the conscious mind and the soul are in harmony, thoughts become more understanding and empathetic of others, more patient and kind. While incarnated, you are constantly given opportunities to show your thoughts are aligned with your spirit. Every moment contains that choice. We are all imperfect, but being self-aware greatly improves the odds of success in overcoming patterns of the past.

Between lifetimes, the soul studies and reviews how it handled the situations that it faced during this and other lifetimes. Here are a few of these universal truths recounted by people from between life regressions and NDEs:

- You are only responsible for yourself and your own thoughts and actions. You can try to help others by sharing knowledge and encouragement, but you are not responsible for the choices they make.

- Birth and death is the revolving door between the Earth and the spirit realm, a passing from one state of awareness into another. Since your soul is eternal and cannot be destroyed, you should not live in fear of death.

- You are never given more challenges than your soul can bear.

- The two most important things in life are expressing love and gaining knowledge.

- Do not take everything so seriously, as most things are not as important as you think they are.
- Happiness is a result of choice. Seek to accentuate the positive aspects of a situation. Your true nature, as a soul, is one of joy and love.
- Do not wait for life to happen to you. If you want to do something more with your life, begin it now.
- Decisions are often made from a place of fear. Choose instead to trust in the Creator and your spirit helpers, knowing you are always being guided.
- Even small acts of kindness can have far-reaching effects.
- If you don't love and accept yourself, you can never love anyone else properly. No amount of affirmations from someone else can overcome self-rejection.
- Anger held inside can be very harmful to yourself and to others. Anger expressed can be even more harmful to yourself and others, so practice forgiveness and learn to release negative thoughts.
- Try to focus more on the present. Your mind is like a hamster in a wheel when you obsess over the past or worry about the future, and gets you about as far—nowhere.
- You are never alone, and you are always loved by those in the spiritual world, even if you are unaware.
- Life is mostly the little things, one after another, as each small activity becomes part of the continuous film of your time here. Be aware that many things can be done with a sense of gratitude and joy, like pouring a cup of coffee, inhaling the crisp air of winter, watching a hawk fly overhead, or walking in nature. All these are an opportunity to engage with your inner self.
- You came to Earth with a mission, a blueprint that is important for your soul. As long as you are alive, your mission is not over.

- Compassion means you do not judge others for where they are on the ladder of soul development. The path from ignorance to wisdom is a long and difficult journey we must each walk alone, so have empathy for those who have further to travel than do you.
- Because thoughts are an energy with a creative force, prayer does have an effect on others and the world.
- Be grateful for what you have. Think about the people who care about you. Think about your health and, even if you have ailments or diseases, how your body has supported you all these years. Reflect on the beauty in nature, the oceans, the trees, the plants, the soil, the animals, the sun, and the wind. Life is a gift to you.

The most common lesson shared by the thousands of people who have reported back from the realm of spirit is the requirement for each of us to be more loving towards others, ourselves and the Earth. No matter what kind of life you have led in the past, it's not too late to change. You still have free will to choose a better path. Patterns not addressed in this lifetime will produce similar experiences in another lifetime. Within almost every situation, choices exist on how we respond. Physically, emotionally, and mentally, we are accountable for the decisions we make on this plane.

Now that we have looked at some of the lessons learned from previously departed souls, or those who were on the threshold of that status, it may be a good time to study what your thoughts really are, from a spiritual perspective.

# *The Mental Realm*

The mental realm is the fourth dimension, a vibrational reality between the frequency of the physical Earth and that of the spirit world. On planets that support life, the third dimension is always paired with the fourth dimension. Spiritual energy cannot become physical, so the fourth is needed as a bridge between the two realities. It could be called the mental atmosphere, as it occupies space around the planet. This is where the rubber meets the road, so to speak. For it is within this realm that all soul-to-soul communication takes place, and where memories from your lives are stored, forever. It is a stage upon which your mind and emotions are the main actors, and the play they put on is used to evaluate your life. Understanding the function of the mental realm can unlock the meaning behind other spiritual teachings in this book, so it is worthwhile to slow down and think about the ideas in this section.

While your soul is within your body, it connects with seven centers, or inner layers, and each of them can send out energy in the form of waves or pulses. The most important ones are the emotional layer and the mental layer, but the physical body and the soul itself can also send out waves of energy. The spirits refer to all these transmissions as thought bubbles, regardless of the layer of origin. When you have a thought or a feeling, it energizes one of these layers to act like a little radio transmitter, sending signals out into the mental realm, this invisible cloud around the Earth. Imagine sitting in front of a computer that's hooked up to your brain and your heart, where every thought and feeling you have gets typed up in a message and automatically sent to whomever you are thinking about. All day long, you are typing and sending, typing and sending. Simultaneously, you are receiving messages. Whatever anyone thinks or feels about you, it is automatically delivered, raw and unfiltered. These thought bubbles sent back and forth are not normally recognized by the conscious mind, but the soul is very much aware of the messages. Thought bubbles are on the same frequency as the soul, and since the soul resides in the shadows of most people's awareness, the information is detected only as a gut feeling or intuition. Those who have specifically developed their sensitivity to these signals are called psychic, and may be able to see this energy around people as auras, and interpret the physical, emotional, or mental patterns being emitted. Animals, also, can read auras, and are good at gauging the intentions flowing off bodies. Our guides and other spiritual beings monitor this energy flow and can read our thoughts as if they were words.

Every spirit has a profile of its contributions to the Earth, and this is what our spirit friends refer to as the Coat of Karma. The fourth dimension is the vibrational reality where your life is recorded and added to the history of all the lives you have had on this plane. But what exactly is life, other than your daily actions, feelings, and thoughts? So, in essence, your Coat is a running record of how your ideas have changed over time. What karma teaches is that waking life is a series of decisions, from beginning to end, nothing more. Decisions about what to think or feel cause your energetic body to send a corresponding tone, sort of like ringing a bell with distinct sounds for each type of emotion or thought. As those tones travel out into the mental realm, they act as an invitation for certain experiences to come your way. The energy you transmit becomes a beacon to similar energies. By ringing your bell with certain notes, you are asking for a response in kind. This is how we learn to avoid sending out the wrong vibrations, and as we become more aware of our signals, the way we experience life becomes more harmonious.

Karma is about balance, a system of cause and effect whereby we learn how to live within a human body in ways that are spiritually acceptable. If your soul does not approve of how you think and act, then life will give you countless opportunities to understand why those patterns should be updated and replaced with more spiritual alternatives. You will continually be confronted with situations that are a mirror to your beliefs. For example, people often have problems in their relationships that share a recurring theme, but within the pattern, there is usually some form of self-discovery awaiting your observation. For me, it was a lack of self-love, which made me feel sort of worthless and unlovable.

To the spiritual world, thought bubbles look like colored smoke rising up from your body and pouring into the mental atmosphere. Bob humorously refers to this cloud of energy as the chimney, and just as a chimney can get filthy from burning certain woods, your Coat gets heavy with energetic dirt when you act, feel, or think in ways that are not in resonance with your higher self. In this next discussion, Bob described the process whereby spirits anticipate what humans or other animals are intending to do, and how they can intervene by putting their own thought bubbles into the mental realm of people. I should mention that it is impossible to capture the way Bob talks in writing. He is very enthusiastic, and he speaks in a way that adds a lot of extra meaning to words and ideas. He is about as far from monotone as someone could be, and will often use his wit to turn serious discussions into funny stories.

- D. I had a question about how you see the world. You can hear things that humans do, so I guess you can hear sound waves. Do you hear them talking and understand the language?
- B. Hmm, well, no, sometimes it just sounds like bubbles, it's like having my ears underwater, sometimes it just sounds like, blub blub blub. But I can read the energies, so that's what I do. I don't understand the words, BUT the words create certain energy frequencies from the individual, regardless of if it's a person, or if it's an animal. Apes, for instance, they talk too, but they send out their intentions, which is like their thoughts and how they want to verbalize it, as an energy wave, and I can read that. So, it doesn't matter what sort of language, of course, it is. Let's say I see a humanoid in nature, and it communicates with another one, I don't necessarily understand the words, but I understand the waves and I can read them, and I can read the intention they are having. If there is someone, let's say, wanting to create a fire, then I can respond and I can send out like, "DON'T". I put that in a mental bubble and then put it into their chimney. That's what we do, we're responding. Because, let's say, here (*referring to the arid mountains of Colorado*), you're not supposed to build fires, create fires. If I were to see someone THINKING about doing that, I would understand, because thinking and talking is almost the same for me. I can read the intentions the SAME WAY. I don't need to hear anything, really. I read the frequency of a thought or a verbal expression. If someone

says, "Oh, let's start a fire, let's make food." If I, or any of the other little helpers in nature, read that intention, and it is not a proper place for a fire, we will send a message, a response. So they detect this action that is about to take place, and we send a reaction to it into a thought bubble, and into their chimney. Some listen, some do not.

D. So, as people go about their day, are their spirit guides and other beings always popping pictures in their mind?

B. Yes, of course.

We are raised to believe the important goals in life are to get a high-paying job, act nice enough for someone to want to marry us, buy a house and a couple of cars, and breed a few more babies into the world. Throw in annual vacations, a fun hobby, holiday celebrations, and you have the recipe for a good life, I hear. There is nothing wrong with any of those things, of course. Everyone wants a comfortable life and someone who cares about them. However, what you weren't told is that the true goal of your life is to master what goes on inside your head and heart every moment while you chase those external objectives. These subtle undercurrents define your success, or your lack of progress. Having a good job is wonderful, but how do you interact with the co-workers? Being married is delightful, but what sort of energy do you radiate when there is a little friction? You may think life is about chasing your dreams, but it is actually about working on your Coat of Karma. When you pass over, it is hung neatly in a closet with your spirit's name on it, waiting for your return in another life. As Ophelia says, we are given an inner filter and are able to control and monitor all the messages we send. If that is done consciously and continuously, life will take on an entirely different meaning and value.

The next logical question would be, how do I go about making the Coat of Karma lighter? Or better yet, folding it so I no longer need to come to Earth? Zachariah explains the way this process works.

Z. Thoughts. This is where you need to be more delicate. The energy of thoughts. People have the understanding that a thought is only within themselves. They do not know that if they think a negative thought, it will affect not only the surrounding, but as well their Coat, because it is silent in their mind. Remember that people on this plane do not necessarily practice the telepathic communication. Other beings more evolved in that specific communication understand the power of thoughts. Here, if you think a negative thought, yet don't speak it out loud, it's never occurred, has it? From a human standpoint, that is sometimes their reality. The power of thought creates not only an effect on the physical plane, but most of all within the mental realm. You cannot escape those creations as you leave the physical body and move into the spiritual power and your soul energy. If someone thinks bad about others, but doesn't say it out loud, it does not just remain inside their head.

D. Is it, in effect, a negative prayer?

Z. Indeed. It creates like a fog on waves. And it creates that mental realm around you. Spiritual beings inclined to be able to read others can see this field, not only around the planet, of course, but around each individual. It is that Coat, that layer, that there is no way to escape, if you like, but also to deal with. Know that higher evolved beings are reading all mental realms around not only celestial bodies, but as well around each individual on Earth. THEY can read the mental realm, seeing what's going on, predicting where mankind is trying to go. Do you understand?

D. Yes, I do.

Z. It's like an open book. People are afraid of it because if you say it like that, they will feel like they are supervised. Again, that equals to a lot of people like punishment and judgement. If you lift forward the other aspect of it, that if they are thinking good thoughts about others, that is acknowledged as well. That is how the spirit realm can see who is enlightened or not. It is shown as, like white dots, bright shining dots from the spiritual realm.

B. *(Christine's voice shifted as Bob took over, continuing Zachariah's thought)* Uhmmm, you know the satellites around the planet? They leave stuff out in space, hanging around like trash. It's the same thing, because when all these negative souls, or souls who did not really listen to their mission, when they leave and they leave all these Coats in the mental realm, it's still there. It's like leaving trash in space.

D. How can that be cleaned up?

B. It's because new souls are coming in, and they don't have a Coat. Some that are leaving will not return for a while. When new ones come in who don't have a Coat here, then the number of enlightened beings will increase.

One of the concepts I had struggled to understand was about thought bubbles. I pictured it as a result of the thinking process, which is part of the logic and reasoning. But Ophelia clarified that the "thought" bubbles we send out can be from any of the vibrational layers within the body, which includes the physical and the emotional. A feeling of joy, for example, would radiate energy from the emotional heart center, just the same as contemplating the colors in a beautiful sunset would transmit energy from the mental layer associated with the brain. Two different locations within the physical body, but both the feeling and the thought are a source of creation within the mental realm. We, as the soul, can control different vibrations within the body, and are therefore responsible for what is transmitted by our body.

D. When we talk about the mental realm, or the realm of logic, the brain, the thoughts that people think are primarily from the logical aspect aren't they? Emotions are more of a sensation?

O. It is a way for your human self to comprehend the two different realities, indeed. Yet both are triggered and set off as a thought bubble. Even though it comes from the heart center, and is created like a sensation, as you referred to, it creates the same dynamic as a pure thought from the brain. So, a prayer can come from both centers, if you like. People struggle with this notion of having an emotion set off as a thought. Again, we are talking about separation and polarity, but they are the same.

D. That is very helpful. I, too, got stuck with that concept.

O. It's the same bubble they send off, regardless of where it comes from. On some level, even the physical can send off thought bubbles, even though they are more like little ones. All layers that operates within a human capacity and understanding has the possibility to send off their thought bubbles, emotional bubbles, or physical bubbles, if you like.

D. That's very helpful to me.

O. They all get stored in the mental realm.

D. So would a pure soul emotion also be a thought bubble that emanates from the heart center?

O. Clarify.

D. Like a feeling of love, that's not necessarily a thought.

O. Yes. Yes, it is.

D. It goes out like a thought bubble, but it's a feeling?

O. Yes, it is the same. It's an energetic form, it's a wave, a frequency. Just different frequencies, my friend, stored in the same reality, the fourth, the mental realm. Just different frequencies. One moves faster, one moves slower. One carries more of a color tone in it, the emotional one. It's a faster frequency. The brain moves slower, if you try to compare it. I'm creating a picture for you.

D. Human emotions, are those faster or slower than the mental?

O. The pure emotion *(Here she means the spiritual emotions like love and empathy)* has the same vibration regardless of where it is, yet encased in the physical vehicle, it tends to slow down. So, its surroundings affect the frequency as it leaves the source from where it has departed, yet the purity within it carries the same frequency regardless of whether the emotion is sent off from pure spirit realm, or from a physical vehicle. But as soon as it starts to depart, it gets confused on this level. It moves through some sort of vibrating surroundings, your atmosphere, if you like, and this is how it gets sometimes lost. The vibration around in the spiritual reality does not carry those tones that interfere with the pure sent off emotion or intent. That is *why* it becomes a pure emotion, or a pure thought. Due to the surrounding on this reality where you are located at this point, everything that is sent off has to travel through...it's almost like a mist. It's a field that is different; that's why it also appears different from this level than it does from a spiritual reality.

D. Your description is very helpful, very helpful.

The mental realm around the Earth, where memories are stored, was the subject of many of our early discussions. Zachariah describes how the Coat of Karma can be cleaned up, and how important it is to become aware of your thoughts and to control what is sent out into the mental realm.

D. Are there other topics you plan on sharing with us in the future?

Z. Yes. The topic about how we create the mental realm, how we are responsible and also at fault if we send out negative energy waves. This is about knowing that we could control the thoughts we are sending out. If a negative thought arise, we have the power of the mind to stop it, to only send out those waves of thoughts that are beneficial for the surrounding. The mental realm is easy for a huge part of the community down on Earth to understand. Thoughts, even though they are carried over waves, are something that people understand.

**The Coat of Karma**
One of the primary lessons the spirit team wants to get across is how your thoughts and actions not only impact you while you are in a body, but how it becomes a larger challenge after the body dies. They have said all memories get recorded in two places simultaneously. One place is within your own spiritual body, like a little video recorder with unlimited storage capacity. The other place is within the mental realm, the vibrational layer where your soul sends and receives information, and this remains with the Earth after you leave. As your soul enters the transitional vibration between Earth and the pure spirit realm, it encounters everything you created while living. If there is a lot of negative energy, it can even cause the soul to become stuck for a while. Then, as if that weren't bad enough, your Coat of Karma holds all these memories, and when you return to Earth again, it must be put back on. So, the next body will assume a lot of the same character traits the previous life had when it ended, along with the burdens of unresolved conflicts with specific souls, and feelings and beliefs that were not in resonance with spiritual vibrations. There is no escaping yourself. The only way to clean the Coat is to have the desire and the will to change yourself from within.

> Z. We will begin with it in an easy form. That you create the passage from when you leave this planet. The passage until you reach the higher realms is the mental realm. That is the part where souls have to cross before they reach their spirit energy, when they release. In this realm; first you release the physical, later you release the mental that is related to this planet in order for you to transform into the spirit form. As you are transformed into spirit, then the mental and physical aspects related to the Earth would have left...or would have...oh, let's see. This is what you need to remember; as each soul leaves the planet, leaving the physical, it will transition through the mental realm. THIS is also the place they go through when they go back in to the planet. Karma

doesn't follow the soul into the spirit realm. Karma is only stored in the mental realm. As you descend down to the Earth again, you will come in contact with every thought, every physical aspect that you have done on this plane. It's like coming in and taking on your Coat again!

D. That's a wonderful analogy.

Z. So as you leave the mental realm, where you create heaven on Earth...or hell, if you like. But what is hell? Hell is the karmic debt you leave. You are fully aware as a soul what you have done as you transition into the mental realm, before departure into the soul energy. Know that karma doesn't follow the soul up into the celestial home where it belongs.

D. That's a very good description, thank you.

Z. As you return, there is no way for you to come back in, and not come in contact with this Coat of yours. **The Coat of Karma**. It belongs and is attached to the soul, and there is no way of returning into whatever realm you choose to travel to without coming in contact with your prior visits to that specific place. Each Coat is individual.

D. So, if a soul incarnates in another planet or location...

Z. *(Interrupts)* Yes! Yes, then it's not the same Coat.

D. Interesting, that is very unique.

Z. Not really. You cannot carry karma from place to place. It is related to where it has occurred. Some Coats are heavier where the lessons are harder, then the Coats are also thicker. It's like a cape you have to carry; some of them are quite heavy.

D. How are the Coats on Earth?

Z. Heavy. It's like a cape. Understand that due to its density caused by what the soul has done here before, for some, it is hard to carry. That's why repeatedly, they have to return to understand and to *want* to change this Coat. If you don't want to change it, there is no way of coming back without repeating the same patterns. That is what awakening means. It's to come in contact with the power of choice and to be fed up with that heavy Coat!

D. That is such a good description. I really appreciate the concept.

Z. Use it if you like, make people understand that when they travel back and forth there's no way to escape their Coat. But also, make them aware that when they leave these two realms *(The physical Earth and the fourth dimension around it)* they return in full spirit into the purest light. There's no judgment of the soul. The life review, or judgment, that we don't like to talk about, only refers to the Coat. Never to the soul. New souls have a problem as they come back and dress again. Old souls can operate in a heavy Coat easier. They don't become the Coat, newer souls become their Coats. That's why it takes a little time to evolve. Soul evolution is to understand that you are not the Coat, even though you wear it.

D. Hmm...that is excellent.

Z. And that's where you can see the difference in how far a soul has come in its own evolution. Look at them and see if they are the Coat. See the soul, see the Coat, and see if they are in one, and understand that this specific soul has a little bit more work to do. If you see a soul that might carry a heavy Coat, meaning...traumas. Not necessarily things that they have done, but what others have done to them. This Coat is not only carrying what we, or the soul has done, but what it has experienced. Those souls you will identify as being pure spirit with a heavy Coat...see the difference in what the soul has done, and what has been done to them. Those who carry a jacket or a Coat where others have caused them distress are in need of healing. There is a way, on this plane, to identify those who have suffered injustices done by others—their Coat is slightly different in color, my friend. Use your third eye to see what Coat it is.

Zachariah, Bob, and I had several discussions about the responsibility of each person to their karma, and if some divine being could take away all the negative karma a person had accumulated during their life, as many Christians believe. They were very firm about the "sins" of people being non-transferable. No higher being is going to wave their hand and let you off the hook for all your unspiritual creations on this plane of existence. However, people often feel unnecessary guilt and fear over inconsequential things. The core structure of most organized religions is based on their ability to "save" your soul from a fate which they themselves fabricated. They terrorize people with threats of eternal damnation, which has become the cornerstone of their belief system, but there is no spiritual basis for those claims. Your actions will be judged, but never your soul, which is pure. Granted, actions have consequences, but the soul will not be condemned for those actions. Your higher self will be the only judge of your life, but with that comes responsibility for your creations, all of them. You, and you alone, are the only one who can undo the errors of your thoughts and actions. Bob gave an amusing comparison of returning to spirit, to someone going into a restaurant and checking their old Coat of Karma at the door. When they leave the restaurant, or incarnate again, they don't want to pick up their dirty, heavy Coat. What our spirit friends are saying is that no one can avoid taking on patterns developed or karma resulting from previous lifetimes.

   B. Well if someone can just come in and take your Coat, then that's just lovely! But an enlightened species, that you are supposed to be, should understand that you are all carrying your own Coat...then... *(Laughs loudly)*...just see how people will respond!

   B. *(Loudly)* Oh, such ignorance! To just stand behind someone else's experience and to not deal with your own! Icons, like Jesus, did not come to take Coats from other people. That is a misconception that HE will just collect everyone's Coat. Lovely, I suppose, because you don't have to carry your own. Some are really heavy, and of course it's easier to just feel like you are going into a restaurant and you leave the Coat...hehehe...the Coat to someone in the door. (*Bob really was amused by his analogy, and chuckled while giving this description.*) Here you go...just take it! And then, when you go out you can choose to not pick it up? Oh, that's just not how it's done, it's not how it works. I'm sure everyone feels like that's a lovely idea.

   B. People need to be aware of that there's no way around taking, or picking up your Coat in the restaurant as you leave! *(Laughs loudly)* Because you've got the number!!!! You've got the little ticket with the number!! Hahahaha! And if you don't, someone has your phone number written down on the note, so if you don't pick it up, they will call!! Hahahaha! There's no way to get around that one, even though some might try! Well, well, well. (*He laughs a little bit, and then gives a big sigh.*)

   The process the soul goes through upon death of the body was an occasional topic of conversation. The message our spirit team wants to get across is that the ease or stressfulness of this transition is determined by the choices made during the lifetime.

Bob, Zachariah, and Ophelia all discussed the difficulty some souls encounter when they leave this plane, especially those who are too involved with the lower emotions or have negative mental attachments. Once the soul is out of the body, it is suddenly thrust into a world of its own creation. All the memories of what it did during life are revealed from a different perspective. All the pain and suffering it caused others, along with all the happy memories and love that was shared are there for reevaluation. Over many lifetimes, the soul becomes better at navigating the obstacle course of being human, so the transition after death becomes easier. In their description of the Coat of Karma, Zachariah and Bob both talked about how a soul is eventually able to fold his Coat and put it in a closet, which is symbolic for having successfully learned certain lessons on this plane. Those spirits are no longer required to come to Earth. They can choose to come back to teach, or assist in some specific mission, but they no longer incur karma as a result of the visit.

D. I had a question about the mental realm. When souls die, when they lose their body and have to travel through the mental realm. If they have attachments to ideas, like say a Christian and his concept of heaven, or a Muslim, or whatever. Are they stuck in the mental realm until they release that, then they can travel on?

B. It doesn't matter where the idea is, it's the idea itself... (*Bob then became confused about the question.*) Oh, what did you mean?

D. Do peoples' belief keep them stuck in the mental realm?

B. Yes, yes. Because it's the thought.

D. So when they release it they can travel on to the spirit realm?

B. Uh, oh, you made the question a little bit too long. Wait.

D. I can rephrase.

B. Please.

D. When a person dies, do they have to release their beliefs before they can return home?

B. It's automatic. Once you have left the mental realm, where you left all your beliefs and actions and thoughts, then you move into the spiritual being and there is nothing following you. There is nothing following you, everything is in pure spirit as you leave that layer. However, some stay on that plane for a while if they need to release more. This is where some transitions take a little longer.

D. Ah, yes. That was my question.

B. You know, there is a little bit of a truth of those souls hanging around for a while. They're not bad, necessarily. They just are too attached to actions and beliefs and they do not return to their pure spiritual being. So they can remain a little while, appearing like a ghost in a closet! *(Bob laughs at this).* But, there is no need to be like a ghost buster! It solves itself when the soul is ready.

D. Is the mental realm around the Earth, like a...?

B. Like a shell. Like an egg.

D. How thick is this mental realm?

B. It's a little bit based on how you...if you have done a lot of wrongs on this plane, then where you leave it is actually a little bit thicker. For those with folded jackets, it's almost non-existent. It's like going through the surface of the water. You don't really feel that, do you?

D. No.

B. No, you don't. But for some it's like going through jelly, sticky. Moving through even slower. Some get stuck. It's like when you see like bugs stuck on glue. Glued on. But this is what we want you to address in your book, that people, in order for them to transcend into the pure spirit, they need to work on their aspects and beliefs and actions on this realm. Otherwise, they might get stuck in the mental! Like a bug on a piece of glue! That might help them do some work before dying, if they knew that they will get stuck like a spider in glue! Oh, everyone would like to rush through like when you go through the surface of the water. That is possible, of course.

D. If a person has led a life that is not very positive, and they decide to change, does it clear up a lot of the past?

B. Mmm. Both past and the mental realm. Both.

D. Does a change in their heart, in their mindset, automatically clear a lot of the...

B. It changes the passage, the transition. That's how they know they managed their assignment. A soul knows how it transitioned the last time. The reward for doing good is first felt as they leave the physical into the mental realm. They have to pass through all the thoughts they had, even if they didn't say it. That can be kind of a traumatic experience for some. Especially if you have to stay there for a while and dwell on it. That's no good. Everyone wants to leave as soon as possible. But if you transition through this realm in the purest way of how you lived, then it's simply like swimming in the ocean. Just passing through, everything will wash off. Then the soul knows it did well.

D. That's very good. Thank you for that. What else would you like to share today?

B. Oh, hmm. Oh, mainly just to be a part of everything, of how the giants *(Bob refers to Ophelia and Zachariah as giants, because their spirit bodies are so large)* are putting forward their messages, and to bring a little bit of insight from a different perspective. And just to be acknowledged for some of the views. After taking notes so many times, I want to share and learn as well.

D. I'm glad you took notes. It's been very helpful.

B. It's important, you know. Otherwise, you might forget the essentials of your mission. Every soul coming into this reality brings their notes on the inside, like a sparkle. I, who work a little bit differently, I store my knowledge in another way.

Christine and I often do the midweek trance channeling out in the mountains west of Denver. I was between jobs during the summer of 2016, so we had the freedom to spend quite a bit of time in nature, which seems to be appreciated by our spirits when they come to talk. During a session we held in a beautiful canyon along the South Platte River, Zachariah was explaining how thoughts are actually creations, a little bundle of energy that goes out and interacts with other energy fields in the mental realm.

Z. Thought is a creation, and it departs from the source of where thought was created and starts to move, like a soap bubble. See and be aware of the journey of the thought. It is easy to look at it as a soap bubble, like when you blow a bubble with those things you had as a child, and you set it off towards a specific destination. But it manifests in the receiving end, and this is something people should know. Be aware that a thought can create so much good, but also a lot of damage, depending on the intention you had with the thought. So, when you send off your soap bubble, you have the power to make sure the soap bubble you let go of are those of light.

D. Does that have to do with the feelings, the emotion attached to it?

Z. It's strongly connected with the intent, if it carries an intent or not. If you send it off without the intention of creating harm, then the bubble has less power to be manifested. It's all about the intention you have with your thoughts, because you have the power to go over and to control your thoughts. The power of thought lies in your intention with it, understanding that a certain thought can just recycle within the source of where it arose. But as you send it off, it is sort of free in the Universe to create, and you lose power over it. That is the dangerous part, because as it is sent off, like that bubble, you lose the power of returning it. When it lands at that specific destination, you, as the transmitter, are in some way connected to it. That is the "return to sender" part of karma. So when you have, with your intention, sent it off, you lose the power over it. However, as it manifests, for good or bad, it also is connected to you. That is the whole meaning of what you send out is what you attract. So it is important to be aware of and understand that not only do you create scenarios with your thoughts, but they can have an effect regardless of distance. A thought travels like an electric wave.

D. It's not diminished by space and time?

Z. No, no. It changes, it's electric. It's like each is carrying an electric code, and that can change as it moves through different layers. But from this specific realm, it's harder for it to leave and go into other realities. It's sort of homebound or closed in a specific region. It can change its structure, but it is still carrying electric codes within that bubble.

D. I guess thoughts aren't necessarily restricted then to the mental realm?

Z. A lot of them get stuck in that realm. The way it looks, the Earth is its own soap bubble, in a way. So a lot of what is going on inside here, which will contradict the general idea that thoughts travel as an electron through space and time, but, in some way, it is restricted here. It's like being encased in a bubble. Thought bubbles manifest a lot in the mental realm that surrounds this plane. It creates illusions in this realm.

D. But a prayer would rise through that?

## The Mental Realm    63

Z. Yes, yes it does. Especially when it is a collective. The power of a group prayer can push through the layers that are surrounding this field. So, the power of numbers directing certain prayer or thought, overcome a lot of the other ones. It's like the white cells in the body, it's a way to kill off that cold you get with a virus. So, the more people join with others, setting the same intention, as in a group prayer, it will affect the virus that others are sending into the mental realm. Incoming souls, that do not have their Coat here, have to travel through this layer of different illusions. So the more people are aware of creating with the power of their minds, the easier it will be for incoming souls to continue working with positive energy on a physical level.

D. Over time, do thoughts tend to dissipate or burn themselves out as they interact with the mental realm?

Z. No, no, they remain. It's like storing a memory in your computer. Unless you actively remove it, which you as a physical do not have the power to do, yet outer beings such as your spirit guides and light beings have the power to remove certain memories as it has moved over the karmic boundaries. So, let's say things you experienced on this plane, such as riots, revolutions and so forth in ancient times. Some of it has been removed from the Earth's memory in the mental realm, as it no longer serves a purpose, as well as equally strong experiences have sort of balanced the karma out. There is no need for it to be stored in the databank, if you like, the hardware of the memory of this plane. So yes, over time, the mental realm changes. It's like updating your computers after the storage has been over-used. But you do not do this, it's from a higher source, where they can let one episode balance out with another. That's why it's not completely filled from the beginning of time when this realm was created. Know that it was not there from the beginning. It was added later as the individuals inhabiting this plane were given the power of will and the power of thought, as their brain capacity and emotional centers progressed and grew. This is when this layer was activated in some way, and it grew. But see it as a computer. Your personal experiences are still stored, which you can access based on the timeline. You can go back and forth and still perceive what you have accomplished and what you have done. But the major, epic occurrences have changed in this specific databank. Not necessarily removed and forgotten, but stored in what would be considered as the general databank...

B. *(Bob came in mid-sentence)*...the vault of different things. The vault for the Earth plane covers all these stories, it looks almost like script roles. It's in the storage unit, in that vault, of the Earth. So you can still read up on it, if you have the keycard to it, but it's not necessarily active, but it is still accessible if you need to read up on it. Also, this would be for the masters who create bodies, so they do not create something similar that will cause the same effect over the evolution of this plane. So, it's a memory of each specific place, and it can be looked at if you look into those specific boxes. It's sort of marked with different ages. They tried with some animals to create a bigger brain, but it's not the same as now. Actually, there was a group of lizards that were very intelligent, but they had too much of an aggressive personality. So the blend with a highly intelligent brain, combined with a very aggressive and very predatory personality; that did not go well. That did not go well, so it's been addressed and it was removed. The individual of the lizard is still here, but it's not the same brain structure anymore. So, you see this a little bit in some individuals still on this plane. It's sort of inherited from that time. It's still a progress of blending the...you can see the problem with this, of course. To give man more brain capacity, like accessing your computer, having more computer memory, with that should come the understanding of how to use it wisely. And when the physical and the mental are not in sync and in harmony with the progress of the hardware, then it becomes a problem. This IS the key of evolution. This is what the light beings are designing, really.

Instead of altering Bob's words, I will just add a comment about what he is saying, so there is no confusion. In several sessions, our spirit friends said the size and configuration of the brain determines how much access a soul has to its higher self. Most animals have access to emotions, to a greater or lesser degree, but only minor access to the logic and reasoning layers. As the brain size, or hardware as Bob calls it, was increased, the mind becomes more logical and analytical. What the spirits discovered, through trial and error, is the larger brain combined with the physical, aggressive qualities of the primate posed a problem. Instead of using the brain in a positive way, humans have followed their ape-like instincts, plotting and planning how to become king of the jungle. There is a new model of humanoid being designed that will be more peaceful. The larger brain will have greater access to the spirit, and many of the primal, warlike qualities of the current physical body will be eliminated. In this conversation, Bob is describing how the spirits attempted to modify a lizard in the past, when they were studying how to structure human prototypes. Since they didn't say, I don't know if lizards were occupied by souls, or given their spiritual energy from the cloud connected to the Master Mind.

D. Could you rephrase that key of evolution?

B. It's the key; the key to evolution is the blend of increasing the hardware, the access to the greater source, combined with the physical, which in some way are also related to their brain. So, like the lizard, it did not bode well. It was an experiment, but because of their nature being very aggressive, and the quality of a higher developed brain, it did not blend very well. There was a conflict within these beings down here at that time. And now, there is a blending problem with incoming souls in current vehicles. You can see it, because we referred to it before as more of an intelligent being coming in. However, the physical bodies down here are not ready for bigger hardware, the computer inside. So this is what needs to be changed, and this is what the master plan, the key to evolution, is all about. It's the measurement of a bigger computer, a bigger hardware, and also those who are in charge of that specific download, meaning the physical body.

D. Is the human body going to be changed? In what way?

B. Yes, yes, it's going to be less combative. Because of the experiment that took place before you, where the brain capacity was enlarged, but it did not balance with the physical. So this time, in this specific vehicle that a human is, it will change. The personalities that people come into will soften, and it will be less combative. And also, they will be more inclined to share knowledge in order for them all to progress and create the mental realm differently. But, the physical vehicles down here have to change, and you CANNOT do that overnight. You can imagine how that will look—it will be very obvious. So this is what is happening, and it is due to the bigger computers, meaning the access to the whole *(here Bob refers to the higher self)* and to their own libraries, and the source, that's why the vehicle has to change. You will have less hair, that's going to be different. SO, there will be less hair on the human body, not that this will be noticed for everyone, but it's going to be different. The skin also will be a little bit different.

D. Are the extraterrestrials helping with this process?

B. In some way, because they are the forerunners to this, as their physical vehicle is better adapted to a bigger brain, in certain ways. And that is what is going to take place over numerous— this is not something that is happening overnight, you know. It's a process, but it's a very interesting design. So, know that there's going to be a difference. And you can sometimes see some of the younger souls that are sort of forerunners in this specific change of the human vehicle. And they appear somewhat stressed, they talk very fast and then get quiet. Because their brains are going much faster than the regular humanoid. The physical is not yet ready, fully, to be in that blend. A lot of these young souls coming in have signed up to try new ways of coming in here with more of their soul energy in their backpack, a bigger computer.

D. What part of the Earth are these souls mostly incarnating?

B. Oh, let's see. Canada is a huge country where some advanced souls have come in, a group of individuals who are not necessarily interacting with others. They are in colder climates. It's actually better for these new beings to be in a colder climate. You should know that the climate has an effect on how the brain and thoughts operates. Too much heat and too much of the sun actually promotes more of a, mmm, ah, mmm, not aggressive necessarily, but just a lack of self-control. The other group participating in this specific experiment is a group in the island of Greenland, close to Canada. And it's because of the colder climate, so the bigger computer has the ability to not create as much harm, because their physical beings are more still. From the mid-equator and going a bit down, the vehicles are less receptive to their inner hardware, their inner computers, if you like. It is that measurement, of course, where the physical vehicles, like the lizards, where there is a tendency that the physical is not fully receptive to an increasing computer inside. If you choose to go to that specific area, you will not be given the same opportunity to access your higher mind, that bigger computer inside. It's like having your old, first computer versus like Windows 10, that you can relate to. SO, if the body is not prepared for a Windows 10, it will not get that. That is to talk in your terms, so it makes some sort of sense to you. However, it is something with the colder climates, so those groups in Canada are the next to be given, hehe, like a Windows 12 or something. But it will not be shown yet, because those are yet being born. But the parents have been extremely well scanned, so they are prepared for these more advanced individuals. But, it's not like everyone coming into Canada will be given a new computer, like a Window 12. It's not! It's still a bit of a project.

D. Are there going to be a lot of old computers leaving?

B. Yes, it is that whole change, that cycle of evolution that is going on at this specific time, and that is where some computers will be removed. It's easy to make that happen.

In one of our earlier sessions, Zachariah explained, quite well, I think, the importance of recognizing how our thoughts and ideas create within the mental realm. This was one of the first requests he made regarding what material we should present to the public. And it remains a theme the spirits want understood.

D. Are there any other ideas that you would like to share?

Z. I want you to make people aware of the field we talked about in the beginning *(the mental realm, the fourth dimension)*, where the conscious mind creates the reality. As you inform on this, it's easy to understand the concept of heaven and hell. It is the same field. If you talk about hell, then you have created that reality in the same field where heaven exists. Focus on teaching people to create wisely within this field, as it is their free choice. It is the same field, it's not up and down. Those who talk about hell have created it in this field, and it is their reality.

D. So, it is essentially an individual's perception, as a result of their thoughts and beliefs?

Z. Yes, yes!

D. So one should elevate their thoughts toward higher ideals?

Z. Yes. It is the same field. You create this field based on your conscious ideas. If your conscious mind is drawn to negativity and darkness, then yes, this field will be such.

D. So, the thoughts are the creator.

Z. Yes, in this field. This is the field we pass briefly. We do not need necessarily to stay here every time we depart, but it's surrounding the Earth plane, and some remain to stay here for a longer time. This is where the higher realms can decrease (*beings from higher dimensions have to lower their vibration in order for us to connect with them*), it's that meeting point. And this is also where the Christ energy can be perceived from the human mind setting. You create this field. If you picture this to be a Garden of Eden, then it will be so. If you picture religious icons in it, it will be so.

D. Are people's thoughts, essentially, one long prayer? And are their prayers answered by the impact of their thoughts entering this energetic field?

Z. Know that prayer also comes in different ways. Some prayers are not light and on a higher level, or higher vibration. They still create the end result in this field.

D. Yes, I guess that was my idea. If you think either good thoughts, or negative thoughts, both types are actually still prayers?

Z. Yes, and they will be manifested in this field. So regardless of what you pray for, or what you intend to create in your conscious mind, it will manifest at this field. This one (*Christine*) has manifested a bench in marble, overlooking the sea from a cliff, because she sees this realm as a station to rest before she continues. That's all she sees in this field.

D. Is this a place she would return to, from time-to-time?

Z. Only as incarnated, while in meditation. She has no desire to visit for longer periods of time when not incarnated. It's a stop, if you like, to catch your breath before continuing on.

D. That's some really good information you've given us today, and we very much appreciate all this.

It is often either unfortunate incidents or increasing age that compel people to become more introspective. Thinking back over your life; the dreams once held so dear, the goals and aspirations, often bring up feelings of sadness. Even if all the things you hoped for came to pass, there can be a sense of loss when looked at in the rear-view mirror. At a certain level, this doesn't need explaining, because no matter what happened, be it good or bad, it is now only a memory. Because it is hard to find and maintain a balance in life, most days are a mix of many different emotions and states of being. At any given time, you may be aware of being happy, agitated, hungry, analytical, worried, optimistic, bored, in pain, curious, joyful, and so forth. The question becomes, how do we use the knowledge about the spiritual order of things to improve the value of our lives?

Waking life can be broken down into pieces, such as family, work, friends, interests, hobbies and idle time. You may not think of it in this way, but from a spiritual perspective, there is little difference among these groupings. The important part lies within your mind and emotions during any moment in the day. You have control over how you are responding to situations and people, and therefore, can regulate the type of thought bubbles you are sending out into the mental realm. Being angry at a rude driver, or being angry with your child, will impact each of them in a unique way, but the effect the energetic outbursts have on your Coat of Karma may be quite similar. In either case, you are tied to the effect the anger has on the recipient. In most situations, the mind and emotions are being used much more subtlety than in screaming matches with other people. It is these quiet undercurrents and common conditions of the mind and heart that we need to examine closely, because that is where patterns of behavior are established. Knowing that we have to re-experience our life once we pass should be a reminder of how important it is to stay true to your spiritual self. As each moment slips by, all that remains are the memories of how you acted and what sort of thoughts you transmitted. That and nothing more.

**Craters or Pebbles**
Just before this book went to print, I asked Zachariah if there was anything he wanted to add or clarify. There was, and he went into a very detailed description of how our emotions and thoughts come back to us, as a form of teaching. When any of the spirits use Christine's mind to communicate, she doesn't remember the words, but often sees the images they are trying to convert into language. During this next discussion, Zachariah projected an image that I think is very helpful to the idea of how we create our own reality. He uses the analogy of thought bubbles becoming

raindrops you send out into your future. What we found amusing was that he actually showed Christine a picture of someone launching arrows instead of raindrops, but he must have decided to soften the message while it was being delivered. What Zachariah showed her was an image of someone walking in a straight line, from birth to death, and when they have emotions or thoughts, it is like shooting arrows up into the sky, very slow-moving arrows that are going to land on the path directly in front of them somewhere, sometime. The force of impact will cause either a crater or a little bump, depending on what you have learned in the intervening time. Some arrows, or raindrops, come down quickly, while others are shot way into the future, even into other lifetimes.

D. Well, as always, I'm wondering how you feel about the book. It's been a few weeks since we talked.

Z. I am pleased. It has progressed as we wished. Let me see *(long pause)*. You might clarify somewhat about the power of thought. The power of thought, my friend, is somewhat mysterious because it travels like a wind. It's hard to understand the effect those have on the manifested reality.

D. Yes, it is.

Z. This is somewhat an illusion, if you like, because you HAVE created with your thoughts already. But man doesn't see it as a manifestation, as it travels in a bubble. The manifestation can take place several years later, the origin forgotten. Know that as you send off your thought bubble, you lose power over it. It does not necessarily mean it will manifest the day after, but depending on different cycles, it will manifest accordingly. But they will all manifest. Know that ALL WILL MANIFEST. Man just doesn't know when. You send them off like raindrops, almost. When they hit the ground is unknown, but when they do it creates new events. Let's say it in a picture for you, let the raindrop land on the ground. How it manifests is dependent on the cycles and events that take place prior to the manifestation. That is why it can never be known when the manifestation takes place. There are several variables that are operating. Just because a thought was sent on a Monday, doesn't mean it manifests on a Tuesday.

D. So, do all thought manifest?

Z. They do. BUT, they can manifest differently based on how you operate in between when the thought was created and the actual manifestation. Let's say you created somewhat of an anger thought in your teenage times, not knowing what you were doing, not reflecting on your actions, yet the bubble is still sent off. If you later learn certain lessons, let's say in your 20s, then when it manifests in your 40s, let's say, it has somewhat lost its power. That is why the power of your thoughts, combined with your actions in between when the thought took place, creates the manifestation. If you have not learned anything from that anger you sent off, then when that raindrop lands, it does so with a boom. Yet, if choices you have made after that thought took place mirror a spiritual enlightenment, let's say, the manifestation will still take place, but will not create a crater.

D. In that case, what form would anger, when it returns, come back as, or what would it manifest as?

Z. As a mirror to you. If you have not learned the lesson, then as that raindrop lands and manifests, it creates a boom, a crater if you like, sending off the same rage you sent off one time, but it will be towards you. However, this is the importance, because people will remember what they might have pondered upon, later. Hmm. How can I make a picture for you? See this raindrop, you send off a thought in rage; you are fifteen. When you turn 20, a spiritual enlightenment takes place. Let's say you lose your parents, so you become an adult early on. Knowing the change within your own evolution makes you understand the importance of not being in rage, because of events that took place around you. The thought you sent off at 15 still in some way exists in space, but because of actions you handled in a certain way, then that raindrop will simply be a bump on your way. You have the choice to create constantly, combined with your thoughts. Your actions are not powerless in between when the thought takes off, to its manifestation. Do you understand what I am trying to tell you?

D. I do. I was thinking about my own youth, I was very angry, I had a lot of anger.

Z. Yes, but you learned. You became humble. You need to go back and look what made you humble. Once you understand, or remember what changed you, then even though you sent off a variety of bubbles in anger, once they manifested, they have somewhat lost its power. But if you had not learned when you encountered the possibility to become humble, if you had not embraced that lesson in the way you did, then those missiles you sent off as a teen will have created craters for you. People might want to have more of little bumps, instead of craters on their path, let's just say that. This is important. If we take the example of a teen losing its parents in their early 20s, if that had not been embraced by growing up and taking responsibilities for their life, if that had not taken place, then the manifestation later on would have been severe. This is important to understand, that even though your actions or thoughts took place from a variety of different backgrounds and events that occurred around you, you have still the power to change your path so it is not full of craters, but has instead little bumps. You are not expected to understand your thought, the power of thought, from when you come in. No one expects that of you.

D. Okay, as an example, if you are angry at someone and you send out anger thoughts like that, are you likely to encounter situations where someone makes you angry? Is that the way it would manifest?

Z. Yes, it could mirror in that manner, indeed. The important thing is that people will remember, you all remember, prior thoughts and actions that you might not have been too proud of. As you come in here, you are somewhat cut off from your spiritual being, –that is why there is little blame from childhood actions, let's say. As you progress, you are constantly being reminded of your soul power, and the power of thought and your karmic debt to this plane. If you choose not to intervene with those prior actions and thoughts, then you will have a life review, as you refer to it, that will reflect your lack of learning. Even though you as a child, up till the age of about three to five, you are connected to your soul particle and your memory. Once you move into the environment of others, such as school, gathering friends, a filter moves in. This is the first lesson. It is the fact when you move into social groups that your first challenge arises. From that point, you are analyzed, and you will reflect upon those actions and thoughts that occurred. Do you understand?

D. Yes, I do. That's very good.

Z. Just see it as you shoot off thought bubbles like missiles into the future. Even after they are sent, you have the power to change, in some way, how they manifest. So, if you do not control them before they are released, you still have the power to alter how they are experienced in the future, if you have learned the lessons related to the original thought or emotion.

D. Well, from your perspective, what are some of the worst thoughts people can send out, or what causes the most future damage?

Z. Fear. Negative thoughts normally are always originating from fear. It could be the fear of not being appreciated. Fear of being without. Fear of losing the grip of your feet. Negative patterns sent off into the atmosphere are always part of the thought bubbles that have an origin of fear. When we say fear, it doesn't mean, necessarily, fear of spiders. We mean fear related to the emotional safety. The emotional has the greatest grip when it comes to fear. The mental fear is somewhat not very much in existence, but emotional fear, that has a big grip on thoughts and actions on this plane.

D. Alright. Well, thank you, I will put that in the book.

Z. I wish there to be known that even though you might remember a prior thought that you sent off to someone or something, if that has not manifested yet in your reality, you still have time to create the result of that manifestation, –if it becomes a crater or simply a little bump. That is what I want to say about the power of thought. You send it off into the future, if you like, but you still have the power over the manifestation. You are not powerless in the meantime.

D. If someone was really angry at another person for several years, what attitude or change in their belief would help, even if they felt the anger was justified?

Z. What would help is when certain events take place for that individual to encounter similar experiences that caused them to become angry, in order for them to understand why people acted or discussed in a certain manner. In order for awareness to take place, one must either experience oneself, or be in the presence of a similar activity. As a similar activity, for instance, occurs, then you have at that point the power of your mind, again, to remember how you acted in the past. At this point, you have the power to react differently. As you do, the first bubble sent off will lose its power. You are never left with only one choice. It will repeat. It will repeat during your lifetime, and it will repeat as you return *(next lifetime)*, if you chose to not create pebbles on your path. If you continue to create craters, feeling like the world is against you, when you yourself created those craters, then indeed, it will repeat. The Coat of Karma is right there when you return. Not such a big mystery. But know that most actions you see around you, that you react on, such as ignorance, lack of responsibility, lack of empathy, they originate from fear. People who lack companionship, for instance, can act out within the spectra of fear, feeling they are not worthy of companionship.

D. Ah, yes, I am familiar.

Z. Yes, you are. You will meet people in the same modality, feeling how they are not worthy of companionship. How you choose to interact with that feeling is a choice. You can send off anger to others, so they don't want to interact with you, or you can do the change within your own system, and that will be reflected in the meetings with others. You are a living proof.

D. That's very good. Thank you for that information.

Z. Oh, you are much welcome. This is the only part that will be discussed *(I think he means how choices can alter your future)* and will be part of future scriptures as well, because it is of importance and it will be mirrored in different topics in the future to come. It will always be a part of your books, the power of choice between actions, thoughts, and emotions as well. Emotions are a part of thoughts, even though it doesn't come from the chimney, as the Little One would say. A thought, people feel like a thought only comes from the head.

D. Are the two primary the emotional and mental?

Z. Clarify.

D. Thought bubbles, the origin?

Z. Yes. Let's just say, to make it simple for you, because both the emotional spectra and mental can send off thought bubbles, as well as the physical, which is a part of your actions. However, they manifest somewhat differently. The frequency they carry varies between the two, and they travel differently. The emotional can travel further, and can move...OK, I will say this to you. The thought bubble from the chimney tends to manifest faster. The other one, which has a greater power because it comes closer from your soul particle, it can travel indefinitely, and it can create and will bring you more expanding scenarios, for good or bad. Don't worry about describing a difference between the two, –that will simply be confusing–, just think of the way it is sent off. If you are asked, then yes, indeed, you are sending. I say, even though it comes from the emotional center, it is still carrying the same vibration as a thought, yet it has a different lifespan than a regular thought from the chimney. Greater power coming from the emotional.

D. With that logic, then I guess something coming from your heart center, like love, would be stronger than other emotions?

Z. Indeed. What do you think prayer comes from, emotional or mental?

D. It should come from the heart.

Z. Indeed it does. There you go. Greater power. This is also why, if you are focusing on sending off your thought bubbles from that spectra, then it's normally travelling without dirt. We will clarify this further in later scriptures. Don't get too confused by this.

D. It's very good, though.

Z. Simply describe the process. That even though you might have sent off emotions, thoughts, about someone or something, just because it didn't manifest the day after or week after, it's still follows you. But in the meantime, based on your actions and new thoughts and emotions, the first one will change in the way it manifests.

D. If you were angry about what someone did, would the act of forgiving them pretty well negate the original anger?

Z. Yes, that is true. One of many ways to change the manifestation of your thoughts. Remember this, share this.

D. I will. Thank you so much.

Z. Do you wish to ask a further question?

D. The only other thing I wanted to get a little clarification on was why souls are made to forget so much of their heritage when they incarnate.

Z. You know the answer. If you remember, then no learning takes place, –why come then? If you remember from the second you come in, what will you learn? The greatest teachings come from the time when you start to socially interact with others. For some, this meeting becomes a shock. For others, it appears like rejoicing in spirit. The first lesson occurs around...that barrier is around the age of six and seven. And then there are levels of teachings that come in, filters that you must somewhat master. And that is why you are here. You are passing through barriers, filters of experiences. If you come down here fully in connection with your soul, then those filters will simply be non-existent, because they are an illusion. They do not exist in the spiritual reality. Illusions created here require you to be a part of that game, part of the illusion, and that can only happen if you forget. Once you have encountered certain barriers, or an amount of lessons, then the awakening takes places. Filters are still in your path, or craters that you have created up to that point. In order for you to be surprised by the levels and barriers you encounter here, you need to be in that place of surprise. That is why you forget. Eventually you remember, at one point. The barriers are still there, the craters might have become pebbles, but if you remember everything when you come in, then there will be no pebbles or craters or thoughts to manifest differently. The power of choice, the power of free will become powerless, meaningless, if you remember everything. It's a chain reaction. You are here to practice free will and the power of choice. In order to do so, you have to be disconnected.

D. That's a wonderful explanation.

Z. I'm happy that you approve *(he kind of smiled as he said that)*.

D. It's hard not to!

When someone treats you poorly, the wise thing to do is forgive them and move on. Moving on means you quit thinking about it and charging the mental realm with fresh energy. If you die clinging to anger, resentment, self-pity, or sorrow from the action or words of others, it tends to bind you to them and to the emotion, as an unresolved issue. By forgiving them and releasing the emotional ties, you free yourself in the future. They may still have the negative karma, but you are not obligated to engage in a future situation to help you overcome the attachment.

I gave Ophelia an opportunity to clear up anything she felt was not covered properly, and she brought up the issue of the recently departed getting stuck in the fourth. She wanted to reassure those still alive that their loved ones are not permanently locked in some energetic reality. Religious instruction almost always includes a vigorous finger wagging about souls being condemned to some eternal prison if they don't follow the rules of their organization, which is nonsense from a spiritual perspective. Ophelia doesn't want our discussion about the transitional reality around Earth to be interpreted as a similar fate. Souls are not judged, and are not sent into isolation or tortured for eternity, no matter what kind of miserable life they led. They will have to face all their mistakes, but that is their burden of karma.

D. Is there anything in the book you would like to see improved?

O. We do wish that there be somewhat of an address about the connection to loved ones, briefly, of course, because it's not in your reality, and it's not where your strength lies. However, it has been mentioned, from a higher source, that it is of importance for people to know that their loved ones are not stuck in the fourth reality. No one wants to believe that someone they care for is locked or stuck.

D. Do very many souls get stuck in the fourth?

O. Not for long, though. However, there is a tendency, if one has not mastered their mission, so to speak. They are encouraged by their spiritual guidance to continue on, yet, it is never pushed. If the soul is not ready to move on, the spirit guide will simply take a step back. Never leave, simply take a step back. This is important for people to understand, that even if they might feel, because of their actions they know they have done in this lifetime, if they fear they might get stuck in the fourth reality as they read this book, you need to make sure they understand that there is always presence from their spiritual guidance. One is never left alone, yet growth comes from understanding within one's self. As people read this book, they are all very much aware of what they have done, and you wish them to be encouraged for change, but also that there is no judgment from the spiritual realities. They are met, joined, and accommodated from this reality. What we wish for, is for actions to change on this plane. In some way, it will raise prior actions, if you like. That is also important that you deliver that message. Only because one might have faltered in the past, one's whole lifetime is not to blame. You still, even with only one day left on this plane, you still can change and not get stuck. This is important. If you meet someone later in life who might have acted in a way that they know is not in favor of who they are as a soul, there is still time. Time does not exist, simply actions. The greatest blame is the one one puts on oneself.

D. That's very good, Ophelia. I will be sure to include this.

Because of his unique perspective on so many things, we thought it would be appropriate to let Bob present the final observation about the mental realm. From the second dimension, he is able to see quite clearly what goes on here on Earth. He can read people's thoughts and observe what they do, which often leaves him feeling a bit confused about humans in general. He would like for us to quit taking ourselves so seriously, as most things are nowhere near as dramatic or important as we think they are.

- B. I actually encourage people to laugh more, as it helps them to understand the little drama they create for themselves. Teeny tiny. No judgment, of course. But still it is so...people really put a lot of attention to the things that are not important and make a huge deal out of it, instead of just letting things go and being amused.
- D. I agree.
- B. So much drama over things that will never leave this place anyway. Things that will never have a meaning or a purpose or even be in a discussion on the other side. Yet still people linger on. Linger and linger and keep on, almost burping the same food up and down, up and down.
- D. What advice would you give people to release all that?
- B. Oh, I would like to say, these people are spinning in their own little bowl. What they do need is the ability to see themselves objectively from above. Almost as if they are those little hamsters spinning in a wheel. And if they see it as whatever they are doing, it doesn't really leave that little wheel. It's just repeating. I would say a lot of it has to do with a lack of other engagements in life. If they were to find meaningful things to occupy their minds, it would help. People need to be intrigued by things. If they're not, they just keep spinning as hamsters in that wheel.
- D. Well said, my friend.

# *You, the Spirit*

Our spirits were each created as a little spark and placed in a nursery, where the long process of learning began. Every dimension has its own nursery and training program, designed to produce spirits who can carry on the work within that function. When a soul is created, it is given a pattern within, a color code that binds it to a particular dimension, and also lays out the role the spirit will have as it develops. Zachariah compared this programming to DNA, in that every spirit has a place and a purpose within the body of creation. Almost all who come to Earth have a home in the fifth to seventh dimensions, and within that home, a part of your spirit always remains. One of the ways spirits learn is by sending part of their energy, which we call a soul, into various living beings, on Earth and elsewhere in the Universe of matter. After every life, the soul returns home, and whatever knowledge and experience it collected during the trip is merged with the higher self, which adds a little to the size and brightness of the spirit. Each mission to Earth begins with a plan of what your spirit wants to accomplish, and what aspects of either the physical, emotional, or mental you want to work on. It can take a great many lifetimes to understand all the lessons this planet has to offer. At that point, your spirit can move fully into a position where you are guiding a group of younger spirits, or into technical work related to the purpose originally given to you by the Creator. Just as you are always being helped by more advanced spirits, part of your responsibility is to teach and help others. No spirit works alone, as we are all links in a great chain that begins and ends with the Master Mind.

You are the soul portion of your spirit, working somewhat autonomously in your assigned vehicle, while your higher self continues doing whatever it normally does in your true home. Because your spirit split part of itself off to make your soul, the energy available to your higher self is lower by the percent sent into the body. Those spirits who have a soul out on a mission can be a bit slower and not as active, but upon the return of the soul energy, your spirit will be back to normal. Based on research from many therapists who conduct between-life regressions, the majority of spirits who are incarnating on Earth are studying and practicing different forms of energy manipulation within schools on the fifth dimension. When the little spirits are birthed as a spark, they get assigned to a particular dimension. Their evolution will be within that dimension, or one related to it. In our talks, the spirits have mentioned a variety of specialties, from taking care of little sparks in kindergarten settings, to designing moons, suns, planets, life forms, DNA, gravity fields, atmospheres, and other unimaginable things. Most people on Earth today are evolving within the fifth dimension, but the sixth and seventh are also well represented. No matter what role your spirit has been assigned, every activity requires study and learning, as each evolve and gain responsibility at their own pace. For those coming to our planet, there may be occasional visits to other realities or dimensions, but until the Earth lessons are understood, the spirit will continue to take on new lives.

Anyone who has been around children understands they are all unique personalities. The soul within the child is a fragment from a larger spiritual entity (its higher self), who has lived as numerous personalities on Earth. When a soul comes to Earth, it is not a blank slate, but comes wrapped within the Coat of Karma, the propensities of its former lives. The spiritual world is also full of personalities, at least on the lower levels. While a sense of humor and joy are found throughout the dimensions, as spirits move up into the higher councils, many of the Earth-like characteristics disappear. They become larger and more transcendent, but not as bouncy, as Gergen once said. I suppose by the time you reach those levels, there is not much that would surprise, so detachment becomes a natural way of being. They do radiate a tremendous compassion and love, however, and that is always evident during our sessions.

In the next discussion with Zachariah, he explains the way the spirit is formed and how it progresses from a little spark to become what the Creator intended.

    D. Let us explore further the path the departing soul takes as it moves from the Earth through this mental realm to the higher planes. Once it reaches the higher planes, is the soul free to do as it chooses, or is it committed to following a pattern that existed during and prior to its incarnation?

Z. There is a web where the soul resides, and within that reality free will exists, yet you cannot move within this web freely. So, your question is dual, in some way. Free will exists, but each spirit follows their own line in the web. And you cannot move between lines. If you see this web as a spider web, then in the center is the source. This source is beyond what the mind can fully understand. It's the infinity of all, and if you see this as a ball of light in the middle, then the spider web radiates from that source, like strings. Then within your own string you have free will, but you can only go back and forth within your own string.

D. The string then represents a pattern, a specific pattern that each soul or creation is...?

Z. It's like a program, almost like DNA within each soul, and this structure within the soul energy is how it returns back to its correct string. It can never get lost as it travels because it belongs in the same string.

D. I can picture that. Something I've always been curious about; within the realm of the creation, is good and bad recognized as polarities that must be explored?

Z. Only in certain worlds is bad perceived. Some realms don't have that structure of good or bad, it just is. In some way, it is related to the density. The density on Earth, for instance, and other places as well, promotes this polarity thinking of good and bad, black and white, to occur.

D. Yes, I understand. Is that the reason certain souls choose to incarnate in a world of polarity?

Z. Yes, it is to look beyond and to remember that on a spiritual level in their string, close to the source, there are no such things as polarity, good or bad, it just is.

D. There must be a reason that such worlds exist, and souls are cycled through these worlds to learn about this?

Z. It's a part of evolution, to go through different levels of learning. Polarity is one aspect of learning, and there are others. Here, one of the foundations, or lessons, is the polarity. Another is linear thinking. It's very primal, yet it serves as a tremendous learning. Projects here are considered evolution at a higher pace, if you choose to work with them. If you choose not to, then you come and you leave. Which is okay, it's also part of evolution.

D. When you say you choose to work with them, what is "them" you are referring to?

Z. Polarity, for instance. When you are aware of, that on a higher level, polarities as good and bad do not exist, then when you enter or encounter situations or people where you move into the polarity thinking or feeling, then you need to address it as a lesson coming your way and not become it.

D. That's very good. Once the soul is back in its place within the web and eventually receives a feeling that it should reincarnate, describe the process whereby the soul leaves its place with the web and returns to a physical form, or a mental form if it is on another world.

Z. (*Sighs*) There were a lot of words there. I will try to break it down. What you wanted to know was how the soul was notified of an incarnation, is that correct?

D. Yes, and how much free will and choice are involved in deciding where the soul goes?

Z. Some strings only go to Earth, they only go here. I'm trying to describe a picture to the best of my ability here. If you see this source and the strings, some strings are only attached to the Earth plane, whereas other strings are a little bit more fluid, they move, and can sometimes go to different places. Still, permission needs to be given, so it's not that the Earth strings are without free will and the other ones can choose and pick. But if I focus on the Earth strings, it's almost like a calling in that string, and those souls who respond to that calling have the choice to incarnate. Know that in this string there are some who have never left, who still need a bit of encouragement. As I see the strings, those souls are closer to the source, almost departing from it. I wish I could make you see this picture. It would have been easier.

D. Is it inevitable that all the souls on the strings will eventually pass through the cycles of incarnation, or do some choose never to incarnate, even though they are on that string?

Z. This is something you don't need to talk too much about. However, if you see this source as the birthplace of souls, and how it pops little sparkles, which is the soul energy from the big source, into these different strings. The purpose is evolution, in all of them. If you focus on the Earth strings, those sparkles who do not listen to the calling will be reversed back into the source as non-functional and will be reorganized, to again be sent out into their specific string. I don't like to compare it to a factory, but to the conscious human mind, it's an easy way to make it understandable. If you see a factory where you create toasters, and the toasters leave the main factory on the belt ready to be distributed to stores, they are tested to be sure they are properly functioning before they are sold. Those who do not pass the test that is meant for this toaster will be moving back on this belt and will be fixed, in order for it later to go out on the belt again. I'm sorry for this interpretation, I do not like to compare souls to toasters, but the image is similar and I wanted you to see it. There is no judgement of these toasters, because it can be fixed. Just know that it is a recycle that sometimes takes place.

D. Speaking of recycling, the souls that do move forward and work on evolution, at some point there must be a completion to their mission. Do these souls, who have acquired knowledge and experience, then return to the source, or are they always an individual identity, of sorts, outside the source.

Z. I'm looking at this picture, and from where I see it, the source in the middle of the strings is the birthplace. As the soul evolves, it never goes back to the birthplace. I cannot see the endings of the strings. I know...I'm not sure if I'm allowed to explore it at this time, or ever, from this point of view. But what I can see, and say, is that the birthplace is not the same as the ending place. What I see here is more of a nursery source where soul energies are split off and created *(given unique purpose)* and then divided into different strings. I don't see it ever going back into the same source, which would indicate recycling. This may be confusing for you.

D. No, that sounds like infinite expansion.

Z. That's more how I would explain it.

In another session, I asked Zachariah about different orders of creation. I was interested to know if there were some beings who did not have a separate sense of self. But later, in thinking about it, I realized my question made little sense. He did the best he could to answer, by telling about other entities where the brain structure is different, so the soul can easily communicate telepathically with others of their kind. He mentions a wheel, which is how they describe the shape of creation in our reality. The center hub is the Creator. There are concentric rings expanding outward that represent the dimensions. Beyond the spiritual dimensions are the universes where form and matter are located. There are twelve universes, organized like hours on a clock. Our entire Universe, our fish tank, is around 5 o'clock. So our Universe is identified as fish tank 5 in all subsequent sessions. They gave the other fish tanks numbers that correspond to their location around the perimeter. Zachariah also said there are many types of physical bodies on other planets. Most exist in their own reality, having no awareness of other types of beings. Much like we humans have no knowledge of other extraterrestrial entities.

Z. What is your question?

D. Within the order of the spiritual beings, from the Creator down to the human soul, there are many types of beings, I'm guessing, some that have independent egos or a sense of self, and others that don't. Is this true?

Z. There are beings that have a split brain, meaning they can move between them. One is more, primarily, for operating the vehicle. Whereas the other is more into communication, telepathically and so forth. There is a wall between these two brains and this individual can move between them. The human has one, the brain is not partitioned. Other individuals carry different possibilities to exist.

D. Within the created Universe that's connected to the Master Mind, are most of the creations directly from the Master Mind, or are other beings responsible?

Z. Let's put it in terms that can be comprehended from this level. If you see the Master Mind, as you call it, as the central core within a wheel. From each direction of the wheel, there are special groups that are always in contact with the core of this wheel, yet operates individually. None, on the outside of the wheel, know about the others. Only a few, I would assume, because they operate individually, but are all connected to the Master Mind, the core, the creation, that makes the wheel move.

D. That's very good. I was wondering if there were individual entities that work perfectly in harmony with the Creator.

Z. Indeed. Some work with the elements. Gravity is one of those. *(He then gave a bit of information that became too technical for this wave of knowledge)*

**Bob in the Library**
All spirits have a book, or record, of everything they have done since being created. After every lifetime on this planet, or other places where they may go to learn, the spirit journals about significant learnings and experiences. It is actually stored in an energetic form, but it is easier to visualize these notes as pages in a book. Each spirit has their own book, which no one other than their guides can look into without permission. The memories from your past lives are condensed into general knowledge and understanding, so a lot of the minor details are stripped out. Your spirit has no attachment to the bodies it occupied on the third dimension, nor most of what it did during its sojourns to Earth. Humans have a tendency to worship the ideas of things, such as fame, money, beauty, and other material objects, not realizing these have no meaning except as tools for learning different spiritual lessons. No amount of worldly possessions or notoriety will bring happiness to a human who is not in harmony with their spirit. But to those who are in tune, they view these things as ephemeral and not a source of their identity as a spiritual being.

The journals that each spirit compiles is kept in the Library, the central repository of knowledge within the fifth dimension. The Library is vast, and parts of it are hidden below the main Library in what Bob described as vaults. Spirits are only allowed to see information related to their level of development, and some records are put in areas that very few can access. Bob told us about working in this Library, and explained his duties of maintaining records in two of the vaults; the Earth vault, and the vault for the sixth dimension. The design lab on the sixth dimension, where Christine and I work, stores documentation on solar systems, cores, and other types of form and non-form creations. These records are kept at the Library, and it seems that Ophelia and I gave Bob the job so he could learn about those subjects. He actually goes into quite a bit of detail about his chores in the vault and what he observes.

D. Do you, as a soul entity or being, have an Akashic record, a history of your existence? Do all of creations have a personal record?

B. All. All. That is the master plan by being created. It's that everything is born with a purpose, a journey, as well as a specific goal. When the soul is born, they are all in school to see where they want to go. Some becomes travelers of incarnations, some are more like observers, some take notes, and some become only guides. Umm, uhmm, some are the keepers of records. It's like being in a huge library and taking care of the boxes to remember where everything occurs. Some are actually a little bit familiar with this *(He smiles like he has a secret)*. Oh, in the Library, in the cellar, there are many boxes of knowledge that I have stored. Not all mine, of course. But being here is a huge honor. Sometimes you can look into the boxes. Some are locked. If they are locked, you're not supposed to look into it. This Library is a central place where information on all parts of creation, incarnation, planets, and how beings are moving through the different dimensions are stored. It's also about the creation of solar systems and galaxies. They are divided into different sections where some are more about, oh, let's see if I can talk about this *(he pauses for a moment, listening to Ophelia)*. Yes, I can. Ophelia says, "Yes." Yes, I can.

B. Okay. This Library that I have been working in, in the basement, it is grand. It stores all the knowledge of all different beings. The masters have boxes that I cannot look into. I work with the boxes from this plane. This is where my notes can be contributed to the baby library. Ahhaha. Little helpers in the Library. Let's see. Your boxes are full of...I was allowed to look into your boxes. You've done so many interesting things for intergalactic, galactic planets. Interesting. I don't understand, really. When I open your boxes, energies are in them. Some boxes have planets *(He later clarified that to mean energetic models of planets)* in them, and some have papers. My box has papers. Your boxes, ohohoh, so many fascinating things for someone like me. You were the one who gave me this job. *(Smiles proudly)* I'm very grateful.

D. Which job was that?

B. To work in the Library. You gave me this!

D. I'm sure you earned it.

B. *(Laughs)* Ophelia approved. But, there are vaults down here I don't go into. But I am allowed in your vault, and the vault of this dimension, the Earth. Oh, there are so many vaults! I see everyone going around here carrying boxes. It's like having your own security code to different places in the basement. Thank you. This is what I do to spend my time.

D. Are you simultaneously there and also on the second dimension?

B. Yes, yes, yes. You never leave.

D. How much of your energy did you leave on the second?

B. Oh, about half. Half, because the other half is in the Library. In the Library, this is where I compare notes, you know. From the boxes that you allowed me to look into, and what I see.

Bob originally had all his energy on the second dimension, his spiritual home. When he was given the job in the Library, he essentially split off part of his spirit energy and projected it into the vault, where it stays most of the time. As spirits progress, their energy increases, so he was later able to split off what he calls his "traveling energy," and goes to lectures and labs where he studies on the sixth and seventh dimensions. Currently, he operates with about 30 percent in the vault, around 10 percent on the second, and travels with the remainder. This traveling part accompanies me during incarnations as a guide and joins us during the channeling sessions. All spirits can divide and be doing several things at once. As you are reading this book, your higher self is still working on another dimension. We will cover this topic in more detail later in the book.

D. Will you be able to, with approval of course, give us information from those boxes?

B. Yes, yes. If Ophelia says yes, yes, I will. Ophelia said that I could describe this Library today, so yes. I will be able to look into the boxes with no lock on, and that are available to you. There are many boxes here. There is some sort of order, of course, on the boxes. It's like you can take one box forward and you can try with your finger to open it, but if it's not opening, then it's not for you to see. I'm proud of my vault because I don't let anyone come looking into boxes here. As well as they don't let me go sniffing around in other vaults! It's all about records, of course, and guarding. This is where we will access more from the vault.

When Christine is channeling someone, she is sort of hooked on to where they are focusing their attention. So, while Bob was connecting to the part of himself in the vault, Christine felt as though she were standing next to him. After the session, she said Bob had been pulling boxes off the shelves to show her, and may have forgotten where he got them, which explains his next remark.

D. That's very good information. Do you have anything else you would like to share?

B. I need to return. I need to attend to the boxes. It's a little bit of a, hmm, sometimes when I take a box out and I look, I forget to put it right back and it sometimes creates a little bit of disorder in the vault. So, I always try to be very careful with the information. I need to make sure everything is where it's supposed to be. Otherwise, when you try to find something, it's impossible, if you put the box somewhere else because you, hehehe, didn't really pay attention to where it was. So, there's some order here that I need to attend to.

D. Are you the only one in the vault?

B. In this vault...Ophelia comes sometimes. But this vault, let's see...I'm keeping information in this specific vault. The information, in this vault that I am in now, is from your realm. The being that you are. But, each reality has their own vault, and the Earth vault is not here. It's a different vault that I have access to, I have the keycard. I have the keycard for two vaults *(He uses the idea of a keycard to explain how access to certain knowledge is restricted)*. There is one more that I can see, but it's not really that much fun, it's merely plants in that one. It doesn't really give you that much, it's more like a storage unit, where they have plants from different places. So you can touch them and look at them, but they don't really say that much. It's a place everyone can go and look. You're not supposed to mess it up, though. If you take a plant out, or a little thing out of one box, you have to put it right back. So, it's more of a museum. It's not really to learn. Well, learn, you can see what's existed on different places. There are actually plants that are more in energy, it's not fully solid. You're not supposed to touch those because they are not really...they are in a sort of a glass bowl. It's more like a little museum. So, I can go there. But you don't really learn that much, I just look at stuff. There are rocks in there, crystals, actually. I do like those. In this vault, there are glass bowls with crystals in them and other things. I do like those, because they show where there have been places of pure crystals, the planet itself or the star was a different crystal. A little bit from each have been saved. There are several glass bowls with labels, it's like a museum. You can go and look if you like. *(It was both amusing and endearing that he invited us to come visit, as if it was a walk to a nearby store.)*

D. Well, thank you for sharing all this information. We'll let you go back and tend to your boxes, if you like. It has been a real pleasure.

Bob has mentioned several times that the advanced records in the vault are stored on the higher shelves. As he is still learning the more basic ideas, he only has access to certain levels of knowledge. Since he is quite small, he needs a ladder to reach the bottom rows, but it only has two steps, and he is very eager to examine the contents of the boxes on the third shelf. The assignment he mentions is a little test Ophelia gave him to see if he could build a color and sound map of certain objects. He also talks about how he meets with my higher self in the vault to discuss things that he should bring forward during our trance sessions. Even though we don't remember, all of us still exist and are working within our home dimensions, So, my higher self continues to visit with Bob in the vault and can also be simultaneously in our lab. It's a little hard for our minds to grasp, but that is exactly how it works. It's like spiritual multitasking.

B. Do you want me to ask a question?

D. Oh, sure!

B. When will I get my third step?

D. Uhh, I think you're going to get it pretty soon.

B. Yes, maybe for Christmas? You know, I'm working on some sort of project, that's why I asked. Because I did leave my little assignment, and it's in the review. So that's probably connected to the third step?

D. So, what's in the third shelf, in the boxes?

B. I don't know!

D. I've never shown you?

B. Well, you took them down. But you know I can't reach, it's always supervised, and I don't understand it. So, no, no. But you know, we actually meet a lot when you sleep, in the vault. Because it is about you allowing yourself to know certain things. You show me certain things when you sleep, your soul, your higher self, and you say, "This you can talk about, this you can show me." And then I said, "OK." And sometimes I don't really understand what it is, and I ask, "How do I explain this?" *(Laughing)* I also have a little agenda in asking, because I don't know, and I want to learn. But you say, "You don't have to explain," because you can read my mind. So you laugh and say, "Don't worry about that, my friend, just show me and tell me, then I will understand. Eventually I will put it all together, like a puzzle, but you have to give me the boxes, you have to show me and you have to tell me certain things." So I do. That is it. It is about helping your conscious self to remember. So, it is actually yourself, talking to yourself, through me. Which is kind of strange, when you think of it! I repeat what you say, many times.

**Windows of Opportunity**

Each of us has a similar objective as humans, and that is to remember our mission. We plan our lives with certain markers and opportunities for development, which Ophelia discussed in one of our December 2016 readings. While it was a little bit personal, the concept is quite valuable for everyone. She tells how the soul comes in with specific opportunities programmed within its life path. These challenges and situations are tests to see if we have learned certain lessons. If you pass the test, it will open a window and give you access to new types of energy, promoting soul growth. If you fail, or do not grasp the window of opportunity, there will be other windows later that have similar lessons. She makes an important point about how relationships with people change as you progress spiritually. People do not learn at the same pace, and those who were once close companions, may become incompatible as you progress.

D. Hello, Ophelia.

O. Hello, my friend. How are you feeling this glorious day? We are very pleased with the process. You have opened only one of several windows. More are still to come in your own personal development. Don't be afraid to open them, be curious, curiosity will lead you to open even more.

D. What type of windows are we talking about?

O. Individually, you have more to learn about your soul capacity, where you are coming from, and how you can resonate with those you find vibrating on a less, how can one say, a less complementary vibration. In order for you to not distance yourself, it is important that you understand your own vibration. Doing so will also create another gap, unfortunately, with other people. Let me clarify. As you are growing in your own vibration, the gap to others will widen even more. Doing so will, in one point, give you a higher knowledge of your place in relation to others, yet it will also make you feel more disconnected to them. Know that, that it is as it should be. You are not here to be within complimentary emotional vibrations, as you, in some way, lack that. I'm not saying that you do not have empathy or feelings, you simply vibrate on a different level. You did not choose that type of experience in this lifetime. You simply do not prefer, neither one of you *(Christine and me)*, to work in that capacity. You have done your lessons, so far, and do not need to engage on that level again, if you do not choose so. She will explore this vibration further.

D. Very good. Thank you.

O. These windows that I am referring to, some will be creating an emotional outburst in some way. There will be sadness followed by enlightenment. Some, as mentioned, are personal windows, where others are more inclined to increase your spiritual connection. As you do, layers from your physical being will be dissolved, as well as she *(Christine)* will go through the same process. This is what the transformation refers to. It's not meant for the physical to dissolve, clearly, however it will become less apparent as your soul energy will increase. The mystery within this teaching is that each and every one has the possibility to make their physical vibration, in some way, dissolve, as they move more into their spiritual being. All carry windows that will open if they are interested in the process of growing. All souls incarnated have the windows implemented in their system. This is where some choose to not pay attention to the windows and will remain in the physical vibration. Those who remember and connect with their spirit will also access their windows. Some only have a handful, whereas others, younger souls, have more windows implemented in their being as they come in. The difference lies, apparently, in the fact that younger souls need to have more chances or options for them to stumble upon their windows, whereas older souls need to navigate to find them. So, in your case, my friend, you have five windows. One was opened as you moved into the next vibration when you moved into the meeting of your soul mate, your soul friend, so to speak.

## Reincarnation

In the next series, Zachariah and Bob are discussing the cycles of reincarnation, and some of the activities souls engage in between lives. They made a very interesting point about how souls can actually clean their Coat of Karma, or essentially end the round of reincarnation, by overcoming ignorance and becoming spiritual during one lifetime.

D. I have a question about incarnating souls. In order for a soul to accomplish the cycle of reincarnation, can you tell the major developments it has to achieve?

Z. Clarify your question.

D. What does a soul need to learn in order to overcome the cycle of reincarnation on Earth?

Z. First of all, remember that incarnating here is a choice. So the choice could be that even if you are somewhat done with this reality, you can choose to come back to remember what you learned in the past. With that said, you can choose to come here as many times as you wish, if this is your preference. The highest lesson on this plane is to understand the polarities that operates around you as you come into body. It is to balance the mental, emotional, and physical self. To see it, as such, to divide male and female principles, to discard polarities. As you understand this in ALL realities, –not only in your mental capacity, you have to understand it from your solar plexus–, then you can proceed from this plane, if you choose to.

D. So, does the Coat of Karma essentially hold a soul in this cycle? In general, do people have to resolve all the issues within their Coat before they leave, or can you leave it undone?

Z. It is suggested you do, because you don't want to leave bad trails. So yes, indeed. But again, I return to the fact of choice. Nothing is forced from the spirit realm, yet there is no one else coming in to clean your coat away. So in order for this plane to become pure, it will be suggested to the soul who wishes to remain in the spirit realm and to not necessarily take care of its coat, to return, to clean the atmosphere.

D. Okay, very good. Thank you.
Z. On a soul level, all souls know. Yet when they come here it repeats, so you cannot clean from the spirit realm, you can only clean by coming into body. The whole goal, the purpose, is to leave a folded Coat, then you can come in and still practice if you like, but you can choose to do so without the Coat. The soul is not in charge of telling when it is folded, only the spirit guides and spiritual beings of the council can do a final overlook over all. It has nothing to do with the amount of time spent here. If a soul has a bad Coat and comes in and understands the dirt it put here, comprehending it not only in the mental realm, but in the solar plexus, then it doesn't necessarily have to come back and repeat it again. So it CAN be folded during one lifetime, if those realizations occur.
D. Very good. I have another question about all these souls. You know, there are billions of souls on the Earth. Where do the majority of these souls go when they are off the Earth plane? I guess a lot of them are young souls, what do they do at home?
Z. Ah, let me see. Our friend made an appearance *(Bob came close, and Zachariah noticed him)*. Let's see. I will take this question. As a younger soul returns, the majority of its chores are about reflection, reviewing, journaling, if you like. As you journal, you are told to be objective, to look at the body, not necessarily your soul, but how the body you picked operated. A lot of time is used to journal your experience. There are guides, helpers, who will give their input, and you actually have to show them your journal. Because it is important that you remain objective, to not make it into a little funny novel. So, indeed, it's a way to remain neutral.
D. As these souls progress, as these young souls advance, do they eventually move into creative positions within the higher dimensions?
Z. What takes place is the soul, combined with their friends, take turns, where one will appear *(act)* as a guiding individual from the spirit realm while the other one travels *(incarnates)* in to the Earth plane. That is the next level after you reflect by yourself, or together in a class. But yet, it is important to do it in your own pace, because you can get colored by other people or other souls' experiences. So, the next level is to take

turns, and that is when you have progressed, slightly. It's not necessarily after only ten lifetimes.

B. *(Bob came in, and Zachariah stepped back)* Huhhh!

D. Hello, Bob.

B. Hello, hello. I would like to add something about that.

D. I would love to hear it.

B. Because, you know, it is something. When a soul returns, it can be tired, but it is still asked to journal its experiences. And here is also where those with more of an angelic appearance can take turns in assisting, because there can be moments of sadness. Even if you look at something objectively, if you see you have done something less good, then there is still a feeling of sadness. When you see a soul sitting, writing in its journal, it's always in the presence of a light being. Because, you know, the light being sends warmth and heat, which actually provides a sense of safety and love, in some way. So this light being stands behind the soul, encouraging it to continue with its journaling. I want to add that you're not just left in a dungeon with a journal somewhere! You are actually protected and assisted as you journal your experiences.

D. Do these journals eventually make it into what would be considered your personal book? So, like my life book that you studied, it has my journaling?

B. Yes! Yes, but from all places, not just this plane. Because you, my friend, you've been to all sorts of places. I ask you about it, because I want to know! Because, you know, we help each other to understand the combined work we do on ALL planes.

D. I'd like to ask another question about something we discussed last week, about the progress of souls on Earth. You had said they will eventually progress into becoming teachers, but are there certain groups of souls that never work within other dimensions?

Z. *(Zachariah came back in)* That is a choice. Souls who wish to remain within their own group are allowed so. However, as a soul evolves, it feels the drive, the smell of other realities, and becomes interested in visiting. But, your home dimension will always be the same. You, my friend, will never be a seventh dimensional individual, as that is not how your soul and spirit is created. The creation takes place beyond our comprehension. And the sparkle of soul is sent, if you like, to where it has the best potential to evolve. All souls don't begin similar, as it carries within its own system a pattern of where it belongs and how it should progress. It is the Master Mind behind it all that creates the different soul energies. It's not the same from beginning to end. It resonates where its location is supposed to be, because it carries within, from the day it is born, a map of its own learning, evolution, travels, and so forth. It is a pattern within you that establish where you are located, as well as your journey. As the soul progresses, it is given the possibility or opportunity, as your little friend *(Bob)*, to move and visit other realities. It is a choice and not all accept. There is no force.

D. So souls that are incarnating on the third dimension, are those essentially fifth dimension souls?

Z. The fifth dimension is similar to where spiritual manifestations can take place. It is a level of...how can I place this for you? This is where certain meetings take place. This is where your Library exists. It is accessible from all different levels, if you have the key. However, it is a place of rest, this is a place for recreation, and joyful experience with nature. It is the opposite, or the mirror, from Earth, so, in many ways, a soul feels familiar here. There is a garden where the second dimensional can plant. There is a greenhouse, almost, if I can paint a picture for you. It resonates with the emotional aspects of the soul, the care and empathy. In some way, the fifth resonates with the seventh dimension. As well, the sixth and ninth resonate together. The fifth dimension is a level a soul can remain a while, regardless of their home base, as they depart from the third dimension. It is a place of rest, to be joyful of the fact of the journey, to read, and to study up, before moving on to rejoin and merge with your spirit energy.

D. I know the fourth is the transition—is there anything that happens before they enter the fifth?

Z. The fourth is the transition, where you need to reflect in solitude, slightly, on what you have done. But this is not a long pause, unless you are hindered by your karmic Coat, then you might remain to ponder. The fifth is more a spiritual barrier. You cannot reach the fifth without first passing through the fourth, there is no jumping, so to speak. However, if I take you as an example, you have the opportunity to go directly from the third up to the sixth and ninth when you depart, and it is because your jacket has been folded. So you can, if you choose, return directly to your home base, your source of rest, knowledge and recreation. You never really have a need to pass through the fourth, as you see it as somewhat dirty. You do not need to come in contact with other Coats. Here is where thoughts can remain, actions can remain.

D. So when a person is incarnated, and they connect to their spiritual self through the little star in their solar plexus, what level does that communicate with?

Z. A lot of times it connects directly to the fifth. Souls who haven't been here as long tend to, I'm sorry for the expression, get stuck. For instance, if they meditate, they can only reach into the fourth. As you progress with your journeys, being present on this plane numerous times, you can navigate through the fourth. However, you have not the ability from this plane, to reach higher than the fifth.

D. Can I connect with my home base?

Z. Yes, indeed you can, through deep, altered states reach the sixth, and you can get a glimpse of the ninth.

D. So, my question about the majority of souls on Earth, for example, do they all have *(Zachariah cut in to answer)*

Z. They don't know anything above the fourth. If they knew about the fifth, don't you think the world would be different? They hear teachings about it, this is what the Church resembles as heaven, if you like. But there are levels above, as you are aware. So, to make it simple for you, the fifth dimension is similar to what people perceive heaven to be, the average man doesn't really ponder about the higher levels, the levels of form, light, and the grid. The grid belongs in the ninth dimension. The eight is involved with the grid on Earth as they resonate with elements, understanding conditions on celestial bodies. We haven't talked as much about the eighth individuals, and we will. We have talked about the fifth, sixth and seventh. The fourth is simply a layer where beliefs can be stuck, thoughts can manifest. This is why you travel here, to work on your own contribution in the fourth reality. To teach how to learn about and clean the mental, the mental realm of Earth, if you like. The fifth is related to the higher emotional vibrations of Earth, but it's also where the libraries and gardens can be found.

D. If I may pursue this, if souls are patterned to a particular dimension, and the part of the soul that's incarnated on Earth doesn't really have a home in the third, fourth, or fifth, what dimension do most souls belong in when they eventually progress to where they should be? Do you see my question?

Z. I do. And it is somewhat complex to answer. There is a reality within the fifth, which would be considered a spiritual home. This is the garden, where several souls remain, if you like. Those you know, your family members resonate with five and seven. If you ask, they have memories of gardens, their spiritual home indeed. So the fifth operates somewhat as a combined spiritual reality, as well as the holder of the Library and knowledge. This is also where your friends from the second dimension can visit and create gardens. Teachings take place at this level. From this plane, some souls resonate with the seventh reality. In some way, all levels have two parts; both a manifested reality as well as a spiritual side. So, as you connect with the sixth dimension, you have the ability to travel to the manifested one. That's why you see it as form. You see it as classrooms and physical individuals. However, it carries a spiritual reality as well, hand in hand. So, all levels can be perceived as manifested, even the seventh. Your friend *(Bob)* talked about classrooms, labs and so forth. He only visits the manifested parts in that level. He has not the possibility to visit the spiritual realm of the sixth dimension or the seventh. So, five, six and seven are dual in some way, and you have the ability from this plane to visit the manifested one. As you leave your physical body behind, you travel to the spiritual side of your level. Do you understand the picture?

D. I do.

Z. Eight and ninth are barely manifested, only for those who are initiated in that understanding.

D. I was thinking in terms of the people who will read our book.

Z. Yes, they will resonate mainly with the fifth, because it will feel familiar to them, with the Library and gardens. A lot of religions have referred to these places. It will be easy to adapt, as that has been established. You can add the realities of the seventh, probably, first, as it more resonates with the fifth. The sixth is more scientific. This book should be about the third level, fourth and fifth, primarily. The second is the amusement that will make people understand the levels, and also the care for the land and to pay attention in nature. Those smaller beings that exist on this plane as nature spirits hide in all sorts of matter. You can find them on the foam in the waters, floating by. Playful spirits, indeed, you see them all the time in the rivers, that's why we are directing you to connect to the water elements and the rivers.

D. Thank you for all this wonderful information.

## *You, the Soul in a Human*

What you think of as your current life could be better described as the latest mission to Earth by your spirit. Your body, your birth family, many of your friends, and most significant experiences you have had, or will have, were planned before birth. The lessons you wanted to learn are the mission objectives, and all other decisions were aligned with that purpose. Because of the interrelationship between souls and objectives, you are playing roles in other people's lives, just as they have agreed to play certain roles in your life. Therefore, one of the main considerations you have to address is the Coat of Karma left behind from previous incarnations. This represents all the beliefs and patterns of thinking, along with your debts to specific souls, where you are bound to them from some previous interaction. Each mission to Earth includes the intent to correct some of these residual mistakes.

Planning for the next incarnation is coordinated with a close group of other spirits and all the respective guides. Roles are discussed and agreed upon, Mothers, brothers, friends, even bosses at work can be played by souls with whom you have shared previous lives. Oftentimes, the purpose of working together is to try and correct some personal relationship or character issues from a prior existence. An example might be where one soul agrees to help another with anger, if, in turn, they get assistance in dealing with patience. Once incarnated, we don't remember what we signed up to do, but our higher self and our spirit guides always know, and they are constantly directing us into situations that can promote growth. Zachariah describes the life plan like a pattern in a children's coloring book. We are given the outline and it is up to us to color it in. If we scribble outside the lines and make a mess of the picture, that is our lesson to learn. If we paint our life in dull colors, that is also our choice, because we have the opportunity to use a full palette of colors.

After the soul lays out the basic plans of what it wants to achieve during the lifetime, it then chooses a body that will best serve those objectives. Here is where the higher beings, such as your spirit guide and other specialists, come to assist in creating the best environment for success. Each baby that is available for occupancy has a unique configuration of seven inner layers of energy patterns, which is determined primarily by genetics. The incoming soul can allocate its energy into those layers it wants to work on, with the main ones being physical, emotional, or mental. If you, as an incoming soul, want to work primarily on overcoming emotional patterns, you may be offered a choice of several bodies with a high proportion of emotional tendencies. Because you are agreeing to work with other souls, there are additional considerations regarding geographic location and family units as well. I know that may sound quite complicated, but a great deal of coordination takes place before any mission to Earth is started. And the advantage of being outside of time greatly enhances the odds of picking the right body. Bob, a master designer, explains how the spirit is given bodies to pick from that will match its mission objectives on Earth.

- B. This is also how you are made. The physical vehicle, those who design physical vehicles, also design it to carry more or less of certain vibrations. This one *(Christine)* has a lot of the emotional vibrations implanted in her vehicle, whereas you have a lot of physical vibration implanted in yours.
- D. Does the incarnating soul oversee the body design and development, from a fetus?
- B. Not the individual soul. The individual soul does not design the physical, necessarily. Only those who are allowed to, on that level, can work on the design. So, let's say it like this, to make it easy for you; you want to go down and you want to work on the emotional parts, let's say. Then, the designer of vehicles, they will give you a vehicle that vibrates more easily on the emotional realities on this plane.
- D. I see. It's like getting a pickup truck or a van.
- B. It's like choosing a pickup truck. What do you want to have, do you want to have a diesel car or do you want to have a petroleum? Some want to have an electric one. So it is just based on preference and what the mission is that you are on. But, because of your specific assignment, then you chose a lot of physical vibration in your vehicle this time around. So,

let me look at your vehicle. It seems like about, I would say, 60 percent is the physical vibration and it is somewhat equal between the emotional and the mental vibration. This one *(Christine)* has about 50 percent emotional. It *(her spirit)* doesn't like that at all. It's so unnecessary. On a soul level, you are vibrating very much in a mental layer, because you are the creator of, I would say thought, but it's more of a planning and structure, which demands the vibration on that level to be much higher. So you are not always, on a soul level, very familiar with the emotional capacity.

The spirits call the manifested, physical reality of our Universe a fish tank. Partly because it has boundaries and is finite, but also because our perception is like a one-way mirror. The human eye can only see third dimensional objects, but the spirit world can see us and our thought bubbles quite easily. To minimize confusion, we will not talk about other fish tanks, even though they come up in our sessions. The focus will be on the fish tank where our human bodies reside. From the dirt under your feet to the most distant star light, everything you can see or measure is part of the third dimension within our fish tank. Each type of reality is contained in its own fish tank, and this is what Zachariah refers to later.

Zachariah talks about how the soul records everything in a spot above the solar plexus, where the soul attaches to the body. The physical brain does hold memories, which can be quite fallible, but the soul has its own recording system. It captures every detail of life, without error or omission. The soul maintains a connection to the higher source. In other sessions, the spirit teachers have talked about how every living thing, from a flower to a whale, has a core that both determines the pattern of the lifeform and is also the linking point with the higher dimensions. In a human, the docking point is called the Center Point, and is situated above the solar plexus, below the heart. It is invisible, of course, because it is an energetic pattern within the second dimension. It is the point where the silver cord connects the soul to the body, and when it disconnects, the body dies. The soul collects every bit of information about its life within that central point. That energetic recording is added to the Coat of Karma, which stays within the fourth dimension. However, spirits are able to link to the Coat and review all previous lives from their home in the spiritual dimensions. Zachariah explains how souls can connect to other realities without incarnating in order to learn.

D. I would like to ask, how are memories stored? Where does a soul hold its memories?

Z. The memories are stored in a center that is located, not in the brain, but in the solar plexus area. The solar plexus is the part of a sparkle that follows the soul. We talked about how you leave certain bodies as you transcend into the higher being you are. And as you leave the physical, you leave the emotional and the mental, there is a sparkle that is connected to the higher source and that is located in the solar plexus area. This is where all memories are stored, but without creating disharmony, or, oh, it's just a way to follow the soul, if you like. When they do the reviews, and as they look back on their lives, regardless of where it took place, they activate their solar plexus in order to connect, like a cord, to the specific Coat they want to investigate. You can see it as fishing. You know how you throw the fishing line into the water? You still hold it at one end, but you throw it in and attach it to whatever you want to investigate. So, you activate the solar plexus where everything is stored, and it sends out a bridge, an energy bridge, to the specific Coat they want to investigate. It's like remote investigation, if you like. Does it make sense to you, do you understand the picture?

D. Does the soul, in the spiritual realm, have a solar plexus?

B. It's a center, a spark, which can be activated within the soul energy. The soul is only energy, but this is a part which can be activated whenever one wishes to investigate or learn from a specific reality. They can also use this specific skill, even if they do not want to look at prior incarnations. This is a way to travel, a way to not incarnate, yet to fully move into another reality, and learn from that reality. Sometimes, in order for progress to move forward, a soul which has evolved a bit, will be able to move from this sparkle and experience a reality in a fish tank, without the pickle of being there in a physical body or in another form of being. This is to move progress for that specific soul faster. So see it as, from the center of the soul, after it has progressed for a while, that it has the possibility to, from that source, send out an energy bridge. It's like casting out a fishing line; you can either travel *(project part of your awareness)* on this bridge to experience a reality, or you can go and look at your Coat. So, in that regard, yes, everything is stored within the soul. Newer souls also have this little center, yet they can only look at the last prior travel they did. After a while they can look at more. Some only observe their Coats. Not all are equipped for using it for traveling. So, to make a picture for you, you can see it as it is stored in the solar plexus. But as a soul energy, you do not have a solar plexus, it's a sparkle within the soul energy.

D. Is there a record kept of each souls' activity in the Library?

Z. Yes. And it's guarded, in some way, by a group of spiritual helpers connected to that specific soul. So most souls, when they return, they go through this documentation with their spirit guides. It's not a group activity.

D. What sort of information is kept there?

Z. If we focus on this reality, what is kept for each soul is all the different layers. The physical layer is one chapter, if you like. The physical also relates to actions, how the body was maintained. It's mainly to look upon choices of actions the individual did that made them a cause and effect for other physical beings *(how your actions impacted others)*. Then they go further and look at the emotional. How they experienced—know that these are all connected, but they're also divided in each souls' experience, because you can have a completely well-functioning physical vehicle, but lack the ability to communicate or to express your emotional wellbeing. This book will help all these three layers to be more aligned in unity, to not limp, if you like. Most people feel comfortable in one, or perhaps two of these layers. The humanoid that was referred to in the past, did only activate a small part of the emotional and physical realities within their being. To not make it too complex, most people on this plane only operate in one or two of these. What is needed to be activated more is the mental realm, your thoughts and how you are not slaves to what you should think or what you should believe. This is your part, what you are here to do. Others will work on the emotional part. The physical is another group that you do not necessarily need to address. It's more, oh, one would not say primitive, –but it is, a little bit. You are working to enlighten the mental, to understand, because that is the last one that is left before moving into spirit being. But know that most people operate in only one or two, out of these three layers.

All need to be aligned. In your case, we are working with your physical being, for it to increase to the same level as your mental and emotional part. So, to use you as an example, you struggle in your physical, your biggest part chosen this lifetime, but not in your emotional or mental. Those people or individuals who are captured, or too much in their mental realm, are the ones we need to move more into the emotional. So, even though you are meant to enlighten or activate the mental realm, there is a group that is very familiar and comfortable to just simply remain in the mental realm, and they need to activate their emotional. These are more the scientific groups. Some of the religious people operate on the border, somewhere in between the two. They are sort of indecisive where they belong, really, moving back and forth between the mental and emotional. You know, operating in both.

D. Well, the emotional aspect is both positive and negative, isn't it?

B. *(Bob came back in)* Huh, hmm. You know, one of you *(he's talking about Christine, here)* doesn't really like the emotional realm, that's why she had to be a woman. She doesn't really like the emotional jungle, mumbo-jumbo, like getting stuck in seagrass when you try to swim in it! One of you is trying to avoid this specific realm, that's also why it was suggested that this specific soul would be a female. Because as a female you're sort of forced, really, to be an emotional person, because everyone else around you is. Oh, this soul doesn't like it at all, it's like swimming in seagrass. That's what she said before coming, oh, you should have seen this soul in the meeting before coming in here. "WHY SHOULD I BE A WOMAN? THERE'S NO NEED!" Swimming in seagrass, all sorts of slow. It was almost like the scissor, paper and rock game between the two of you. It was manipulated, that game, of course, because there was no chance that she would win, it was just for show. It was a little bit of a game, just for show. *(Stops himself)* Oh, oh, she's going to hear this, she's going to know it was for show, there was actually no difference. *(Sighs)* Anyway, the emotional realm is something that this one does not really want to engage in, because it just slows the individual down, in this one's opinion. That's why it's also

*You, the Soul in a Human* 105

important to be in that realm. So, know that you struggle in your physical, whereas she, in the emotional.

D. So you were in the meeting?

B. I was in the meeting. Yes, I was in the meeting. I was quiet, observing, taking notes. Because I knew that I was going to participate, later on. Ophelia was there, on one side of the table.

D. I didn't want to be a female, did I?

B. Oh, it wasn't really that you didn't want to either way, you didn't care. Which was one thing that she was pushing, that you didn't care, but she did. But it was actually suggested, because of the experience in the emotional realm that needed to take place, which was not something that was in favor. It was unnecessary, she said, but it was suggested that it would help.

D. Is the main objective to educate about life on Earth and the purpose?

B. The first book is about understanding that you are a spirit, and you come back and forth. And that your actions are actually moved along from one incarnation to the next. It follows the soul. When you come back, you have to do it all over again, at times. People need to be enlightened, so they understand they have choices to do good or bad. That they do not come in as a bad soul. So, bad actions and attitudes are actually manufactured at this plane. All your past actions are like stepping into a pair of your old shoes, –as you step in, you might want to change the shoes. You might say that to someone, do you really want to have the same shoes all the time? You have the power to get brand new shoes. People might like that, especially women, because they like shoes. They will understand, if you say; imagine that you have to go in the same shoes all the time. They can go out of fashion or not be comfortable anymore, so you want to be able to have the option to change shoes during a lifetime. But if you don't choose that, you will just walk around in those dirty, not very modern shoes (*failing to change negative behaviors*). People will see that. Oh, the first book is about giving people hope, and also, to say to people that no one is bad, really, when they come! Cause and effect has a meaning; it creates their old Coat and old shoes, which they have to pick up when they come in. There are some who are barefoot, either because of old actions, or to collect information for the masters. You will recognize those who are barefoot, who suffer a little bit, because they want to understand and move information into the collective records, so the masters know what sort of new scenarios to create for new souls to come into. A lot of the barefoot souls bring this information back to the masters.

In the next chapter, the idea of being barefoot is discussed in more detail, but since Bob uses the term occasionally, it should be understood as those people who are emotionally sensitive. He describes those who operate primarily in the mental realm as "those who wear shoes". This means they analyze things in a non-emotional way, somewhat lacking the ability to engage empathetically with people or the Earth.

I asked our spirit friends on several occasions what should be included in this first book, because of the far-ranging concepts they had covered. Their main desire is that people feel encouraged to find and communicate with their own spirit, and to be aware that everyone is responsible for what they contribute to the world. These really are the basic teachings, but also the most important, as they are necessary steps to other ideas. If someone truly embraces their inner wisdom, it can reorganize their priorities and change the way they view life. Understanding they have total ownership of their creations can give people the will and desire to change themselves. For example, if someone is prone to flying into a rage over the least provocation, and they were to drop dead tomorrow, all those patterns of anger are put on hold, stored in the Coat of Karma within the Earth's mental realm. The soul returns home, but the spirit will have to send another part of itself down in another life and assume the very same patterns that were left behind on the last visit, so the next incarnation will be dealing with the same issues. It will only get resolved when the human feels compelled to make the conscious effort to control the anger, and learns how to distance themselves from negative emotional responses.

Almost every situation has a spiritual component, and this spiritual component is the important part of interactions on this plane. People tend to lose sight of this, completely taking on the identity of the body and forgetting it's just play acting. There should be a constant, vigilant observer within your mind that evaluates your thoughts and monitors your emotions as they occur. It's effortless to hold a small rock in your hand on top of a building, but hazardous to catch at the bottom if it is released. Negative emotions are much the same; easier to control as they arise, than to stop once they gain momentum. The key to maintaining your hold on that rock is to run feelings and ideas through a filter of empathy and true concern for others. Those feelings are an actual vibration within your body, so it is a process of training your emotional state to remain at a higher level.

B. You will talk about this, you know. You will talk about how one can recognize who they really are, even though they are in this masquerade drama, dressed up in all sorts of mumbo-jumbo.

D. Are you going to give us advice on how they can recognize themselves?

B. Oh, many people have a lot of clothes on, it's like a disguise. They hide behind masquerade masks and clothes, and it's because they're afraid inside. But what are they afraid of? It's when people judge them. Other people's actions can actually put on more clothes on another soul, you know. You put on a new hat and then another, and it just gets heavier and heavier. It's about dropping it all to the floor. So, the theme of the first book is to understand the recycling program *(reincarnation and karma)* and to do the best one can, without getting stuck in the mental realm!

In one of the earlier sessions, Bob humorously described the life selection to be like planning a trip. If you think life isn't going the way you hoped, understand that it is the life you picked and you should just make the best of it. Or, as he said, make sunshine in your head. Our lives should not to be regarded as punishments, but rather as opportunities for growth within a greater spiritual plan; a plan our spirit chose for us.

B. You're all here on some sort of vacation, you know. It's like when you are going on a holiday, you don't know if it's gonna rain, and this is the same thing, one could say. Because some come down here and it just rains, and some people are just in sunshine. So it's the same thing. You might think, why did I pick this bad destination? There is nothing pretty here to see, and it's just raining. Who do you complain to? *(He laughs quite loudly, before continuing)* You can't call someone and try to get your money back, or a refund for bad weather! Then you think, if I'm stuck here, what can I do with this specific mission? So you have those people who, even though it rains, they know how to make it fun. They might bring out a game, or do something inside. It's a perception, if you like, about your destination. You can make it pretty, and you can make it fun, even if it rains and even if it's kind of ugly. It's all in your mind. People have a need to feel like they are not being punished. No one wants to make a bad choice, you know! (*Laughs loudly*) Why did I pick that hotel!? Oh, you did, you picked it, you looked in the catalogue and you picked that hotel! But now you're only looking at electric wires, and it said sea view. It's the same thing, the same thing. People need to not feel so discouraged about their choice of destination.

D. That's a funny analogy. I like that!

B. It's something people can relate to. You think you pay for a sea-view and then it's only a sea-view if you hang out your window. And then you want to go down and complain to someone. But here, you know, there is no one to complain to. You do the best you can with what you are given. And there is a reason. You are not just dropped somewhere, for someone to be mean to you. It might appear like that, you know, if you are in a boring place. But it is in the perception of each individual. Some people, when it rains, they don't just sit or go around sulking. They either bring out a game, or make a cookie or something, you know. So it's all in the head, all in the head.

D. That's really good advice. You have lots of ways to make things amusing.

B. It's simple really, it's just making it simple. It's like breaking it down to...hmm, you know, everyone is really good at giving children advice on how they should be, and so forth. But, when the children have grown up, they forget all these magical things they talked about with their children, and they forget to tell it to themselves. You know, you can tell things to yourself. Those with great imagination, even though it might be perceived as a little bit, you know, "What's wrong with him?" But, it's more fun in that head! Inside that head! It is. Don't judge those people who have funny experiences in the head. It's better than those who go around and are just gloomy. It's about encouragement, you know. It's not necessarily to put pointers to people, because there are enough people and institutions on this level that put up fingers and pointers. Go left, go right, stand still, nod! It doesn't create happy people. It doesn't create that space of sunshine in the head. It only creates rain in the head. And if you don't know how to play a game or make a cookie, then you are just sad, because you are sort of, oh, I need to go left, I need to go right, nod. You know, it's about creating sunshine in the head, then people are happy.

D. What's other advice you can give to help people be nicer to one another?

B. Oh, if people are happy in the head, then it kind of goes automatically. Because you can't act judgmental, or with a lack of empathy, if you are happy in the head. So those people who act like that have rain inside their head, they need to be brought sunshine. You can do it with a little bit of humor. You know what always does the trick, it's when you smile and laugh, not at them, but to disarm them. Foolishness, that is the best thing. If someone is really talking judgmental about things, if you sort of give them a little knock on the back and laugh a little bit, and say something like, "Well, you know, we still have Christmas coming up," or, "Wasn't it the best cake ever that this and this person brought to the fika?" *(fika is a Swedish coffee break, where sweets and cakes are shared)* You know, it's just about disarming, really, because then it just falls flat. The Buddhists are aware of this methodology and how to disarm in a way that is not considered an attack, because then it just goes back and forth and there is just rain all over in the heads. You create sunshine in the head, that is what you're supposed to do. So, you can sing, you are my sunshine, my only sunshine... *(Which he then began to sing),* "*You are my sunshine, my only sunshine, you make me happy, when skies are gray.*" THOSE ARE BAD PEOPLE WHO TAKE SUNSHINE AWAY FROM OTHER PEOPLE!! That is really bad, to take other people's sunshine. So yes, I do like that song. I also like the song *(He continued singing);* "*Row, row, row your boat, gently down the stream, merrily, merrily, merrily, life is but a dream.*"

I really appreciate the way Bob talks about acceptance of those things that can't be changed, urging us to focus instead on finding ways to make life more pleasant for yourself and those around you. Shifting attention away from what we feel is wrong with our life, and with others, by putting energy into something that is productive or enjoyable. When we become happier, we are better able to share that happiness with others. After all, as Bob said, it is really bad to make it rain in someone else's head!

Another topic that came up with some frequency is the brain of humans. As was mentioned earlier, there is a new model of humanoid being worked on that will have an increased brain size. Because the body and the brain have to work in harmony, Bob is involved in the early field testing of how to adjust the energy pattern in the new body to accommodate the new brain. There is a direct correlation between the size of the brain and the ability of the soul to connect with the higher self. The older models are going to be phased out and it should result in a more peaceful world, as the aggressiveness and lack of self-control give way to more harmonious societies. Between the demands of the physical body, and the unnecessary involvement people have with their emotions, very little capacity remains in the current operating system to use for higher purposes. Bob explains how the mental capacity of humans differs from the abilities of the higher self.

> B. We don't wish you to be confused, it doesn't serve a purpose. Your brain isn't as good on this level as it is at home. Your brain is better on another plane, you have much more space in your computer than here. It's a little bit less, *(chuckles)* it's not primitive, I would say, but it's functioning much slower here. We can't put too much into your database, because it can't handle it! That's why we put it in different waves for you. Much of the power is actually used to make this physical thing move around, and if you don't have to move around in the same way, then you have more energetic capacity and wisdom in your inner being, like the brain. This is the problem with the human mind and the brain. Because so much of its capacity is just to make the physical function, to make it move, to detect it is hungry. There is so much primitive stuff that is involved in this brain on this level. It's not the same on other places. The brain can have a higher understanding, if it doesn't constantly need to be aware of the physical body and the emotional. The emotional dilemmas are not very common on other places. It's less emotional where you have travelled before, and I think you actually prefer that. You don't like the emotional, because it doesn't resonate with you. You're not trained, really, in it. The earthly emotions are like a sticky jelly. It's a human invention, you know. It exists on other places, but there is much more empathy in the energetic form

when souls go to those places. Here, it's just a huge mishmash of stuff in the being, and the mental is shut down a little bit more. This creates a lot of different confusions that you can witness all around. Because people, souls, are not necessarily *(pauses)*. It's like walking into this costume, and there are all sorts of things you have to maneuver inside that you're really not trained for.

Even though these advanced spirits have impeccable mastery over themselves, I can sometimes hear a clear tone of dissatisfaction about certain situations on Earth. I would not describe them as judgmental in any way, but rather a little disappointed in the way people have been repressed by different groups. In the following passage, Zachariah was very forceful in his condemnation of how the ruling elite keep people in complete ignorance of their spiritual rights and heritage. Our friends and advisors from our homeland want very much for everyone to find the power within themselves, and to remember who they are.

> Z. This is to awaken the average man, to make it into their daily lives, to create new routines on how to communicate to the divine. What is the divine? Why are they looking to the heavens when all is to be found within? Similar to, why are they looking towards a preacher? Same thing. The truth lies, in their opinion, in the distance. Not fully allowed to be touched. Some gaze upon the stars. Some wait for the truth and salvation to come from a priest. Same problem. The truth is told to be in the distance, not fully to be grasped. It is that distance between individuals and the source that this book, the first wave, is trying to eliminate. Similar to making it in their own language, as did Luther. *(Luther, a German monk in the mid-1500's, translated the Bible so people could read it for themselves.)*

> Z. Just look at yourself. What did it take for you to come to be awake? You were asleep. You lacked excitement for being here. This is not only within you, my friend. Many souls lack inspiration and understanding of their path, feeling lost, feeling lonely, feeling like something is missing. What they are missing is that connection, which they are told lies within a far distance from where they are standing. There are all sorts of things they HAVE TO DO, SAY, GIVE, ACT, BELIEVE, in order for them to reach this destination, to reach that power. Similar as the people in ancient times were not allowed to read

books in their own language. We are still facing the same void between those who claim the enlightenment and those who are SAID to be followers. I will point out the word "said" to be followers. If someone is told over and over that they are followers, that they are not in charge of their faith and destiny and life path, after a while you believe in it. It is about igniting a flame, it is about helping people, as you were helped, to move into the inspiration from within. ALL carry a flame that is unique for them.

In order to find that inner connection, both Zachariah and Bob talked, at different times, about paying attention to the location where the soul connects to the body, a point slightly above the solar plexus, but below the heart. It is from this center the highest vibrations available to people can be sensed as flashes of insight or feelings, and should always be trusted more than mental ponderings or emotional responses, as it represents the unfiltered soul impulses. In this next passage, Bob is describing that process. Christine and I had gone to an event where something was said that neither of us agreed with, internally. Since he always follows me around, he was well aware of what was rolling up through our chimneys.

B. There were things said that did not resonate as a truth, and that also became a bit of frustration for you. So if it resonates, you will feel it like a tickle inside the upper part of your engine, near the solar plexus. It will feel like a little bit of a sparkle, like a tickle. If you don't get the tickle, then just ignore it. It should resonate deeply within, and it will be that tickle that tells you when it is true.

D. Well, very good.

B. Indeed. So that would be something of an advice I would give you. Did it tickle when that message came? Did you feel it in your solar plexus area?

D. No.

B. No, there you go, it's as plain as that. It's not necessarily a big magic; everything is not like, oohhh. It's simply a little feeling in the solar plexus area, either a cramp, or a tickle, or it can be felt as a freeze, a little bit like being chilly. This one has a sensitive belly, so she is aware of that when the belly becomes cold.

## The Inner Dimensions

Ophelia and Zachariah talked extensively about the inner realities available to the incarnated soul. We, as humans, have been taught and instructed to look outwards for information, guidance, and authority, while simultaneously being discouraged from being independent thinkers. In contrast, one of the main teachings from our spiritual guides is that attention should be directed inward, where we will learn of our true nature. When the soul is within a human body, it is able to detect, or perhaps feel, different vibrations. There are seven layers available to the modern human, which Ophelia says need to be mastered. Three of them we have discussed; the physical, the emotional, and the mental. I will just add a few notes about the first and second, before Ophelia discusses the entire spectrum.

The first layer is related to the magnetic field of the Earth, along with the elements and the rocks. On several occasions, Bob talked about tuning into the chakras in the feet, to sense the vibrations of the first dimension. It is common knowledge that birds and many other animals can navigate by sensing this vibrating energy field. Humans, as it turns out, also have a crystal of magnetite between their eyes and are able to tune into and feel the magnetic field of the Earth, just like other animals. Because rocks, such as granite, often contain a lot of feldspar and quartz, they too possess their own magnetic field, which is part of the resonance of the first dimension. The core of the Earth itself is a living spirit that establishes everything on the first dimension, just as DNA creates the form of our bodies. The first layer is the densest of the vibrations, and it relates to a feeling of heaviness, as Ophelia discusses later.

The second dimension is where life begins, and is bounded on the bottom by water, and on the top by the more complex, mobile creatures such as humans. All life forms can communicate with each other and their surroundings. Humans, in the past, were also aware of the information emitted by plants and animals, but the ability was diminished when our brain was rewired. Because our attention is so locked on the emotional and mental layers, the fourth and fifth vibrations, we lack the inner fluidity to focus our attention on other sensations that may be present in the body. Water has a vibration, and when we immerse ourselves in a living body of water, like a river or an ocean, we can become aware of this energy field.

Ophelia, in her soft, melodic way of speaking, gave us the following lecture on the seven layers of vibration, which I thought was very helpful in understanding where the mind can focus at any time. The goal, spiritually, is to learn how to exist or use all these layers in harmony, without getting trapped in any particular frame of reference.

O. Good evening. This is Ophelia.

D. Hello, Ophelia.

O. Hello, my friend. It is always a pleasure to be invited in this sacred circle that we provide, where we combine the higher realms and all the layers in between, in order for us to connect with you. With you, that is the physical you, as you exist in spirit through all the layers. So, if I may, I would like to draw a picture for you.

D. Please do.

O. The physical you, meaning where you put your feet, if you see yourself standing, and you can see a rainbow going through you that represents different layers of your being, the center, meaning the soul, or the spirit that we actually prefer it to be called, goes through all these layers. So you have the possibility to connect to all different dimensions, if you choose to. That is the secret of those who are initiating the higher order, or the higher...how can one say...master all the spiritual realms that are contained within each being. So, we have talked about the feet, or one of us have talked about the feet. *(Bob described the root chakra as being in the feet, where it senses the Earth vibrations.)* If you see this picture and move up, coming in contact with the next layer, that could be symbolic to midway on your thighs. Whereas all the layers are connected to your being, you have...oh, how to make it not too complicated...hmm. This is what the ancient civilizations knew about, a knowledge that has been lost over centuries. It exists in all individuals, yet most of them are not connected to this wisdom. There are actually seven layers that you are connected to, seven dimensions from this specific reality. One to seven. One to seven, where your spirit connects through them all. The eighth would be considered leaving this specific reality. The eighth layer and above is not accessible for you at this time.

D. Which level is this level?

O. This is number three. You have access to one, two, three, four, five, six, and seven. Seven would be related to your crown, your central point on your head. Let's see, the eighth is where the spiritual realm begins. Eighth and up are the spiritual levels. In prior times, individuals were actually connected to them all, from one to ten. They could carry ten dimensions from this plane. The teaching of how you have been disconnected actually relates a little bit to this. Where the three above, eight, nine, ten, are not accessible for humans at this particular time.

D. How do these dimensions relate to the Earth level?

O. You can see it as being the center of your belly area. There is a reason why people talk about the chakras. Yet don't get confused about whether they correlate to these dimensions. That's not fully the truth, but it is an ancient remnant from that teaching about several layers within each being. The first, the first dimension can be reached about one meter below your feet. This is the connection to the magnetic field that you are a guest of visiting from this plane. There are no living beings, per se, in this first dimension, yet it is the foundation of all the ones above. The first dimension is where magnetic magma makes stabilizing celestial bodies, as well as those who are guests on that body. It is the core of all realities that everyone can connect to. This is the easiest one to reach for you. As this relates to being heavy, a lot of people automatically do this without really knowing that they are. The heaviness that comes from this realm is to make people pause, to make people understand the importance of their location and where they are at. The first dimension merely exists as a spirit, it has no living beings, per se, and it is merely an energetic friend, if you like, helping guests on their celestial body to pause and to connect to the celestial body. One way to communicate with this level is to simply sit among rocks. Rocks carry the vibration from the first dimension. Not trees, not plants, they belong in the second one. The first are more fundamental to all living beings. With beings, I'm also referring to planets and other celestial bodies. Everything that is considered from this material relates to the first dimension.

O. The second. This is where matter becomes into living form. The first reality within the second dimension is the element of water. The element water is considered a living being and carries an awareness through all that sip. This is the reality where all life begins. That is why those who belong in the second dimension feel very strongly about all living beings, yet they are close enough to understand the first, meaning the rocks. They actually origin from the late part of the first dimension. All dimensions in that borderline to the next one actually carries a dual vibration from two sides, so to speak. So, between all there is...there's no black and white, there is this gray zone between the dimensions where the shift takes place. And there are entities just in that specific barrier between the dimensions. So, in the second dimensions where water takes shape, meaning from the bottom where seagrass, and where particles in the sea emerged from, that is related to the beginning of the second dimension. Moving up, we are moving into more of a living life form. The fish. The fish carry somewhat of early vibration from that layer where first dimension moved into second.

O. The third dimension is this reality, where manifestation from them all can take place, from the ones below as well as the ones above. This is where it manifests. So if you see this layer as turmoil, almost, between these different vibrations from the lower to the upper, then you can see how it can become confusing for some who are not necessarily familiar with all the different vibrations coming from all directions into the physical body. A strong soul knows, and can dissect all vibrations and not necessarily carry them all into one ball, but they can tune in on each and different one of them.

O. The fourth vibration, this is the emotional body. This is also why this correlates to the color yellow. The color yellow is related to emotions. At the highest level, it creates inspiration and it also establish joyful states in a human being, as well as those who are in the late second dimension, which means your animals. They can tune on the fourth vibration; however, they cannot reach the fifth, which is connected to the mental realms. It does not mean they don't understand, they just don't get confused by that realm. They are more in tune with the fourth. The fifth can be tricky. This is where people falter. This is especially true in that barrier between the fourth and the fifth, where emotions meet logic.

D. Is the fifth the mental realm?

O. It is the beginning of the mental realm. The crucial point at this specific time is because a lot of individuals are in that barrier between the fourth and the fifth, where emotions meet logic. And this is where confusion can become a reality. You need to be aware that a lot of people are experiencing their reality here as somewhat locked in this border between the fourth and the fifth. How to follow one's emotions yet stay in a logic reality. The technology that is rushing forward, almost like a wave, a tsunami at this specific time, relates to the fifth dimension. Those who are more in tune with the fourth get confused, feeling trapped between old ways, meaning following emotions, that the soul is actually taught before departure *(before incarnating)*. The fifth vibration is related to understanding and learning. Technology, as said, belongs in this realm. Science, those who are more inclined of learning, rarely pays any attention at all to the fourth vibration. So, you can see the different layers.

O. The sixth is where the higher senses takes place. A lot of those who works with spiritual matters can go directly from the fourth and jump into the sixth. This is where a lot of spiritual guru's falter, as they don't connect with the fifth dimension. Meaning, because a lot of this reality belongs in the fifth vibration, if you go directly from the fourth to the sixth, both being emotional states, then a lot of the wisdom gets lost.

O. The seventh. It is the pure spirit. This is where you work when you do this kind of work. This is what you can combine, it is like the core through them all. I hope the picture helps.

D. Yes, that's very helpful. Could you clarify the third dimension for me?

O. The third is where the manifestation takes place.

D. Is that physical matter?

O. Yes. This is where you belong. As a physical being, a human being, this is where you can manifest ALL layers, if you like. Some, as mentioned, are only in tune with the fifth. Meaning, they miss the emotional realms, such as the fourth and the sixth. The seventh is merely a polarity pole to the first. These seven are all accessible from this plane as a human being. Know though, that most people are either in the fifth, or in the fourth. Those who are practitioners in healing or energy work normally find themselves in the fourth and the sixth. Meaning they miss the fifth. In order for your book and for your message to be successful, you need to be aware of all these different layers that people see themselves locked into. Later on, you will meet those who are in the fifth vibration only. Your work is to make them see the fourth and potentially even the sixth.

D. Why not the seventh?

O. Hmm, that is a wish, of course. Know that the seventh is where you communicate with your spirit guides. This is where you access the Universe. This is what you can access doing regression work, as well as spiritual practices, such as deep meditation. Monks in training normally access this plane quite easily.

D. The creation that happens, that causes manifestations to occur in the third dimension, where do those originate?

O. Hmm. That is a great mystery, of course. The manifestations in the third dimension takes place from all different layers. They are brought in as experiences, staged if you like. And you are all involved in participating in order for that story to unfold, personally as well as globally. This is where the power of choice also manifests.

D. The spirit form that can enter into animals and trees, the cloud, what level does that emanate from?

O. That's not from these dimensions, it's from the tenth and above. That is the pure spirit realm. That's not what I'm referring to with the seven layers. The seven layers are considered more parts of the human creation that you are all, in some way, regardless of where you are on your spiritual journey, able to access from the third reality. They are not necessarily connected, all, to other spiritual realms. So the sixth dimension *(outer dimension)* is not the same as the sixth layer that a human can access. The fourth and the sixth, in this specific teaching, are layers within the emotional being within the human body.

D. I see.

O. So, the seventh are for those who are spiritual teachers. Those who practice their inner wisdom daily, they can reach from their physical being in the third dimension directly to the seventh. They can have a glance, an awareness of something beyond, but this is not where, from a physical being, you can reach. This is why, in some way, this reality is somewhat dense, because you cannot reach higher than seventh. The cloud that you asked about, the collective soul, it sort of hovers, if you like, belonging in the other, upper realms, that is not, necessarily, belonging as levels in a human being. It's not in the creation of a human.

D. Do these levels relate to energy centers in a human body?

O. Indeed. This is why it is also referred to as the chakras. It relates to an ancient teaching where the people knew about these layers. Later it became points, for people to connect to these layers. So, see it as layers. Some refer to them as auras. It does not matter which word you choose, it is the same meaning. Those who are practicing their own higher being in their spirit, they can vibrate, if you like, in all seven points, layers, chakras, or whatever you wish to call them. Most people operate mainly in one or two.

D. Is the third dimension related to appetites of the body?

O. Hmm. Indeed. It relates to diet. It relates to physical problems. It also relates to, let see, why some struggle with the fluid within the body. They need to connect with the second dimension, which relates to the water. They should not tune in on the first, as their body is already too heavy. So those who struggle with lack of fluid, or circulation in their physical being, they benefit by tuning in on water and the second dimension. They should not necessarily tune in on the first, as they need to let go of that heaviness. So, your physical vehicle is actually almost like a thermometer. If you pay attention to your physical being, then you will know where to find your best resource for it to function as properly as possible. So you, my friend, you need to let go, as much as you can, from the first dimension, the reality of safety, the reality of rocks. Symbolic of rocks, meaning anything that is too heavy is not good for your specific physical vehicle at this time. We want you to tune in to number two, the water. Your circulation will improve.

D. That is a wonderful description, Ophelia. Thank you.

Bob brought forward the idea of being either barefoot, or with shoes, as a way to compare the difficulties people face in life. The barefoot, as you can picture, are injured more, struggling with physical, emotional, or mental problems, often for years. They are forced, in some way, to feel. The downside is the toll it can take on the person and their relations, but the positive aspect is a potential for significant spiritual growth. A severe physical problem, for example, can also cause a tremendous amount of emotional and mental stress, so that the entire energetic body becomes involved. If the person is able to focus their attention upwards, towards the seventh layer, meditating to seek assistance, perhaps the soul may grant insight, understanding, and acceptance. Those barefoot people may, as a result, become more compassionate, patient, joyful, empathetic, and peaceful, which would not be possible without the introduction of the physical problem. And finally, those changes to the thought and emotional patterns could help clean the Coat of Karma, resolving issues that may have followed that soul for many lifetimes. So, you see, being barefoot can make for a harder life, but if the problems are handled well, accelerate spiritual growth. Naturally, we all want to wear shoes and have a happy, stress-free life, but your spirit may have chosen differently, for your own benefit.

B. People feel heavy, and you need to show them a way of transforming. If you think of a butterfly, first it is in a cocoon, and then it flies. A lot of people feel like they are still blocked within certain systems and beliefs, and especially experiences. You need to show them it is possible to do that transformation from cocoon to butterfly. Meaning from being in a more dense energy around you to a lighter, happier energy. That it is based on choices, and it's also based on actively wishing for change. And that is not something that is established in the head. It comes from within. People need to release and block the level of the mental, the logic of life. And when they do, when they move their awareness to a different part of their perception, from their head to within, or you could even call it the heart system, then it's a whole different way they can move around. The mental realm, in some way, keeps people locked and closed, and there is not much room for moving around. Whereas if you experience your reality from within, from your heart if you like, then there are no limits. That is a part of your job, to make people relate to your journey and to make people want what you have and how you did it. That is also why you walked a less smooth path up till this point. If you think of walking barefoot and some people have solid shoes. Those with solid shoes do not necessarily come with a lot of transformation in life. Their life is less bumpy, but also with less transformation and growth. Those who walk barefoot feel pain and hurt themselves occasionally, but these people are also those who have the greatest possibility for moving their whole system around. Just different ways of coming down here. Sometimes we choose lives with shoes and sometimes we are barefoot. That's an easy way for people to understand.

D. Do most people operate in the fourth and fifth inner dimensions?

B. Oh, you have the physical being, you know, parked in the third dimension. So a lot of them are only in tune with the fourth, the emotional, meaning they feel everything, but there is no logic. SO, it's like navigating for the blind. Then, we have those who only operate in the fifth, who only follow their head. That means they don't feel anything, meaning they are the ones who are with shoes. So, it can be compared to those with shoes, or with no shoes. But there is clearly not a black-and-white situation here. Only, I would say, those who are in the mental *(fifth)* layer rarely, RARELY, are barefoot! Rarely! But there are people in the fourth that actually have shoes. Like those people who come down and bring with them a very easy life. Very emotional, but yet their lives are not very complicated. Those have shoes. There are not many barefoot who are operating from the mental. Your work is to combine these two, because you're going to meet them both. So you need to learn how to address them, because in the end, the ultimate goal, I assume, is for all to be aware of all the layers, and operate in all their zones, layers, or chakras. So many words for the same thing. Stupid, really. Same thing, same thing.

D. How am I operating?

B. Oh, you're operating well. We only wish for you to not be as in-tune with the first dimension, because you are already too heavy. SO, we need for you to be more rhythmical, and the other vibrations actually carry more of a rhythmical dance, a little rhythm in the... *(He laughs loudly and snorts)* Oh, you do not need to ground yourself! Let's just say that! It's more of being mobile...to move, and just be more in tune with the other ones. You know, birds, they are good for you. All things that fly, they carry more of that quick vibration. So if you want to tune in on something, then you can tune in on birds and butterflies and those who fly. They carry actually a little bit from the seventh. Even though they belong in the second dimension, they have a sparkle from the seventh. Which means they are connected to the whole of their spiritual being, in some way. So, birds and those with wings, there is a reason why they can fly. Because they are in tune with a vibration that is very light and can carry them, and that belongs in the seventh reality. Watch the birds, you can see they don't fly just straight back and forth, they move and they float and go in different directions. This is what we would like you to feel in your body, even though it's big. We don't expect you to fly, but we expect you to be more of a rhythmical individual. So, yoga will do you good, as well as the bath, even though there's not necessarily waves in it! Huh!

D. Is the ideal human able to access all seven layers?

B. Indeed, indeed. And they are vibrating at the same frequency, ALL seven of them. It's not like an instrument that is not in tune, they actually vibrate the same, in the same rhythm. So those who are aware of where they are coming from, as well as the reality where they are putting their feet, they vibrate in more layers, but are not really concerned about the fourth vibration *(the emotional layer)*. They bypass it, because a lot of both the fifth and the fourth can cause individuals to feel locked, or stuck. So, there are layers within the human body, in your design, and these are left behind when you leave your physical vehicle. Hehe, like putting it into a storage unit. You have to go through the fourth and the fifth reality, and how you experienced them, this time around *(Bob means you have to re-live your thoughts and emotions as you pass through the mental realm after death)*. So if you lived a lot in the emotional layer, it will take more time to go through that one. The mental layer might go slow too, but if you didn't ponder too much about stuff, then it might go a little faster. But the process as a whole normally takes about the same amount of time, unless you travel more frequently. Because then your jacket is more like you just step out of it and fold it and put it into the closet.

D. What are the characteristics of the sixth?

B. Those are the ones who work a lot with energy, –healers. The best healers are those who do not necessarily tap into the fourth at the same time. Because they can be detached from their emotional beings, as well as providing emotional healing to individuals. So, those who are far along on their progress as a soul, when they operate in this realm, they can do it without being over-sensitive to things. When you see a teacher in this reality, those who only teach and remain somewhat detached, they are the ones who have learned the lessons in the fourth. Even though you can be empathic when providing services *(energy work and healing)* from the sixth, you should not necessarily tap into the fourth. Because, if combined, it's not necessarily helpful. Some teachers still operating in the fourth layer, they can emphasize the fears people have of leaving this layer, finding them easy targets, trying to attract followers. So the sixth vibration belongs in a higher sensitive order. It is not the lower, connected to the fourth. The fourth is related to emotional safety and fear. That does not exist in the sixth, which is pure emotion where pure soul-to-soul interaction takes place. Those who practice healing on a higher level, they operate, at best, only from the sixth.

D. Hmm. That is a very good description. Thank you.

B. So, that is what I think we should talk about today. That is what could be of use for your book. Because you need to detect and combine all these different beings. And you can see them as either with shoes or barefoot, or being locked in certain different layers. And if you see someone who is too heavy, then you can help them. Everyone says, "Oooh, you have to ground yourself, you have to be rooted." But some people are that by themselves you know, and they need to be more...hmm...like a liquid. It's different for each individual. So, this book will address the masses, regardless of where they are at.

D. That's really good. So, the first dimension, we sense that through the feet chakras?

B. First and second.

D. Second as well?

B. Well, because the second is related to this plane, the Earth plane, so in some way you connect to that as well. But there is, what was referred to as a layer, between all dimensions. It's sort of a gray zone between rocks and living life forms. What separated it is the water.

D. So the emotional qualities of the first dimension, you said they were heavy?

B. There's no one living there now. This is just purely a magnetic field, a body of gravity and an awareness, and it also determines the atmosphere and what minerals exist on that specific level. So when it comes to the first layer in a human, it relates to the same thing. It relates to what minerals exist or lacks in a physical body. It's like the little framework for the physical being. Don't get too stuck on details, because it might only confuse you. Only understand that there are layers within the physical body. Most people are operating in the fourth or the fifth layer, meaning the emotional or the mental, the logical spheres. So, this is what you need to combine. Also, those who operates in the sixth or seventh, you will know them as highly evolved spiritual teachers. Because they are not stuck, as a bug in glue, in the fourth or the fifth. The third is only where it manifests.

D. I actually think I understand that now. It's very helpful.

B. If you see it as this, then you understand the importance of the book, because you have to direct this first specific book to all. Later you will more address a lot of those in the fifth layer. So, you need to make them open up their eyes a little bit more. It's easier to create change in the fourth layer than it is in the fifth. Because the emotions are moving, so they are already in change. Whereas thoughts are not necessarily always moving.

D. Huh, that's really wise, my friend.

B. That is what I wanted to say. So with that, if there is nothing you would like to ask me, this is where I will resign, as they say. It's a pleasure, as always, to participate, and today I was allowed to share some of the secrets from the first dimension as well. Because, you know, being an individual that belongs in the second dimension, and it's not like I live in the second chakra! *(We both laughed at his joke)* It's just that there is a difference, of course, with the dimensions versus the layers and the chakras. Just know that there is a difference. Yet it correlates someway to agreeing. I hope it was not too confusing for you.

D. No, it was actually just the opposite, so thank you!

B. Ah, that is important to understand, there is the big Universe, and there is the small one. The smaller one is the chakras, hee-hee, it's like a baby universe. A baby structure, it's like a ladder, a cycle, a baby version within each of you. And then there is the big one, which is, oh, it's bigger than expected! When you travel to all these different places, it's amazing to see. Once you know the secrets from the first dimension, once you see this is actually where the core of minerals comes from, within all celestial bodies, as well as galaxies and solar systems as a whole, then it gives you an understanding. Because then all sorts of roads open up, and that's what's going to come forward later on.

D. Oh, I'm really interested to hear about that!

B. *(Laughing)* Oh, that's a completely different wave. So, that's going to be amusing. But now you know, now you know that it is from inside, the core, where it's designed and decided what exists on that reality. So, that is it.

D. Well, thank you, thank you so much!

Ophelia had instructed me to connect with the energy of the second dimension through water. Bob had also, on several occasions, told me to take a bath, which I never do, and put certain oils in it that would be good for my skin. The one time I had done so, Christine came in and saw me sort of sitting in the tub. Because I am quite tall, I couldn't actually get much of myself under water, which was quite amusing to her.

D. And how best to tune into the water?

B. *(Ophelia had been talking, when Bob suddenly came in)* Puhhuh...I think we talked about it before, that you should be in the bathtub, that is water for you! *(He began laughing very loudly)* UH HUH HUH HUH!! YOU HAVE WATER EVERYWHERE AND YOU DON'T KNOW WHERE TO FIND IT!! THAT'S JUST STUPID!! OH, WHERE to find the water? You're not in a desert, you know! Huh huh huh, oh, I'm sorry, that was not fair. I'm sorry. But, you know, you do have water really close to you. Everything that we are referring to, with the oil and the water, is actually helpful for you because they all carry liquid. So, you know, I see what you're doing, and you're doing well actually, paying attention, even if you did look stupid in the bathtub! HAHA! She *(Christine)* thought you did. She thought you looked stupid even if she didn't say it! Well, at least you tried. You know, we can't ask for more, really, than that you try. But you like the waves splashing over you. I don't like really when its still, because it doesn't serve the same purpose. That's why you don't see the purpose of taking a bath, I suppose. There's no waves in there. The waves are good for you.

D. I like the waves.

B. Yes, you do! Yes, you do. Float like a cork, you do. Floating like a cork, that is really good for you. Because there are minerals in the salt water that is better. There's no use to put your feet and your body in a puddle where there is no nutrition in the water. So the lakes, they don't really serve a purpose more than to cool the body down. But when you are in the Mediterranean, you like that. It actually both serves the purpose of cooling the body down, which you like, as well as giving it some sort of energy boost at the same time. So it serves a purpose. But you know, we can't have them all. You do have the mountains, and so on, and you do have the fresh air. That is important as well. We are aware that you have different options, of course.

D. Are the mountains and the rocks part of the first dimension?

B. Yes, indeed. Here you tap into the barrier between the first and the second dimension. The second dimension is where you see beings come to life. Especially here, in the mountain areas, the layer between the first and the second is very wide. It's actually bigger than in other places. Places like some desert areas, it's very thin between the first and the second, and that's why there's not a lot of life forms there. No need to be there, because the life forms don't get a lot of oxygen. You know, the first dimension actually provides a little bit of oxygen. You didn't know that, did you?

D. No, I did not.

B. No, you did not. You thought the rock was just something on the ground. This is not the layers, the chakras we talked about, but this is actually the celestial dimensions. The first dimension, combined with the outer ones, provides oxygen. Nitrogen also, in other places. Not this specific body, but other places. It's actually a little bit of an adjustment for what sort of minerals that can be found on that specific reality. You should write this down, you know.

D. I will. That's very interesting!

B. It is. The planet Mars had a different setting of its first dimension. It actually provided a lot of calcium, nitrogen, and magnesium, where plenty was found on that plane. When the magnesium became too much on that plane *(Mars)*, it didn't work well for the little beings, let's just say that. That's why it was not inhabited later on. So at this point, it is regulated from the first dimension what sort of minerals and elements will exist on this plane. Those from the second dimension know what elements exist, because we have more of a direct insight, since we're so close! That's why, that's why.

D. Did you have other things you wanted to talk about when you came in today?

B. It was to explain the different vibrations that you carry. So the physical vibration that you carry, mainly on this level, connects with the mental vibration, as well as the emotional vibration. However, the soul vibration can be detected and heard through your heartbeats. Some people actually don't listen to it, it's almost like they don't know that they have a heart, until it's too late. A lot of this is to make people aware of that they are a multi-vibrating individual, and that they should learn and enjoy to tap into all different realities they carry. And sometimes people are sort of bound in one place and it's about leaving comfort zones as well. I would say though, that you will have the greatest work ahead of you with those who are in the mental vibration too much.

D. How?

B. Because those who are more tapped into their emotional vibration are more inclined to believe in something of a higher good, if you like. And, also, have an easier path to understand that there is something beyond their physical view. The mental vibrating individuals need a lot of proof. My feeling is you will be able to deliver those answers in a future setting, where you can give them the same as you are now giving those who are vibrating in the emotional self. It is all about, really, to detect the soul vibration. That is the whole wish we, from a higher level, want you to teach. But also, to understand truly what that vibration is, and to not judge anyone else who has their soul vibration different than your own. Yours may be in one way, and someone else may seem to be in another way, but everyone has the same possibilities for balance within. Because it doesn't serve any purpose to stand with pointers and say, you know, your soul vibrates only in this certain rhythm, when you don't know that really, do you?

D. No.

B. So, as long as they understand they should not judge how others vibrate. The basic line is that those who vibrate in the emotional realm search for guidance and answers above them, whereas those who vibrate in the mental realm they only look for answers right under their nose, like in a book! So you can see where the difference lies between the groups. There is a division here, and they don't necessarily like each other either, so you can actually mediate in between them. They don't really respect each other.

D. Well, that's true, I think.

B. Because neither understand the other one. However, neither is looking in the right place, to the sky or to a book, because they have to look inside to know who they are, really.

D. Emotions are kind of restricted to Earth, aren't they?

B. Well, yes, in some way. Yet, ah, the heart form *(the higher emotions)* is a vibration that is actually resonating like empathy. Empathy is a vibration, so a part of this emotional...let's say it like this. Again, we're drawing a picture. SO, parts of the emotional vibrations, like love, and like empathy, and like tenderness, they exist, of course, in ALL universes and realities. Yet those more contradicting emotions are more bound here.

In yet another session, we continued our discussion of the different vibrations within the human energy field. I don't think Zachariah appreciated the question, or the way I phrased it, and gave me a little dressing down, so to speak. I wondered if he thought my question crossed into an area of judgement, where someone could abuse this knowledge. The cosmic laws are very clear when it comes to interfering with, or judging, another soul's development. Your personal space is honored by the spirit realm, and can only be accessed with your permission.

D. I have a question. It's concerning spiritual vibrations within the different dimensions. Is there any way to measure spiritual energy from a physical perspective?

Z. You mean, if there is a way for you to see where the soul vibrates at the highest level and in which layer, is that your question? From a physical standpoint? What is it you wish to see, my friend? You have to be clear about what it is you wish for. Why would you like to know this? How can it be helpful for you or the scripture? The questions are more than one, my friend. Why do you wish to see this and what is the purpose for it?

D. To explain the difference between spiritual energy and other energy forms that man can perceive.

Z. That is not visible for the naked eye. Yet it is the sensation that is felt during deep meditation where the spinning within circulates. It is a feeling, a sensation. Those who are with open eyes can see the energy...

*(Bob suddenly appeared and finished the sentence)*

B. Like a chimney. It's like a chimney. Okay, when you see someone sitting like a Buddha and they're in deep meditation, those who have their eyes open have the ability to see the soul energy like a chimney. However, that is not very common. Most people simply sense something has changed in the field around them. Neither of you can see the chimney, so don't expect to see people like chimneys when you are near them. Not even in deep hypnosis can it be seen all the time. It is a skill set that is only given to those who are mastering this technique, to be able to master this vibration within, and how you can come and go. It is not even for those who are considered psychic people, actually. You don't see the chimney, but you sense something is going on. So, your question about how the vibration is different, this can only be detected through your senses. You can compare it to when you were at work. Those people you were around, it felt almost like the energy didn't move, it seemed silent. You can detect the difference because there is no vibration coming from them. Then you know the vibration inside, the soul energy, is not really activated. Don't expect to see the chimney because you will be sad in the head if you do. It's not very common though, from a physical standpoint, to see anything. There are those who are trained in deep meditations for hours. A lot of them are over in the Asian region, they can see the chimney. For others, like yourself, it is simply a sensation within the energetic field within the room. It's almost like it is quiet when there is not spiritual energy, it's almost like it is dead energy. Those who are spiritually advanced transmit a little bit of like Morris Code, like de-de-de de-de-de, like little frequencies. That's why fish in the ocean, they are spiritual beings and they are pure in their vibration, and they detect others from that vibration. So, underwater it is easier to detect the spiritual vibration. It travels differently in the element water than it does in the air. But it's ah, it's a feeling about the change of energy in the room, but you cannot see it with your physical eyes.

D. I was just wondering if there was a way any scientists could make observations about it.

*(Zachariah came back in)*

Z. Indeed, there is a project ongoing in the Russian community about this specific dilemma. Dilemma because they haven't figured out the keys to solve it.

D. Should humans solve it?

Z. There is no need. Yet, due to the strong science community, there will always be an interest in solving it with the outcome of a physical answer. However, as the little friend just determined for you, there is a way to read spiritual energy in a room, which is something that can be done with small instruments that will detect differences in the magnetic field. So yes, there is a way to understand and feel the amount of spiritual vibration on this level, yet there is no need to get trapped in trying to solve it. While it will only confuse because there is no physical evidence to be found, only those that are sensed, or with this little gadget that can read the vibration in an area.

D. Spiritual energy, then, must cause some sort of magnetic flux in the nearby environment?

Z. Indeed, indeed it does. More in different regions, that is why you are in this region. There are remains of spiritual energy which can be found by those who are on the path of trying to solve the mystery. It's an energetic vibration that can be found in some way, using gadgets, similar to how you read the ground. You can use it in a simple way, like with your pointers *(dowsing rods)*, if you like. Yet it will not give you the answer to make it proven to those who do not believe. Yet, more and more will come in contact with the fact that everything radiates energy, and that everything is connected, within and without.

Zachariah and Bob have given us a lot of information on where memories are stored and used in both our bodies and in the spirit world. They also talked about the two ways in which humans can connect with their higher selves. One, the mental, is located in the head. When messages are sent and received from the mental, there is a potential for them to be contaminated by other energies. However, the connection from our central spark, above the solar plexus, is the direct link to our spirit, and is the location where our inner knowing is felt. They also pointed out there is, what can be likened to, a web of possibilities that emanates from this point. Previous experiences or thoughts actually cause future occurrences to become more or less likely. Multiple energetic lines radiate from this center point and connect, like bridges, to future occurrences. These bridges can be strengthened or weakened, like magnetic attraction or repulsion, based on experiences and thoughts. Guardian spirits read this web and intervene if they detect a probable future that is not beneficial to the growth of the soul they are guiding.

    D. I would like to know more about how memories are stored during a lifetime and after a lifetime.

    Z. It is actually stored in the same spark within the individual. It is still an energy form that creates a pattern of all experiences. It stores in the central area slightly north from the solar plexus. This is known as the chakra where joy and inspiration is transmitted to individuals. As each experience takes place, it creates a ripple of energy waves throughout this center, manifesting in new scenarios, if you like, that could potentially follow their first action. See it as a web where one action creates the wave of energy to a potential next effect. This is always stored. The brain is a human function, it's not where anything gets stored as you move from this specific plane. The souls restore their memories within this spark in their own energy form.

    D. What about the Akashic records?

    Z. The foundation from this web within each individual gets transmitted into this, what is perceived as a book. There is not actually a book form in that way we perceive books. It is stored in an energy form, but from this level (*for humans*), we talk about books. But it is stored actually as an energetic form. Think of that sparkle that we mentioned to be in the soul. As the soul returns home, it carries this little web of experiences. Some are old, and some are from their present visit. It's like layers in this web, so it's not just one dimensional.

    D. I think I understand.

    Z. Thank you. As you return to the spirit realm, this is removed from the soul so it can be analyzed, together with your spirit guides or by yourself. This is also stored individually as an energetic form in their specific record where their information gets stored, as well as a collective Akashic record, that you call it. There are groups working with this as each soul returns. See it as a little bit of a transmitted chip within the soul that gets... *(Bob jumped in and took over)*

B. Like surgery! Okay, it's my turn! It is removed, like a little surgery when they return. They can take it out and put it in a little glass bowl. It's when you get home, this is where this little chip of memory, the web, the layers are removed from the soul to be analyzed. It's not for the soul to carry it around.

D. So the soul does not carry with it all memories and all experiences?

B. No, not with it. *(Made a tisk sound)* Let's see, it's more like it's removed when they return and it's downloaded into sort of a genetic bank for that soul, and also for a collective group.

D. Okay.

B. But the memory is still there.

D. Okay, that is helpful, thank you. I also wanted to know and understand if the subconscious part of a person is the same as the pure soul that remains in spirit form?

Z. *(Zachariah came back in)* You are slightly right. The subconscious is a part of the memory from this specific little chip that the soul remembers from each travel they do. That gets moved into part of the brain. However, it never remains as the soul leave the specific destination they are at. But it is stored within the subconscious. This is how spiritual people access their home base easier. They can activate both these centers. One is part is in the brain and one is in the middle of the chest.

D. So the part of the soul that incarnates, or attaches to a body, is it always energetically connected to the pure soul that remains in spirit?

Z. Yes

D. And is it able to communicate with that part of the soul?

Z. Yes, through that part in the brain. The sub-conscious center that is connected in the brain. The emotional aspects and actions are connected to the center in the chest area. Do you see the difference?

D. Yes, I do. Thank you.

Z. The evolved souls activate both centers, and all aspects of their nature. Meaning they can communicate mentally or they can travel, actually, to different destinations of their choosing.

This is how she *(Christine)* moves. She uses this center in her brain, combined with different mechanics that are unique for her. But she can actually activate this part in the brain, and it is from this center that she moves to other realities. This is also where she receives most of her communication from other realms. This is why she is clairaudient, because it's closer to the ear.

D. Is it in a particular gland or part of the brain?

Z. Yes, in the back of the globe, back of the head is that center that all individuals on this planet have. Yet not all activate them,

B. *(Bob abruptly took over)* Because it's unfamiliar to some, and it's, ahh. I see this ones' brain *(Christine)*, wait a minute...There are several things in the brain here that needs to be looked at it. It's like lights inside that's going to turn on differently. We will not confuse you with this specific brain, because it's actually a little bit different. Because of the work you are doing, she needs to be connected to different realities. They are going to turn on different lights depending on what group is going to communicate with her, through her.

D. In a normal person's brain, is there is anything they can do to help activate the communication?

B. Do you mean the mental, the chimney?

D. Yes, with their higher self.

B. Oh, yes. This is where each soul is unique. Some are more inclined to be better receivers in the center, in the chest area. And some are more in the brain. The subconscious center in the back of the brain, the back of the head above the neck. It's kind of easy, actually, to see these different people. You can see how they interact with their surroundings and see which center is actually active in that individual. Those who are very far ahead in their journey here, like some monks in secluded areas over in the mountains, they are actually always active in both these centers at the same time. They don't have a difference in their receivers, really. So it's very different. Most are stronger in one of these two. Let me explain. When the soul leaves the Earth plane, it actually seems like everything moves into one sparkle, so it's not two centers that follows the soul. It's only one sparkle *(he appeared as if looking and reading information in front of him)*, and it seems like the light in the brain center is turned down, and moves automatically to the heart center. There is one place in the energetic web where the soul puts everything into this little bottle, looks like a little cookie, in the center. When they go home, they leave this little cookie for analyzing. It's like dissecting a frog. Where some beings are concerned, specific actions can be removed from their memory card. It's like a surgery team looking at these little cookies people bring back. It's like taking out the raisins in some cookies because it's not supposed to be there. Taking them out. (*Certain extraordinarily negative actions are removed from both the soul and the collective memory, to only be evaluated by higher spiritual beings*).

B. So, I take a lot of notes on how people manage in these different centers. If their spirit guides communicate with them, I see a light in one of these centers. Hopefully I see two, two lights. The light in the center area almost turns orange, whereas in the back it is sort of reddish. It's like a stoplight. I can determine the frequencies in a human from these centers. This is where their spirit guides can observe and help their individuals. The human transmits like little fogs from these centers and their spirit guides can actually read these little fires coming out. Then they know where they need to assist. So spirit guides look at these two centers and know where they need to bring more attention to their person.

D. And these two centers are both in the brain? (*This session was held outside, on a mountain west of Denver, and I couldn't hear some of the comments because the wind was blowing. The recorder, however, picked up everything*)

B. No. No. One is in the brain, the other is north of the solar plexus in the chest.

D. Which one is red?

B. The one in the head. They're almost the same color, it's just that the one in the center is more like an E.T! hehehe. If you look like an E.T. then you're doing well! Uh, huhuh...it's orange, pulsating almost. But this is where the spirit realm can see what the individual is planning and they can intervene if they want to. Like, let's say that, uh, you have all heard about how the guardian angels interfere before accidents, for instance.

D. Yes.

B. They can actually read, mainly from the chest area, what actions are about to take place. And if there is a little bit of a trouble ahead, they can interfere. And they move into an area in the head to send a signal for the individual to go another way. So actions are transmitted from the chest area, from that center. And if a soul, spirit guide, reads that there is something the individual is about to do, and they can help, they send a signal to the mental center so a new thought comes in. This is how people feel like they have guardian angels over them. When something happens where they just suddenly did something else, and they don't know why.

D. Well, people do have guardian angels, don't they?

B. Yes, they do.

D. Are you a guardian angel?

B. *(Smiles)* Kind of, oh, a little bit. Because you are barefoot, I make sure there's not that many rocks, necessarily, in front of you. So I sweep them away, almost like curling! That's what I do! Because there doesn't have to be more than there already have been. So I swoop, sometimes, in front of your feet, because you are a little bit tender, and your feet have always been a little bit of a problem. You picked a path with more rocks than you needed, actually. In regard to being a guardian angel, sometimes I try to push you onto another, more smooth, path. But you're stubborn as well, so some paths that you have chosen were more rocky, and then the only thing I could do was to use my little swoop and just brush like a curling *(the winter sport)*. Curl a little bit, as best as I could.

D. Is there a class of guardian angels that never incarnate?

B. Oh, you know about them. But they are like big birds. They have wings that surround whole areas of the Universe under their wing. Oh, lets... You can feel them when they come, because everything gets lighter around you. It's like time standing still almost. *(Voice gets very faint)*

Zachariah talks in great detail about inspirations that come into the body from the spirit during situations when we are presented with choices. The soul wants to lead us in the right direction, but we often allow the mind or emotions to override the more pure impulses from our very own spirit. Because each of us has a place in one of the spiritual dimensions, our spiritual energy will resonate more with that vibration. Christine and I work on the sixth, an area of logic, so human emotions have always seemed a bit foreign to me. Those who are at home on the fifth or seventh will have more of an emotional leaning, and struggle a bit with the logical approach. Neither is better, but are simply polarities that should be balanced. It is possible to be reasonable and empathic at the same time.

D. There are a lot of fascinating subjects in this *Wave 1*.

Z. *Wave 1* is primarily about choice, the choices that are in front of you; it's merely a way of looking at it, if it is a challenge, or if it is a choice to grow and to step aside from any sort of pain one might feel it comes with. That is the struggle of being in a human form, as it tends to put an angle on it, an angle of being a struggle and a challenge, more than a curiosity. Very few think about WHY it has even come in the first place. One never looks at why certain things attract to certain individuals. It is not chance.

D. Can you describe the energetic process that drives that?

Z. As you come into this reality, you prepare yourself from a variety of different topics. Anything from physical, emotional, and mental, you get the choice to pick, if you like, combined with the spirit guide. Some choose only primarily one realm to operate within, yet it is suggested you pick two, because of the polarity between two different experiences. So those who choose within one reality, let's say the emotional, rarely progresses as fast, if you like, because there is nothing challenging it. You are sort of locked, or in a safe haven, if you like, because you do not have another angle to a dilemma that might arise. So you pick, normally, from two.

D. What would be a counterpart to the emotional? Would it be physical challenges?

Z. Primarily the mental, as people tend to analyze too much. Instead of going with the first instinct. THE FIRST INSTINCT CAN NEVER come from the mental realm. It is the primary instinct that originates from your solar plexus, where your engine lies, where your soul energy is the strongest. If you see it in your body, how you blend in the solar plexus area, which is considered an emotional center, that is where you are the strongest to your soul power. As you move your experience, let's say, upwards into the mental area, which begins from the throat and up, then it can change, –the original understanding becomes something quite different. That is why the concept of "follow your gut feeling" came about, I assume. But it's not in your belly area, really, it's somewhat misleading to say that it's your belly area that responds to something. It's actually in the solar plexus area.

D. Does that represent your higher self?

Z. Indeed it does, my friend. You're doing very well, you're paying attention. As you moved into this reality, you chose to make your solar plexus somewhat asleep, yet your mental realm and physical were quite well operating, with some dysfunctions in the engine area, as you know. You've always preferred to be in the mental realm as you travel. That is more connected to the understanding you are familiar with. You are highly logical. Know that when we refer to these different realities, we are referring to it from this plane, the Earth perspective. As you move into your reality, which is merely connected to the mental capacity, it is very different. All different realities operate within more or less one specific vibration. Your home base *(the sixth dimension)* is more logical, mental, a higher understanding, not necessarily the higher feelings.

D. Would the higher feelings be better represented by the seventh dimension?

Z. Indeed. The sixth and the ninth operates primarily from the mental. The engineering. In order for it to progress in a certain manner, it is primarily operating from that reality. However, light transmits or travels through them all. Sound is related to the emotional, because it is like a heartbeat, a heartbeat and a rhythm triggers the sensations of care. Light triggers the mental progress. Put them together and the creation on different realities grow. None can exist without the other.

Jeshua, who is from the upper vibrations within the ninth dimension, has come through a few times to teach. He is organizationally the highest member of our current spirit group, although he has discussed another member from the tenth who will be present in later waves of knowledge. Since he is my main guide, a lot of what he said was personal or related to the project, but his advice on how to connect with him is applicable for anyone wishing to work with their spirit guide.

J. You have the ability to communicate with me directly, if you choose to, without sitting in a setting like this. *(Channeled sessions)*

D. What is the best way to do that?

J. You need to sit in your own power. You need to meditate. Because this is when you will get the insight of who to target *(which spirit guide)*. You have to bypass the logic mind. It has to be a wish, and that desire is solely within your control. You have the power to do so.

D. Can you tell me of any lessons I learned in a previous lifetime? *(As my guide, he would be familiar with all my lifetimes)*

J. Regardless of what you find in your past, to still honor the way you are and what you've become, to not discard a less favorable part of yourself, to see it as a whole, a learning. Don't be ashamed of who you were. It does not reflect who you are now and who you can become. That is the lesson I will give you. Regardless of how you felt, with the experience you gained in this life, it can only enlighten you to move from that still point in order to achieve greatness. It will actually be helpful to some individuals you will meet. Shame doesn't help progress. It's the lowest vibration before fear.

D. Thank you for that. Shame does make one feel small.

J. Indeed. As big as you are, everyone can encounter the feeling of shame. If they dive into that feeling or experience, they can get trapped. Grow from it, accept it, know that everyone has a point within that triggers the same feelings.

D. Very good. Thank you. Are there any other lifetimes that contain information that would be helpful, since you're being kind enough to do this?

J. There is a life, besides the one you've already been told about, where you worked with Zachariah in the temple. However, as that knowledge was lost, there came a time, in the 1300s in Tibet, where others have placed a similar knowledge, and you became a keeper of it.

D. I remember that came up once before.

J. Indeed. That was a time of solitude, dedicating your life to guarding those scripts, twelve in numbers, one for each known dimension. The mysteries within them, how you can travel between them, what you will experience as you connect the twelve dimensions within a physical experience. That was the key that ancient civilizations taught.

When Jeshua comes through, which has been rarely, the energy present in the room is very powerful and his voice almost frighteningly forceful. It can be very tiring for Christine when these higher beings come in, as she provides the battery they draw on to speak. Jeshua is the only member of our team who has ever mentioned any religious figures. He describes how the spirit world created the incarnated soul of the historical Jesus. This came up during what an unrelated question, so his observations are being included, since he would not provide unnecessary concepts. I am well aware that people have specific ideas of who Jesus was, and what he represents, but the spirit world only sees how much of the true teachings have been suppressed.

D. All twelve dimensions are no longer available to the humans, are they?

J. At this point, it is mentioned, up to seven and nine. Seven are the most known, eight and nine sort of floats above them all. Ten, eleven, and twelve have been forgotten. Back in those days, in an era before known history, it was well known how to carry within your physical vehicle the cosmic dimensions. At this point, nine is the holding of form, as it operates as the last known dimension. You will read that Jesus was a nine dimensional being, when he was actually a twelve dimensional being, the last one carrying all twelve within a physical experience. Due to the occurrences that took place, the last three dimensions decided to take a rest from the human vehicle. There are still those who try to connect, and quite well manage. Those who have the ancient scripts. Tibet is one place where this knowledge is kept. And in Egypt, there were findings underneath the Sphinx, never released to humanity, as it was considered to operate against the Catholic Church. The Catholic Church, Christianity, acknowledge nine dimensions, in some way, feeling like they have a patent on the other three.

D. So, was the historical Jesus we commonly hear about, was that the same as the Jesus you are referring to?

J. Yes, the last to carry the twelve dimensions within his physical vehicle, trying to radiate all of them.

D. Do you have any direct knowledge of him?

J. Because he carried a piece, if you like, from all dimensions, we are all familiar with him. And because he was the last one, we followed him. As he returned, that soul, oh, how can I make you understand, his soul was divided into the twelve dimensions as he returned. He was, in some way, made. His soul was an experiment to see, during a dark time, if man would recognize the light. So indeed, his soul was bigger, in some way, as it was patched up, if you like, from all twelve. He resonated with all vibrations, and as he came home, parts of him were divided back into where it belonged. So in some way, all twelve dimensions incarnated in him as twelve observers. Do you understand?

D. I do, that's fascinating. So when he returned home there was no remnant then, or spiritual remnant?

J. He returned, all twelve returned into their own home base, reporting their experience within this physical vehicle.

D. So what portions of the bible accurately reflect his teachings?

J. The part where he simply appears, with no words, radiating knowledge to those who had open ears and minds. That is true. He rarely spoke. That is a misperception in some way. He simply appeared and knowledge zippered through him to those who stood near him, like a battery. You knew, if you listened, if you were as quiet as him, you knew. He had the ability to recognize the soul in front of him, as he carried all twelve dimensions within. If he encountered a soul vibrating on a lower frequency, then he allowed the first and second dimension to communicate. Those who observed him could feel his aura, like a cloud almost, radiating. He actually preferred not to speak, even though he did. But those who were initiated in his circle, they simply observed his energetic fields as they moved from him like waves to those who were near. Allowing all twelve to speak through his presence.

D. The reference to the twelve disciples, is that an allegory to the twelve dimensions?

J. Smart, indeed. There are keys hidden in the bible. That is one. Not all is fiction.

D. Within this work that we're doing, how should we address the church today?

J. You should address it similar as it was made in that time. The Romans did not understand. Similar, you have the same crowd, the old ways within Christianity, science as well. You should know that this is a time to radiate knowledge and the more you spread, the more will hear, similar to how it was in that time. So you see, this scripture and the words, it is made to unlock human consciousness of good, a memory of a presence of the divine that was taken, in some way hijacked, if you like, by both the Church and the science community. If you make people aware of who he was and what he came here to do, that he was not proclaiming supremacy over others, like Church proclaiming to be the ultimate connection to the divine. That was not the teachings.

D. The tenth, eleventh and twelfth dimensions, are those something that we can have any knowledge about?

J. Not at this time. You will as they will move in. Don't be confused. Stick with the information you have, it is profound. It is meant to set the wheel in motion. At this point, you address the beliefs systems of the regular man; the access to the divine within each individual, never parted from the source, regardless of what you wish to call it. It is not only for a few. The Church recognized the power he had, instead of focusing on the light he shared. They were baffled by the power over man, not recognizing that it was a mutual respect, connecting soul-to-soul like a web. They misjudged it and saw it as a power of controlling souls, instead of connecting them.

D. That is a very profound way to look at it. To give people comfort they are never alone, I would like to discuss how thoughts and prayers can be heard by spiritual beings on your level.

J. Give them the symbol of creating soap bubbles, as they did as children. That is a way to send out their prayers, up into the heavens for their spirit guides and loved ones. Also, understand that some would like to know how to communicate with the level of loved ones. Spirit guides might feel too far, too vast, or vague, even. You should refer to not only spirit guides and angels, but also the communication with loved ones who have past. Soul companions meeting somewhere in-between. This will give comfort, because this, for some, is all that they need. A spirit guide might seem vague for those who are embarking only a few times on this reality, yet everyone has lost someone they wish to communicate with. Don't forget that in your book. It is a way to know that you are always connected. Those who are more awakened will read about the connections to their spirit guides and higher realities. Yet some have not come that far. You don't want to leave them behind within this scripture. As you communicate on events and so forth, that should be a part of the information that you convey to the public, OF THEIR RIGHT TO COMMUNICATE WITH THEIR SOUL COMPANIONS AND THEIR HOME! It is a right as much as free will. It is not a choice for only a few, it is each person's right. That is what makes us somewhat disturbed, that rights have been eliminated from the conscious mind within humanity. Obligations, of course, are there, REMAINING MUCH PRESENT IN THEIR MINDS, but the rights, their spiritual rights, this is what I am referring to.

D. What are some other spiritual rights?

J. To feel loved, to love yourself, to recognize the strengths in others without competing. That is a spiritual right, the law between equals, respect, instead of putting it (*others*) down, recognize your equal. Grow together, bond, instead of separate, being strong on each side. The spiritual enlightened people understand and recognize strength in others without understanding or feeling how it is a downfall for yourself. That is unity.

D. That, too, is very profound.

J. That is how the council in the ninth operates. All are equally strong, lifting and benefitting each other. It is a circle of unity. A spiritual right is to understand and love yourself as well as others, boundless, free, with no limits of how you are and why you have come. Your path is unique.

D. That's really good. Thank you.

J. Oh, you are most welcome, my son.

*(Bob came in at this point, as Jeshua left)*

D. I have another question you can answer. I was asking Jeshua about, you know, when people think about someone that has passed on and their spirit is in another vibration.

B. Like dogs? *(I don't think he followed my question, but I laughed at his response)*

D. Yes, anything, even pets. For example, if I think about you, how do you pick up that thought?

B. Oh, it's like a bell. It resonates within me, it's like, ling, ling, ling, ling, ling, ling. It's like a bell and I know that you are trying to reach me. So it comes as an impulse, like a little bleep, bleep, bleep, from your being, either from your solar plexus area, which is completely pure, or it can come from the mental area, which is more creating as a wish, an analytic connection, in some way. So if you're focusing on sending your wish to us, from your solar plexus area, then you will feel us in your whole being. However, if you only send it from your mental capacity, then you would only communicate with us with certain pictures, which will be more limited, but we can still communicate with you that way. However, if you fully want to engage, then you have to send out that wish and energy for us to communicate directly into your solar plexus area. So, you do that and I will hear you. So will the others. Don't send, don't–, don't be like a chimney. The energy comes from the core, from your breast region as well as solar plexus area. Feet should be solid on the ground, both feet solid on the ground. And you just imagine that you just send out a huge wave of colors, not only yellow, but you send out the whole spectrum of colors from that area. And you feel how your energy is expanding, and then you welcome us in. That's when you will see us, as well as feel us. If you only try to communicate up through your head, like a chimney, then we will certainly be able to put pictures into your mental realm. But you will not necessarily see us and feel us fully, but you can communicate with your thoughts. If you want to fully communicate with us as well as those who are on your home base, then you use your solar plexus area. Different.

D. Yes, I'd like to know how to do that.

B. I just told you! *(Laughing quite loudly)* HAHAHA HUHUH You're a little slow in your computer there!

D. Well, when you send that out with colors, do you visualize where it's going?

B. Indeed, when you send it out, you see how it's spread out like a whole wave going in all directions in front of you, and you ask for, in the beginning you can ask for one of us to come, and we will travel on the color wave that resonates with us, and then it will directly connect with your solar plexus area. You have your eyes closed and you ask for our presence to be known, but you also have to send out the wish for us to come. This is an easy trick for you to communicate with us. And you will not only sense us in your own being as we move into your layers, energetic fields, but you will also be able to communicate with us. If you only use the chimney, then we will communicate with pictures, and you would think that that is good enough, which it is in some way. But if you fully want to embrace your family, or fully engage with all of us then that is how it is done. Feet on the ground, steady, straight back, that is what you do.

D. Then you send it out, a full spectrum?

B. And you send it out, you puff it out, a full spectra of all the colors that you can think of. All the different variations of colors are good. And you send it out and you ask for one of us to come, and we will pick the color, the wave color, for us to communicate with you.

D. If I include that in the book as a way to communicate, there's no danger that people will pick up beings from the fourth dimension that might be lurking around?

B. If they only use the chimney. But as they communicate directly from their own source and their own soul particle, it's no danger. Colors. NOTHING BAD CAN TRAVEL ON COLORS! Whereas the chimney can be dirty. You know a chimney, how it looks. It can be gray and dirty. And if it's gray and dirty, there can be all sorts of other gray and dirty. But if it only comes in colors, nothing bad travels on colors. So, you say that to them. It's almost impossible to send out gray and black from that region, within your being. If you do so, then you're responsible. But it's almost impossible to come from that part. There's only colors in that region. STUPID, if you try to do something else. It's almost impossible. You don't need to worry about that too much. Nothing bad can travel on colors.

D. Awesome! Thank you.

Ophelia also described a method to communicate with your higher self, and even though it was directed to me, it is universally applicable. When I was young, I had very bizarre experiences that I never could explain. Every day, sometimes almost continuously, I would have strange visual distortions of zooming back and forth. Whenever I ever looked at something and locked my eyes on it, within seconds it would feel like I was inside a spring, and the image would start zooming out, and my peripheral vision would become black, like looking through binoculars backwards, and then it would zoom in like it was coming very near. Back and forth, back and forth, until I became nauseous. I had no control over it and could not stop it once it started, it just kept going with its own cycle. It eventually would stop, for a while. But it went on almost continuously, from when I was a baby till early teens, then sort of tapered off. It has occurred only a few times as an adult. I asked Ophelia about this experience.

O. When you were a young boy the energies rotating, if you like, inside were stronger. Now it has been sort of slowing down. It will return to the way it was when you were a little boy.
D. Is there anything I can do to help that process?
O. Yes, you can sit still and try to welcome the vibration and the rotation that you will sense like a spinning inside. This frightened you at one point. At this time, you are an adult, and you know that it has the potential for you to connect with something divine. As a boy, it scared you because you did not know how to make it stop. You will start feeling it in the lower center of your belly and it will move like a wave up through your solar plexus. As it reaches the center of your chest, that's where fear, prior, kicked in. This is where you will now persevere, and you will connect to that power within. Sit in that power and fully embrace it. Your breathing exercises can be helpful. The breathing needs to be very deep and connected to the Earth for it to have the effect we are referring to. No shallow breathing. The breathing is to go down into the Earth through your feet, up through the base, through your spine, through your inners. Transform at one point in your solar plexus area. This is where it starts to feel a bit uncomfortable. Continue the breathing in the same pattern and it will continue to vibrate and it will continue to rotate. You might feel like your whole physical will rotate, it will not. You will simply follow this vibration, how it spins inside of you. This is where you have power, if you exercise this, to have an OBE, to leave your physical body if you choose to. That is what we wish to say about that.

# *Earth, 2nd and 3rd Dimensions*

No discussion about the third dimension is possible without including the work of spirits on the second dimension. When we think of DNA, we are thinking about the end product of the labors of many brilliant spiritual beings on a reality that exists vibrationally not that far from ours, although still invisible. I never really understood how creation comes about, until we began having fascinating and amusing dialogues with Bob. He has completely changed the way I view the Universe, our planet and all the nature that surrounds us. Every plant, animal, fish, cloud, tree, and bug has been carefully designed and modified over countless millennia, to be a success in its environment. It is truly embarrassing to realize how much of their work is being undone as we humans thrash around in the community greenhouse; chopping, poisoning, and eliminating the laboriously planned and skillfully executed balances built into nature. Earth would be a barren rock without a single drop of water, if not for the creative talents of the spirit world, and of course, the Master Mind. In some sessions, Bob has wondered aloud about why he invested so much energy into a project, only to see it taken away. It's like spending your whole life lovingly building a home, only to have a passing vandal burn it down because he wanted to roast a marshmallow. It causes such a sadness in all dimensions, especially the second, that it is mortifying to think about. And, to add to the embarrassment, every single thing that lives, except humans, contains awareness from the Master Mind, who created us all, so nothing goes unnoticed.

The beings with a home on the second dimension have a near-physical body, meaning that they can occasionally be glimpsed, if they want to be seen. Bob, and those who are like him, take designs that come down from the higher realms and work on them in the lab. Then they do field testing, getting the design into a final form to introduce on certain locations in the third dimension.

Wherever life is found, the second dimension is involved. Even the fifth dimension has beautiful gardens and ethereal animals, courtesy of these little gardener spirits. There are many different types of beings found on the second. Bob described some of the little helpers as very tiny "light bearers", because they restore and repair color patterns in plants with the light energy they transmit. Others are observers, who report back to the labs on the second and eighth.

B. Did you see them? Did you see them on the river, you know, like little foam? It's the small ones, teeny tiny, they're like fairies, almost. You see them as bugs, but they're not bugs. They have wings, but they're not bugs. Don't see them as like a dragonfly, they're smaller, like a bug, but they're actually spiritual sparkles from the second dimension. So I will talk about the second dimension, as this is somewhat of an expertise area for me. So, I'm sort of solid, you can see me as a person. But there are all sorts of sparkles and levels within each reality. So here we have those that simply sort of sparkle in sunlight. You can see them, you see something in the air and you feel like, oh, maybe it's the sun, maybe it's dust. It's not dust. It's not dust, it's them! The small sparkles from my world. They are as important to this reality as the big ones. They're shy, a little bit. Most in my group, we are a little bit shy to the bigger ones. The sparkles, they don't merge with things like stones and plants. They can merge sometimes, like with a leaf. Those you see like foam in the river, those are actually bigger. You would probably consider them like bugs, but they're not.

D. I have a question, then. What people see as fairies and gnomes and little creatures like that, are those also second dimension? Are they different from those in your group?

B. You don't see them in the lab, because they don't have hands like we do. So, as it was mentioned, from the creating force, the Master Mind, –if I talk about my reality–, from the Master Mind it is created different levels of manifestations, if you like. Some are sparkles, and they actually observe elements and shifts in the wind and so forth, because they can float easier. I don't float like the wind, I would fly if there was a storm, but I don't float in it. So, these little sparkles are mainly observers. It's like those things you see, you have them in this reality, those things that flies over and take pictures *(like a drone)*. It's similar, but they are more disguised. If the sun is on you can see them, and you see them and think it's like a dust, but it's not, really. Those are in resonance with wind, rain, sunshine, and they float and they observe, reporting to the eighth, in some way, because they *(the eighth)* are the masters of the elements. Though they are nature spirits, in the sense of the word, they observe shifts. So, you can say they are like our eyes and ears, before we take action in the lab, for instance.

D. So you don't really interact with them?

B. Oh, you can hear them, if you are trained to, because they download information through different vibrations of light.

D. Do you get information from them?

B. I'm not trained, really, to communicate with them. But there is a group within my group that works a lot with understanding the shifts in the elements. But we all took that class at one point. It's not like you skip any classes as you progress.

D. So, the little creatures that help the plants, that people see as fairies and things, is that another class?

B. Oh, the fairies. The fairies can actually be, in order for it to manifest so a human can see it sometime, it can actually be several from those sparkles that join together in a cluster and they create a form for humans to see them. So, it's actually several. If you look too long, it will actually dissolve. And why is that? It's not just one entity, it's several. So, when you think you see something, and you look at it and it dissolves, it can either be that there are several, like little sparkles, those who observe the environment, or it can be that it is shy and it actually moved into a solid form and hid. Because there is this fear of being detected and so forth. We actually take classes in disguise, but as we grow, we become more bold and we want to be seen.

D. Do you?

B. I want to be seen!

D. Well, I suspect you might, but others?

B. The people in my lab, they are still a little bit shy. So if you were to see them in nature, those who are a bit shy, they will just sort of blend into a solid form, a tree or a rock. And you thought, you know, didn't I see something? And you kinda did, but then it's gone. But if you pause and just look around where you thought you saw the little creature, it might come back. But if it doesn't, it's just shy. I, on the other hand, like to be seen.

D. I would like to see you.

B. Ummhuhu. You have seen me! In other lifetimes, where the conditions within your own physique and your own mental realm was different, combined, then you saw me more clearly. But the world in general was not ready for those types of knowledge, and you were in a setting where this wasn't their reality.

People take almost everything for granted, never pausing to consider the mysterious way things come into existence. The second dimension is responsible for creation on all planets in our fish tank, with the Earth being among countless places where life exists. Bob is only one of a multitude of second dimension spirits who joyfully work as creators, caretakers and gardeners, tending to all the things they have put here. There are many specialties these spirits can pursue, which is largely determined by their predestined pattern. Unlike humans, all their activities and goals are useful and helpful to other entities. Bob is a specialist with the engine *(digestive system)* and the liver in animals. Bob's tutor, Gergen, who is like a father to him, is a master of DNA manipulation. Bob's twin spirit, Ia *(which he pronounces as EE-ya)*, works with light energy on the inside of life forms to assist with healing and repairing damage or injuries. Evolution is entirely a product of our unseen friends in the various dimensions, working together with the Master Mind. When instructions are sent down from the higher realms, these little individuals are the ones who ultimately create and modify the plant and animal life on Earth. As an example, Bob takes a little credit for the coffee bean, as he was in charge of the team that brought it forward. He also had a role in developing the earthworm, and is quite distressed at how commercial farming knowingly kills off these creatures. A lot of speculative theories have been proposed of how things come into existence and change over time, but I am aware of none which reflect the truly spiritual nature of the process. The beings in the second dimension have been creating life on Earth since it was a baby planet in the nursery.

Bob was born within the second dimension, and occupies a form which is nearly solid, from our perspective, and similar to a human body, but smaller. The bodies of those second dimensional beings start out quite tiny. Bob calls them sparkles, and they do grow and age, but not within a framework of time. Growth is measured in experiences, or cycles of learning, and as they move along in their cycle they appear to grow older. He is currently studying and learning about form, and will probably soon move into a role within one of the councils on the second dimension. When he was a little sparkle, he stayed within the second dimension, but has now developed to a point where he travels, as he calls it. This is the process where he can project a part of his consciousness into other dimensions. Bob is able to project about thirty percent of himself into the Library, and also about sixty percent into the labs on the sixth or seventh where he is currently studying. Since he is my guide, when I incarnate, he dedicates part of his traveling energy to follow me. He is perfectly aware of the different locations, and he can focus on all places at once. Besides his incredible knowledge about the Earth, he has a delightful personality and the way he perceives things is unique and entertaining.

An aspect of the beings who work on the second dimension is their ability to merge with objects, which Bob calls "blending." This is actually part of their learning experiences on the Earth, as well as on other celestial bodies. Just like our soul can slide into a human body and then leave again, our friends on the second dimension can merge their energy into rocks or other life forms, and step out any time they like. Bob is about one and a third meters high, and from his descriptions, other types of beings in his dimension can be quite a bit smaller. Most of them are shy when they are out on the Earth repairing damage or collecting samples. Since they do not like to be seen, they can just disappear by stepping into a tree or a rock. He works in a laboratory that is joyfully buzzing with talking and laughter. He said I would consider it disorganized, but they do seem to enjoy working in groups. Even though most of the second dimensional beings are somewhat reserved, Bob is more outgoing and curious. That is part of the reason he was picked by Ophelia to study how form is created on the sixth and seventh dimensions. Ophelia tutors him in lectures and labs on the seventh dimension, which are related to light energy. If we take a planet, for example, the core pattern is made from light, sound, gravity, and vacuum, which cause certain elements to manifest. This work is a combined effort between the sixth, seventh, and eighth dimensions. Christine and I *(our higher selves)* work in a lab environment on the sixth. I was fortunate to get Bob as an apprentice, and have been teaching him about how we use energy to create different types of manifested objects *(I don't recall any of this, of course, but have learned to accept their statements as truth.)* Based on what he has told me, we have been together for a long, long time, in Earth years. And he has always followed me as a guide when I incarnate. As a guide, he learns and evolves. All spirits are given a blueprint to evolve, not just the souls incarnating as humans.

B. I've been with you before, you know. My notes are not just from this lifetime.

D. Have you ever incarnated?

B. Not in a human form. I've visited, of course.

D. Do you work with any of the animals?

B. Umm, you know, the elks are a favorite group of mine. They are intelligent. There is more inside them than just a creature on four legs. They are the ears and eyes of the second dimension. I do not approve of how humans sometimes treat them. We do not approve.

D. What type of animals have you incarnated as?

B. Not as an animal.

D. What then?

B. I was here in a...oh, it was before I traveled *(projected part of himself to other dimensions)*. Those do not exist anymore. It's a little creature, with a shell, almost like a small turtle. It was merely to see how I could operate within another being. This animal does not exist anymore. The animal I blended with, which is not the same as incarnated with, because I could come and leave as I chose. It's very different. And this particular creature did go underground as well. There are actually, all around you, things that you perceive as dead obstacles, like rocks, but actually contains an entity observing the surroundings. They are there in disguise, and I wanted to see how to be disguised. There are things in nature that are more than meets the eye, you know. So you can come to Earth on different layers, or levels, or planes. Everything does not need to be in an incarnation to evolve in the form of being a child, young adult, retired, and so forth. So when I went down, my level was different. And we will address this for you more in detail, because there are ways to come to this plane without going into a human body or an animal form.

D. Do you have anything else you would like to share?

B. Well, I'm happy to make myself known to more people, and have some of my expertise shared, really. Because, a lot of times, everyone says, "Oh, look higher up, look up to the angels and all sorts of other beings, way high up." But they forget to look down at their feet. We're just sort of below the feet, if you like, we're really close.

D. How long have you been with the Earth?

B. I came around the time when the great changes of weather occurred. There was a time when there was a huge cloud surrounding, encasing the planet. Tremendous rains. I was observing only. There was a time before, no...the dinosaurs were gone.

D. So this was after the dinosaurs?

B. After. After the dinosaurs. Dinosaurs were a project of an intelligence that is operating from a different star system. So, I came after.

D. When you're on the third dimension, how do objects feel to you? You can sense a tree and a rock?

B. It appears energetically, in some way, because that's what I can read. The people in my lab, they can read if something is wrong, because they see it as an energy. Even though it is solid on this plane, we see it in an energetic form. So we can see, let's say, that a tree is supposed to have a certain variety of colors in its color map. If a color is missing, that is when we can come in and try to adjust and correct. So, we see it as energies, even though you see it as a physical object. But it is created in a physical vibration. So we can create things that are going to be physically manifested for those who are on that plane. However, I can also see something that is only in an energy form, which is similar to what existed prior to another form had taken its place. Let's say you have a city that is built up. I can still see what the original intent for that place was, based on not manifested things anymore, because they have been removed. But I can still see their spirit, if you like, because it is still stored on that place as an energetic memory. I can still see it.

D. That's fascinating.

B. So we see things in energetic forms. But, if I see, let's say, two trees, I can tell if one tree is only energetic, it's not there anymore for anyone to encounter. I can see the other energetic tree exists on the physical, –it looks different to me. This is sometimes where people can say they can see different realities, like layer on top of layer. Then they tune in on the energetic memory that once was there. It can also be certain things that, you know, I'm talking from my perspective of course, with trees and stuff, BUT, you can also see certain occurrences that took place, because it's stored like a memory, like an energetic chip almost, what took place. Some people who are psychic or very in-tune, when they come to certain locations, they can see EXACTLY what took place.

D. How far back in time?

B. Oh, it's not that far back. It's not like from the beginning of time! It would be all sorts of crowded!

D. It somewhat fades over time?

B. Indeed, it does. You see the manifested one, which is currently existing. Then you see one that, let's say, is from a hundred years back. Not existing anymore, but it is still vibrating as a memory on that specific place. And as it goes further back, it fades. So you can see, somewhat in rewind, what existed, and I'm talking about trees and plants and stuff at this point. Rocks, they tend to not really move unless someone is building something.

D. What about in the future? Can you see what is to come?

B. I cannot.

D. How long will you remain with the Earth...how long will you stay here?

B. I come and go, you know. The mission has changed over time. Now I, because we all evolve, I want to evolve by communicating with the souls that I interact with in spirit form. There is a community of us that wish to learn from souls that are from a higher species coming in. And I am fortunate to be one of those. Well, uh, this will be where we end the session for this specific topic.

D. Thank you for joining us. It is always a true pleasure to be with you.

B. Ah, it is from our perspective as well. It's a way to learn how to communicate through a third vehicle and to feel that you are involved in a process that could lead humanity forward. My concern is for animals, and I wish there to be a higher awareness and empathy for creatures. Not just those who are cute. There are creatures in nature, like insects and bugs, that are highly valuable to this ecosystem. Like the bees.

D. We will add that to our book, if you like.

B. Uhmm. Yes, please.

Bob talked about how the second dimension will use certain planets as greenhouses, where plants, insects, and animals can be placed to see how they progress over time. These planets are not programmed for evolution, so whatever they place on there can grow with no outside influences, and then be examined to see if it meets the objectives they wanted to achieve.

B. I know of planets that are more like a big greenhouse. You can visit and put your project, just release them there, and they will just flourish, if you like, and you can go have a look-see, to see how they progress over time, because they are not going to be interfered with by other activities. So whatever you put there, and whatever destiny or life purpose you had for that specific creature or plant, if you like, that will come to term, because there is not any outside factors that will interfere with each individual, each entity here, because it is like a greenhouse.

D. Well, it's good there are places like that out there, otherwise you might get discouraged.

B. Because some of them are put through the process of evolution. Let's say you create a beetle, and you want to see how it becomes after a certain amount of time, in order for you to maybe launch it in a reality where it will encounter certain outside effects. Here *(on the greenhouse planet)*, it is not interfered with. So you want to see how this specific beetle operates after it has progressed for a certain amount of time. And let's say you want it to be a very active beetle, and you see that, uh-oh, the evolution it went through made it become like it's retired, it became lazy, so then you readjust. It's a way to see, without it having to be interfered with other things, and a lot of it has to do with climate changes as well, so it's not only humans who interfere, of course. But here we see the individual or entity itself without interference, and then we put it where there is interference. So, that's what we do.

## Earth, the 2nd and 3rd Dimensions

I was curious how Bob came to be in several places simultaneously. He once said he is always in the Library vault, and another time he mentioned never leaving the second dimension, so he was able to give a very good explanation of how spiritual beings split themselves. Each of us who are incarnated do the same thing, because part of us is here, and another part is existing elsewhere at the same "time."

D. Okay, I have a question about you, Bob. I know you operate on both the second and fifth dimensions, but where is your true home?

B. Second.

D. And how did you get part of yourself on the fifth dimension, in our vault in the Library?

B. Through Gergen *(his teacher)*.

D. So do you, in some way, split your soul?

B. In some way. It's a transformation that occurs when you move between layers that you are allowed to move in between. Some need assistance. But it is a way of projecting part of you. So it's like I project a part of me to the vault, for instance. And I'm projected there, but because I'm solid in many ways, I appear like the other ones who are projected there, similar to like Ophelia's big class. I project myself because I am allowed to, but I'm always connected to the second dimension. The more I progress, the less I leave behind. So I can project more of my energy, let's say, to make it easy for your human computer, which is not very big, let's say it like this; when I first started helping in the Library, I was like 50 to 60 percent in the second and I just left the rest, like 40, in the vault. As I was allowed to move to your lab and to go to classes above, I left like 10 percent in the second. I constantly like to have about 30 in the vault, because it does tend to take up a lot of my capacity and my paying attention to details within it. I do want to be thorough, so I don't want to leave less than 30. However, the rest I'm splitting up, I don't like to take the rest *(the 60 percent)* and split that up between six and seven, so I take the rest and either go there, or there *(to sixth or seventh)*. Now, I'm leaving like 10 in the second. And that's why when I get home I need to withdraw back in a lot of my traveling energy, if you like to call it that, because I kind of miss things at home. I do like to travel, but sometimes I feel like, since I'm not really that present, I kind of loose touch with...I have friends you know, who don't travel, and I don't want to appear like I don't care what THEY do. So I like to go back now and then just to show that I'm actually still the same, even though I'm traveling more. A lot of them are like little gardeners and they operate on the third, so I try to go back and see what they do.

D. You need to get a little helper to take notes for you!

B. I do have, you know, little students. They sort of keep me updated on certain things, but it is hard. I would say it's easier for you to understand that I project myself.

D. I do understand that. I was curious which dimension you were created on. Thanks for clarifying that.

B. Home is always in my lab, and with Gergen and my students, and my friends. A lot of them are gardeners.

Almost all Earth based cultures that existed before the mainstream religions destroyed them had a knowledge about nature spirits. Bob confirms that not only do they exist, but are much more common and diverse than you might imagine. This multitude of different spirits serve critical purposes on our planet. Bob makes several interesting observations in the next session. He says that some cultures knew of the existence of the little nature spirits, and were able to see them *because* of their belief. Then later, he explains the mystery of how animals seem to know ahead of time about natural events like earthquakes and tsunamis. Because all animals can telepathically communicate with nature spirits, they are told of these upcoming events and where to go to be safe.

B. You know, I did take notes when I was in Ireland. I like Ireland. I like the nature spirits in Ireland and Scotland, because they are funny, they are like little balls in nature. Nature spirits. So I do have a warm heart for that region, the islands.

D. Yes, I hope to go there some day.

B. There is also a place north, the Faroe Islands, that not many people go to. There's a lot of nature spirits there, and I spend time in that area contemplating about my notes and stuff. It's a place that is still untouched, if you like. Hmm, there are a lot of energy spirits in the region from Ireland and Scotland and up. Even Iceland has untouched areas for nature spirits from my realm to move around more freely, and they are welcomed there. In most places, there's not a lot of understanding for creatures from the second dimension. Because they can't see them, so they do not exist. Which is a misconception because, you know, it's like not being able to see the ocean, even though it was there and you could hear it. That's what we talked about before, about how you can hear something, and even though you can't see it, you know it exists. It's the same with the second dimension. Indians, natives that live here are aware, and there's also groups in South America, and the Aborigines in Australia. Native civilizations know we exist even though they can't see us, and once they know and appreciate us, they can see us.

D. That's a good secret!

B. It's because they know how to look through the rocks.

D. What are your responsibilities in the second dimension?

B. It's about creating balance in the waters, that is one of my responsibilities. Also, the minerals, which is like the quartz, it's put into certain places in order to create energy shifts in nature. So it's about creating balance in elements that are existing in nature.

D. Is the center of the Earth a crystal?

B. It's more of a fireball. It's a crystal, but it's more like a liquid. It's not solid like a rock. It's a living entity, actually. It's a red liquid. It's a little heater, almost, like a generator inside. It's not a crystal. It's red and a little bit moving, so it seems to be of liquid form. But not liquid like water, but more like your Greek yogurt.

D. How do souls, like yourself, develop in the second dimension?

B. Oh, some are still learning how to blend with solid materials, the rocks and the trees. They are the children, learning still how to blend with solid material, to come and go, and to observe. So they begin with learning how to blend and to observe. And some are moving further, helping animals, communicating with them. Helping them move to safe spaces when there is like earthquakes and so forth. You know how they can understand when they're supposed to go when there is like earthquakes and tsunamis, for instance? That's when they get told by the teenagers *(refers to those in the second dimension who have evolved from sparkles at the childhood level)*, but the teenagers also have teachers. So there are those that only work with communicating with animals, and also making sure that when there are shifts in the Earth, like from magma, that it occurs correctly. Because there are still shifts going on, in order for the continents to move slightly, a little bit. So that is also something that these spirits are involved with. I work to blend mentally, energetically, with incarnated individuals such as yourself. I also take notes, and I store them in the Library. And I take notes from my colleagues working with the rocks, because we don't want the children to be locked into the rocks! So there is this manual on how you exit rocks and how you go back in. There are these notes about our realm as well, because that is another vault.

D. Do the continents move slowly, or do they sometimes move suddenly?

B. Oh! That is up to the masters! Because they can move quickly, actually. It is a little bit misleading that it is just moving bit-by-bit, slowly over time. It has actually, in the past, gone much faster. And that is when you can see certain animals are in places they're not really supposed to be. You can find a tropical animal up where there is snow, for instance. There are signals, but man chooses not to pay attention because it doesn't fit into their reality and their own books. But there have been occasions when it has gone much faster. There are actually individuals *(animals)* found in the African continent that are winter creatures, as well. So it has gone faster, and it is based on some sort of master design, I'm sure. It was something with the climate that needed to change. There was something with the atmosphere, and ohhh, when seasons came in. A change of seasons. Also, where life was to flourish more.

D. How many other incarnated humans do you work with?

B. No, no, there are others who work with humans. I only work with you. I don't know how to move around that much, because I've only started to learn how to communicate through a third person. I don't know the others. I can see them, I can observe them, but I don't communicate with them. It is set and decided before departure in the meetings. I work with our group only.

D. Well, we're glad you are working with us.

B. It's like a family thing, you know. It's like you're part of a family tree, even though you are different. It's like *(gets real loud)*, I'm a little bush next to your tree! I'm a little bush, so you can see the bush didn't go that far, stands next to your tree. *(This is*

an amusing way of saying he is small compared to me, and because we work together, he stays very close.)
D. But you're such a powerful little bush!
B. So yes, the bush sticks to its tree. *(Laughs)* It's like, there I am! So, that's sort of it. It's not such a big mystery, really, but we also want to be heard. And not everyone can hear us, so we can call, and we can call, but no one hears. I know others who also work with some sort of communication. The hardest part is trying to work on this level. Animals are always receptive, whereas an incarnated soul in a physical body is harder to reach. It takes a little bit of training. Animals are always aware. They hear us differently, so it's easier. It's a reward, really, to try to energetically blend with another energy form inside a physical being, and try to communicate as best as possible.
D. I had a question. What sort of souls or spirits do animals have? Is it like a group soul, like a deer, or an elk?
B. It's the same soul. There is, in each individual *(Bob calls animals, "individuals")*, a little spark of the soul. Yet, it's different from the soul in a human, because if you see like an elk family, it is actually the same sparkle that maneuvers and works all the different bodies. It's like a collective spirit. It's bigger than another kind of spirit. It's more like a big cloud coming in and it sort of blends, or just maneuvers from that source. If you could see this cloud, it's just a little above the animals and sort of maneuvers them in a group, if you like. So all are actually connected to this big cloud above them, and the big cloud is the soul, of sorts. It resonates to a part in the big central mind. It is almost like a brain, a central brain where this cloud operates from, through little animals. So there are souls in each of them, they just belong in, or are a part of, the same cloud.
D. That's a very good explanation, very interesting.
B. And they communicate, they are more inclined to their mental centers, because the cloud belongs as part of the Master Mind.
D. Does that Master Mind exist in the pure spirit realm?
B. Oh, it's like a central, in the middle somewhere.
D. Is it in the mental realm?

B. It's not in the mental realm. Don't mix this up with the mental realm around the planet. This is the source of creation, so this is where the Master Mind belongs. You can think of it in this way; that there is a Mother energy in this central creation, then there is also the Master Mind. And there are several organs. But the question about the animal, its soul comes from the Master Mind. They communicate through them telepathically, that is why it's from the Master Mind.

D. Are you from the Master Mind?

B. We are all, in some way, from the Master Mind. But that is where I receive information, because it's telepathic, almost like radio stations sending information through waves of impulses. It's like the Morris codes, that is sort of how it would appear for you.

D. Is that how you sense it?

B. It's like de-de-de-deet! De-de-de-deet! It doesn't say anything to you, does it? So you have to be in tuned with those radio signals, otherwise, it's just like de-de-de-deet! And it doesn't really say anything to you.

D. Well, the mental realm around the Earth...

B. Very different. It's not the Master Mind.

D. What lifeforms contribute to that?

B. There's no lifeforms in the mental realm, really. It's where the soul experience creates images in themselves. It's not a lifeform, per se, in that realm.

D. Are these images only coming from the souls that inhabit humans?

B. No, the Master Mind is in animals, and the animals experience things. Just because they are operating from one cloud doesn't mean they don't experience things. They also leave a record, which is created and stored within the mental realm. But it's not like leaving a jacket, really. They just move into a spirit form in a different way, because they don't have the soul that's going to go through, pondering about things they did. But every experience they have gets recorded in the mental realm. That's why we don't want you to eat them. And that is why you're not supposed to shoot them and treat them badly, because that also creates a little bit of garbage in the mental realm. We talked about this. There are the Coats, but also

these other experiences that needs to be cleaned up a little bit.
D. I was curious about what types of creations leave memories in the mental realm. What about trees, do they too?
B. Yes! Yes, trees! *(Gets quite loud)* That's why you're not supposed to just shuffle them down! You don't have to have all this paper anymore. You don't have to create paper from trees. You should just let the trees live, because they also create good oxygen in the air, which is needed at this particular time. And it's also because of the second dimension. We work with the roots. We can feel, you know, sniff the roots to know if it doesn't absorb and send out oxygen and things correctly. It's a whole chain that is affected if you cut down trees. We do not approve.
D. I don't either, it's bad. Maybe there are too many humans.
B. At least the jackets need to shift. Out of season! *(Laughs)* Hehe, it's like last year's jacket, –you don't want to have that one anymore! It's a little bit like that.
D. That's funny!
B. So, we will meet and talk about this further.
D. Thank you for joining us at this time. I know it's not our scheduled time, but thank you.
B. It doesn't really matter, it's the intention of trying to reach us that we respond to. We poke this one, so she always knows when we want to talk. And then she says, "Do you think we should have a session?" Oh, wonder who had that idea? It's like, who do you think told you? That's how we operate. And we do operate in your dreams, that's why you both need more sleep than normal at this particular time. And it's a way to recharge and rejuvenate, and the cells need to heal and to do their magic inside and create harmony on the inside as well as the outside.

Our societies teach us distorted ideas about other living creatures. Native cultures were more aware of the spirit that lives within plants and animals. The western materialistic view is one where plants and animals are just objects without feelings or senses. As our spiritual friends have told us, all life forms have access to the emotional vibrations. The creatures that move around require more spiritual energy, but the ones that don't move, like trees and plants, also have feelings and consciousness.

Scientists know elephants feel sorrow over the death of their family members and friends, and will cry when they feel sadness. Everyone who has cared for a dog recognizes they have emotions. Lesser known are the studies done on plants and trees by researchers, such as Cleve Backster, who have proven that plants recognize people and exhibit anxiety or calmness when certain humans come into a room, dependent upon how those humans have treated the plant in the past. Trees are aware when deer or other animals come by to nibble on their foliage, and those that can produce tannins will immediately send it out into their leaves as a defense. The tannins taste bitter and, if the animal keeps eating, will tan the inside of its digestive tract, impairing digestion. The interesting aspect of this is the communication between trees, because when one member of the tree family is stressed by a deer, for example, all the nearby trees will respond at the same time and also send tannins into their leaves. Anybody who has spent time in a forest knows that deer always move along as they forage, never stopping very long at any one place. Trees are sentient beings with enough spiritual intelligence to communicate with other trees and to be aware of activity in their surroundings; the deer, of course, know this. Scientists, on the other hand, don't see how communication is possible in a senseless object without a brain or lips, like a tree, and loftily dismiss any studies that go against a materialist or nontheist view of life. The spirit occupying other life forms is equally undetectable as the soul in your own body. Descartes' observation of "Cogito ergo sum" *(I think, therefore I am)* applies to all living beings, not just humans. Our casual disregard for other creations around us is not appreciated, or approved of, by the spiritual world. A sense of respect and concern for plant and animal life is an immutable aspect of empathy. Compassion is directly related to soul development.

Bob is quite clear about the source of all the spirit energy being from a common pool, an extension of the Master Mind. I was curious about how this energy comes to be united with the physical form. I asked him to clarify that issue, which he does in the next dialogue.

> D. Before you go, I did have a question about something you had talked about earlier. The little bit of master mind that is put inside all living creatures, –how does that get in there? Is that something you work on?

B. Like a sparkle. No, we don't do that! How does a soul get in, one might wonder? It's an intervention that takes place, designed by those who operates with blending certain objects for certain things to operate. I would say it's a quicker process when you do it from the Master Mind, because it's simply sent off. You can see both, both are sent off from its source, like a sparkle. Even if a soul goes into a human body, it also comes in like a sparkle. However, the other one, from the Master Mind, can be sent simply by an impulse, and it can be exchanged over time. It can be refilled, if you like, it's not constant. When a soul moves into a body, whatever percent has been delivered in that specific vehicle will remain the same. Whereas a sparkle from the master mind into a plant or living life form like a tree, it can actually be refilled or even removed. So, that's the difference. It's simply sent like an impulse, I would say, like a heartbeat almost. It's a less of an intervention. It's more of a, how can I say, it's an easier process than the incarnation of a soul, even though both are sparkles.

D. Is it controlled by a group of spiritual beings?

B. I would think so, yes.

D. So the experiences that the plant or animal has, the Master Mind records that?

B. They can follow it directly, not the same way as with a soul, because the soul reports and stores within its own soul energy, in its own particle. So the spirit realm can analyze the chimney on the soul in a vehicle, but they can't analyze the soul's experience within. However, if the Master Mind wants to read a sparkle in, let's say a tree, they can directly connect and read the experience from within.

D. That's wonderful, that's a perfect explanation.

B. Oh, you're welcome. It's not so tricky, it's just a little bit different.

D. That depends on how small your computer is.

B. Ha! Huh, that's true! You might want to upgrade. Hehehe.

In this next session, there are a few things Bob mentions that need a bit of clarification. Bob is a scientist and takes a lot of notes about things he observes and ideas he has while traveling around. He has been taking notes on Earth for untold millions of years, and is happy to now be able to share some of his knowledge. What is amusing about this reading is that Ophelia was the one who allowed the messages to come through, and she presented them to Bob in a bowl, so it was like drawing for a raffle. Since he didn't know what was on the notes, he got pretty excited and started talking like he was a game show host, which was both charming and amusing. Within the first message, he talks about skin problems both Christine and I have had. In her last life, as Alicia, she had a very serious skin eczema, while I had serious acne problems as a teenager in this lifetime. Later, he makes a reference to cups, which relate to a comment Ophelia made many months earlier. She talked about the difference between bringing knowledge in a barrel and dumping it on people, or giving the same knowledge in cups, a little bit at a time, so it is easier to process. One of the most remarkable things to me about our sessions is the perfect continuity and memory of what they have put forward. They have never made a single error or contradicted themselves about any topic or point of discussion. No matter how much time has elapsed, in our reality, they never forget previous talks. Because they in some way operate with a group mind during our sessions, Bob remembered Ophelia's comparison, and wants one of the cups of knowledge to be about how the animals and plants all contain spirit, and should be treated with empathy.

D. Hello, Bob.

B. Oh, It's my turn. Let's see what I can tell you today. Okay, there will be messages drawn from the bowl of wisdom today! Ophelia says there are going to be notes drawn from the big bowl of wisdom that is locked in our vault in the Library. Today, some of those notes will be drawn from that bowl. It's like those games you see on TV, you know, when there's a bowl of notes and you can draw one and there's like a little quote of wisdom you read. You know, those games.

D. Alright. Well, let's see what we can find!

B. Okay, I see there are...one, two...six. Six notes. SO, let's see, there are six notes in the bowl that I am going to pick from today. So, which one will we begin with? Number three. Oh, huhuh, this is the note number three. (*Long pause as he receives the thought bubble Ophelia sent to him.*) It is about your physical journey. It's about your body, and why you picked this body with a little bit of problem. Let's see, let's see. Oh, you both connect to this specific problem with your skin. You both are aware of the skin on your vehicle being sort of weak in that specific area. You took this mission, this time around, with a little bit of a problem in your skin, because she did the last time. So now it's your turn to understand that weakness can come from feeling like the body isn't really that attractive. It was for you both to experience the same thing, really. The physical, oh, there's more on this note. There's something about your diet, and something about your feet. You also learn more about the physical vehicle and you report back on how to improve future physical vehicles. Interesting, indeed. Because when the new energies are coming in, then the physical vehicle has to be improved. So you picked a body that was a little bit more dysfunctional, from your perspective, less properly functioning on different aspects. You also picked a place where you put this body, where it would be less likely for it to heal properly. This is actually where you both report back something about your physical vehicles and skin related issues. You report back on a more energetic form, I would probably say, in your dreams. But it is something that is reported to a higher order. With future bodies, they are most interested in improving the physical vehicles. The skin on these new physical vehicles will actually become not so dry. They are going to improve the skin quality. So, know that you both, in different orders, picked these kind of bodies where you report something that is related to the physical skin.

D. Oh, good. Thank you.

B. So, that is note number three. We will put this aside now. We could potentially look more, if we are interested, since it is already open. We are a little bit on overtime here, so we will look into the fourth note. This is my note.

D. Your note?

B. My note, because I have been taking notes on numerous occasions. So this is my contribution to this project. This is my note. I do want one of the cups to be about the empathy for the animals. I do want there to be an awareness of, that there is a soul, not only within those animals that are moving around, but also, there is a soul in some way in everything, like the trees and the bush and the stones. Because all carry a small portion from this collective soul. And I want there to be an awareness of, that even if you kick a stone, you know, there's still something that can be living inside it. And I want there to be an empathy for where people put their feet, because if you are not kind to the planet and to where you put your feet, then it affects the whole you, because your feet are like big sensors. If you think of the TV and the satellites, you have this big dish, and everyone is like, "Oh, look to the heavens! Look to the heavens!" But, you know, it's the same satellite receiver from the feet. So there is one satellite everyone talks about, "Open up the crown chakra", which is like one big satellite disk. But there is also disks under your feet. So if you see it like that, it's easier to understand that if you are healing where you put your feet, then it's going to be easier to heal what's above you. And it is something with the atmosphere we are a little concerned about. It is about the pollution in certain countries where the knowledge is very low about the effect of factories and so on. And that is a concern. So, if we could put forward a little bit about the care of the feet, and the care of the planet. See it as a project and you want to come back here. You have your Coats here, what do you want to come back to?

D. That's a really good point, Bob.

B. I was actually involved with what kind of plants and trees were supposed to be in certain areas. So I am a little bit familiar with the trees and the moss. Do you know the moss is a living creature, do you? *(Bob laughs and gets very loud)* Huhhuh...You think it's something green and soft that sort of happened!! *(Gets quiet again)* But it's not, it's actually a living being. If you put the hand on it, and close your eyes, you can actually communicate with it. That's a little bit of a trick to communicate with realms that are sort of below. The moss is a little bit of a... *(Bob trailed off and didn't finish the sentence)*

D. Does each type of life form have a different group soul? Like a deer and a chipmunk?

B. No, no. They're all a part from the same over-soul, the cloud. It's all part of it, it's just different portions coming from this soul. It's actually not different between an animal and a tree, even though there is more in an animal, as it has to move around. So there is more of a percentage and more of an awareness from that cloud in those moving around than those standing still like a tree or a rock. But if you have moss on the rock, then it is actually a little bit more of an awareness in that specific rock. You can look at that if you like. If you see rocks with moss on them, then there's more of an awareness in that region.

D. Huh, fascinating!

B. Ah, but it's all coming from the same cloud. It's just different levels of awareness and different levels of operating. If you move around, clearly you need a little bit more power than if you're standing still *(He laughs at this)*. Yeah, you know, it's just different, but it's from the same cloud.

D. Well, even the human body has access to that cloud, doesn't it?

B. Yeah, mentally, mentally they do. That's why some can communicate with animals, and some actually make fun of those. But they tune in to the awareness that belongs to animals. SO, yes, if you are open enough, you can all communicate with the rocks and animals. But some practice this more on a professional level, tuning in to this awareness. This awareness is something that is the same on all other places *(beyond Earth)* where there are life forms. So, this plane, this planet, is not different than other planets. It's more mobile between different celestial bodies, whereas coming into an incarnation as a soul, it's another way of moving, and it's more of where you belong, really. *(The soul is locked in a body during that lifetime)*. Whereas the other one...it's also almost like a cloud moving silently between different celestial bodies and dimensions, tapping into, silently, like undercover almost, silently tapping into what they want to look at. It's like a living being, this cloud.

D. Does it extend beyond the Earth?

B. Yes, yes it does.

D. Is it connected directly to the Master Mind?

B. Yes, yes, it is. That's why it can move between, silently, without any interference from other...it doesn't get affected by change of atmosphere and so forth.

D. The human body, it has a lot of functions, like the heartbeat. Is that controlled by the Master Mind?

B. I don't know about that, really.

D. Does the incarnating soul control the body?

B. Uhhh, they blend and can have the ability to change the vehicle. However, the vehicle itself is designed from a group of individuals. That's why you are reporting about what we talked about, the skin and so on, and changes. They create these little bodies and vehicles for souls to tap into. Ah, but it is a...ok, let's say it like this. When I blended with certain creatures in the past, I did not have the same ability to affect that individual or that rock. As a soul energy coming in, you have more of a possibility to change and improve, but also go the other way, like if you eat badly, for instance. You have in the beginning a perfectly good body, but if the soul doesn't care and honor that vehicle then it can go the other way. So the soul has more of a power to work with the physical body than when I blend with a creature or a rock, because I can't really affect that being, I can just sort of visit, because I'm not attached in it.

D. That's good. I appreciate that description.

B. So the soul has the ability to work more directly with the vehicle. It's different.

D. We'll include that in one of the cups.

B. Yes. That's one of the cups I want to share. I want there to be an awareness that you have, as a soul, the power of choice when it comes to the vehicle, and there's a connection through your feet. *(To the first and second dimension)*. And also about the living beings that exists—there is an awareness in everything around you.

D. Very good, thank you so much for that. I think we've gone through all the notes, so do you have anything else to add? *(Some of the six notes delivered had information that will be included in later books, as they related to another wave of knowledge)*

B. You know, it's those little things that people miss around them. Because there's always someone there. It could be just something simple, they recognize something in a rock, or they see a face in a tree. And those who stop and ponder about it, those are more in tune, of course.

Because of the incredible intelligence that Zachariah, Ophelia, and Jeshua have about various topics, I occasionally probe to see how much they will reveal about mysteries we humans are always contemplating. Due to our primitive and violent nature, there is a limit to what they will divulge. However, within the next discussion, Zachariah mentions something that contradicts one of the foundations of physics and astronomy, which is the assumption that the gravitational force is a fundamental constant.

Zachariah gives detailed talks about gravity, stating gravity is an independent component that is added, by the spirits, to the living core of planets and stars as they are established. However, there is another gravity field external to planets with different strengths throughout the Universe, which can also be locally adjusted by the same group of spirits to achieve certain objectives. He also described how gravity within the planet is not uniform and can move around within the shell. A great many ponderous theoretical equations have been written using a fixed constant for the gravitational force, instead of an unknown variable. Not proper, one could say. Personally, I have always thought the big-bang hypothesis to be completely without merit, as well as the concept of black holes, since both were devised as mental abstractions to satisfy mathematical equations that are only locally applicable, astronomically speaking. The theory of general relativity, as published by Poincaré and plagiarized by Einstein several years later, includes assumptions about gravity that are not correct. Within the vacuum of space, the gravitational field is something that is controlled by the spiritual entities on the eighth dimension. They adjust gravity during the cycle of evolution within solar families to control orbital motion. But gravity is also an element within planetary bodies. On a quantum level, gravity is part of the atomic structure and is related to the creation of a quark and the electron. Contrary to popular belief, mass does not create gravity. Gravity is needed to create matter. Gravity is an element needed to bring into existence the quantum elements which arise from the cosmic light energy field. Albert Einstein's greatest deceit was his imperious decree, in special relativity, that the speed of light in a vacuum is constant for all observers. Then Einstein followed that line of reasoning to make the asinine conjecture that gravity is created by the curvature of his so–called unified space–time. Generations of otherwise intelligent people have fallen for his flights of fancy. Fortunately, our spiritual friends have promised additional information on this subject, which I am eager to hear.

- D. The energy that builds the Universe, where matter is first materialized, is this the frequency of our dimension, and is this the building block?
- Z. Is your question is how material manifests, and the origin?
- D. Yes.
- Z. That is what will come in later books, my friend. But to give you an understanding. The frequency, the vibration, moving

like waves through space, as it connects to celestial bodies that carry a certain amount of gravity, will give the possibility for manifestation in various levels. This field, the Earth's celestial body, is made in order for numerous manifestations to take place as different vibrations are moving in. You, as a human being, being one. I wish I could give you the picture, my friend. You will remember this as you meditate more. The vibrations that are moving like waves, or fields, if you like, like a web through the atmosphere in space, as it draws near celestial bodies that carry a high percentage, if you like, to make it easier for human ears to understand, a higher frequency of gravity. Gravity is not constant, it's different depending on where the celestial body is, as well as its atmosphere where it is contained. Not even within your galaxy is the gravity the same.

D. I was wondering about that, if the gravitational field was constant?

Z. No, it's not. Within the solar system of yours, down here, it is somewhat similar.

D. Are there life forms on other planets within our solar system?

Z. Hmm, not at this point. At this point in the solar system, reaching out to the planet Pluto. Except for the planet that comes and goes that is not constant in your solar system, there is no known life forms as you know it. However, there are planets orbiting into this solar system during certain times that carry physical vibrations, shown as manifested individuals.

D. Do other planets carry non-physical vibrations?

Z. Indeed, indeed.

D. Is there activity and life forms of that nature?

Z. Indeed.

D. Would those be considered to vibrate differently?

Z. They're vibrating on a higher frequency, meaning it goes faster, if you like. This vibration is slower, meaning, because of the slow movement in vibration on this plane, you are able to see all the vibration causing different manifestations. Rocks carry one vibration, even slower than a human, or the living force. But they still carry the same—oh, let's say, they are still bathing in the same puddle of gravity and the percentage of gravity that is contained in this solar system. Gravity is not constant. As you move through other realities, you have the possibility, –not to change gravity, as that is part of the creation–, but you can, if you are able to move within space and time, adapt to different frequencies of gravity. Gravity is a mass that makes it possible for different realities to manifest, due to the vibration that contains or encircles that specific celestial body.

D. That's very interesting. Thank you for that description. I have another question. Do light and sound travel in the same manner, like waves?

Z. Mmmm. The difference is the light is more direct, not in a curve like manner, whereas sound moves in a rhythm. Depending on the frequency in sound, it creates certain waves which can vary from very small curves to big ones. It's actually a highly advanced technology and science. Each galaxy and solar system carries a different vibration of tone within, depending on what the original idea of that life form was.

D. Once something is created, does it need continuous input of light and sound to maintain the form?

Z. Light.

D. So light maintains the form?

Z. Light maintains the form. However, sound keeps it in its original intent. So, let's say, we can say more, that light is the engine, whereas sound waves keeps it to remain in a certain form, so it doesn't float. Let's say, to make it easy for you; we have a solar system, the light energy keeps the motion, if you like, the sound barriers keep all in its place, so nothing leaves its original intention. The sound barrier surrounds each celestial system. The light is to remain within, to create a certain input from the sun in order for it to move at all, the engine, the motion. You should know that surrounding the celestial reality of a solar system, for instance, there is this barrier of sound, almost like it is encased in a protecting, vibrating shield. One does not wish for things to move randomly around. So even though the Universe itself is constantly moving, it is still that shield of vibration from the sound that encase and protect the creation and intention from the start. Can you see the picture?

D. I can. I do have a question about the motion of planets around the center-point, the force that drives planet motion around a sun. Does that force come from the sun or is it part of the planet's energy?

Z. It's combined. To give you a percentage, if it's easier for you, one would say about 70 percent comes from the sun itself. That's the importance of having its component in correct amount, depending on how many planets you WANT TO PUT AROUND IT. The core of each celestial body resonates, –and this might be confusing for you–, the resonance actually creates a tone. So each celestial body within the solar system actually carries a different tone. You were not far off with your meditation in order to try to capture the different sounds from your fellow friends in the solar system. *(Christine and I once held a guided meditation using Tibetan singing bowls to mirror the vibrations from the planets).*

In the next discussion, Zachariah is describing how the spiritual energy travels and can tap into physical bodies to have experiences, but the physical body cannot exist without the spiritual energy within. If you think about it, what he is saying is the raw materials that make living organisms would remain in the first dimension without the infusion of spiritual energy from either the Master Mind or a soul. Second dimensional patterns of DNA cannot function in the third dimension without the presence of a higher spiritual being. While we are incarnated, we look all around for physical evidence of the spirit, but the only place it exists is within ourselves and other living beings. It is the invisible force that makes your heart beat and becomes the awareness of your mind. Although its manifestations are all around you, discovering it is an inward journey.

D. I have a question about the patterns of life on Earth. The animals, trees and other lifeforms, are those patterned by other spiritual beings, more advanced spirits, using a source field provided by the Creator?

Z. Interesting that you asked that, as this is what our little friend has come to discuss later on. However, patterns are merely frequencies or vibrations. Physical vibration is created on a lower level. It blends with the spiritual vibration, the spiritual...oh, let's see how I can draw a picture for you. Everything on this level vibrates in a certain melody, or pattern. From the spiritual realm, it almost looks like you are glowing in different ways. Those who have more vibration, who are more in-tune with their soul memory and power, they vibrate almost like a disco ball. However, let me explain it to you. The physical vibration is created from the level of where it occurs. Whereas the spiritual vibration is tapped into it. Over time it has been a little bit of different results when these two blends. We will leave out the mental vibration at this point, because it merely creates a confusion. So if you see the pattern of the physical as being created from the level of this plane, it is not necessarily created from the main source, as you referred to it. The spiritual vibration travels and is not necessarily in need of the physical. The physical vibration, in order for it to function, needs the spiritual, however.

D. Does that apply to all living beings?

Z. In different grades, in different levels, in different blends. There was a time on this plane when the majority of humankind were more like the disco-balls, they were more glowing. As for the spiritual vibration, they were aware of it tapping in, so the physical was more of a way to move around. At this point the physical, and again we leave out the mental vibration, the physical has somewhat taken over. Meaning it's creating a shadow over the spiritual vibration. These two need to be aligned, almost like a symphony.

D. Is the human body different than other animals?

Z. Indeed. Indeed. It is more dense, it is more craving for other attentions. More craving for—instincts are stronger, in many ways, here. Meaning spiritual vibrations travel sometimes without hitting their destination. It doesn't mean that a human individual lacks a soul, it only means that they are not aware of the spiritual vibration. It's like they can't even hear their heartbeat. If you listen to it, the heartbeat is your soul talking to you.

D. That's a good way to explain it to people.

Z. It is always problematic to describe the unseen for those who only see the physical. Be aware of that you will be pushed to answer things that there is no way for any humankind to answer. You might have to refer to the same as the priests are doing, asking, "What do you believe in?" It is the same thing, you know. That is why you will probably, in some way, have an easier way with those who are religiously inclined than the scientists. On other occasions, the scientists will more easily understand what you are referring to. Use your judgement on how you deliver your message to the both groups. Very different, yet both lacking the sensation of their spiritual vibration, if you like. One is looking outside to see the spiritual vibration. Looking for someone to descend from the heavens in like a vehicle, or like an angel, when they have the heartbeat inside.

B. *(Bob suddenly came in to finish the discussion)* Oh, it makes no sense. Because, you know, those people only look outside for their heartbeat to function. Whereas those who are more in the mental realm, which are the science people, they are very much in their mental home-base. It's like a little dungeon, really. They are only looking for the words, and what they think they can touch. So one only wants to talk about what they can touch. The other one is looking towards the heavens for something that is not really there to be found. It's actually found inside. If you tell them to listen to the heartbeat, and the heartbeat is that individual they are searching for outside, it might be helpful.

D. That's a good way to put it. Welcome back, Bob.

B. Thank you. So it is my pleasure today to talk more about the vibration, and the vibration of the physical reality that you see here on this plane. Everything is manifested in different frequencies in order for it to appear, or manifest. So, this is a little bit of the secrets from the second dimension, and it is almost like being in a lab. You are in a different lab. The lab that I am in is to create different solid vibrations for different things to appear. *(His lab on the second creates flora and fauna.)* Like a rock or a tree, who's not moving around, they carry a lower frequency, if you like. But, if you want to manifest something that is more of an intelligence, then it demands a different structure to it, more organized. Whereas YOU, huh huh, you are more creating solid things like stars and planets, and how they move around in different ways. I work more with the solid mass once your things are already in place. So after things are in place, and everyone has done their job by creating atmosphere and gravity and so forth, the people from my reality comes in and we create the different settings, if you like, on what is made to be manifested. I'm STILL yet to work on those levels that carry only energetic realities. I'm not there yet, I'm not there yet. I've only heard of them. I see them in the boxes *(In our vault, in the Library)*, that you create some realities that carry no solid form. So, I have no idea how they are going to play out, but I'm sure it's fascinating! So what we do, is that we work in a place somewhat like a lab, putting the final touches on things. If you see a flower, a flower is a delicate, very tender creature, yet it carries an awareness that is based and tapped into an emotional layer. It is not necessarily a mental being, but it carries an awareness. However, the frequency is much lower than when it moves into those more solid, movable, manifested creatures.

D. Is the cloud...?

B. *(Interrupts)* No. Oh, well, the cloud is sort of what we can use. We can take...OK, let me give you a picture, my friend, since this clearly isn't easy. If you see my lab, and I work on creating different awareness's in the form of rocks or trees, it's very different, you know, depending on where you go. *(Earth, or other planets)* But I can use different amount from the collective cloud in order for me to create. So, in some way it is energetic work, but it is not necessarily, ah, we do not create simply energy forms that are not solid. It is about patching things together *(adjusting patterns of DNA)* that also resonates well with the atmosphere. There are groups who work with atmospheres surrounding celestial bodies that you have already placed. There are many different groups, my friend, working in order for something to appear like a creation. It's a Master Mind behind it all.

D. With a flower, or an animal, does the Master Mind provide the pattern that you then use with the building blocks? Is it an interaction between the pattern and the Master Mind and the material? *(My question was not clear, but he picked up on the interaction part and gave a very nice bit of information)*

B. Yes, since you're asking, animals and trees and flowers, they communicate on a similar level, yet a human mind doesn't see this interaction all the time. Those who study forests and animals can actually see an animal avoiding a place where the energy...let's say a puddle is not necessarily clean. You will pay attention to it, but the animal will not drink there. How do they know that? It is because they communicate on the same level on their somewhat smaller mental vibration. So if you see the human mind, let's say that the human mind, the mental brain, has, let's say ten strings, then flowers have like one, and animals have two. That means that an animal can communicate with their surroundings like trees and rocks and puddles easier. With the ten strings, it is harder to move down to one.

D. I see what you're saying, yes.

B. Oh, good. That's very good, because sometimes it's hard to make a picture into words. Sometimes it's harder to put words on what we're trying to say, and it is a struggle.

D. And then I have to explain it to others, so I have to have a good picture in my mind.

B. Indeed! Indeed! This is how you can remember it. And I'm not saying that the human mind has ten strings. However, refer it to ten energy waves, like layers, whereas flowers only have one. This is the mental vibration we are referring to. An animal carries two, so an animal can easier tap into the flower, if you like. You can see how animals, they don't eat poison things, for instance. How do they know that? Scientists actually look at this. Why do animals know certain things that the human doesn't? It's because they communicate, in some way.

D. Is that within the cloud?

B. The cloud only supervises how much from it will be tapped into each manifestation.

D. So, were most of the lifeforms on Earth designed by people or entities like yourself?

B. Indeed, indeed. In the lab, in our lab. Everyone has a lab, everyone works in labs, if you like. The manual comes to us from the cloud, and we follow the instructions. BUT in order for it to operate where it's supposed to go, we have to make adjustments, so it resonates with the surroundings. The codes are all in the layer of the cloud, the codes of creation, like a manual, to make it simple. I will give you another picture. Let's say you want to create a bush. You are in the lab and you tap into the cloud and you search for a bush. But you also need to pay attention to the atmosphere, the surroundings on where you want to place this bush. So, you are creating a bush on this plane, and first you need to be fully aware of the conditions on this plane. You can't create any bush here, because it will die. We are more aware of the conditions on physical bodies, celestial bodies. So you want to create this bush, and you need to take the manual that resonates with the conditions where you want to PUT the bush. So there it is. It's not very mysterious, really. It's just basic knowledge, in the galactic way of thinking. Sometimes you can see, because conditions changed on this planet, bushes and stuff that were put in very suitable conditions to begin with, suddenly did not work AT ALL. Dinosaurs as well, because the conditions changed. They were once manifested here and placed, but the conditions at that time were different.

D. That makes sense.

B. Indeed. Everything has to resonate with whatever you put there.

Within the second, sixth and the seventh dimensions, there are many actual working labs where energy is used to create things, and there are also training labs and classrooms where the principles are taught to the younger souls or others who wish to learn. Bob attends lectures and goes to the teaching labs on both dimensions, but the labs he is talking about next are the working labs. The beings on the second dimension, like Bob, have a more solid spiritual body than those on the fifth and above. Those on the higher realms can sometimes move between dimensions, which he sees as someone suddenly appearing and then later, disappearing. Since he can't do that, he finds this mode of travel fascinating, and is a trick he would like to learn.

D. I know you work in a lab, but how does that compare to Ophelia's lab, the work they do on the seventh?

B. It's just very different. Ophelia's lab, oh, let's see. I've actually been there for a little tour once. I'm going to see if I can talk about that, just very briefly, of course. It was like, you know, when little school children go to the museum, you go in some sort of order, in line, and you're not supposed to touch, but you can see. So they work a lot with light, it's very bright in there. It's a lab where, oh, I don't know, but it's something to do with light energy. Very yellow, very vibrating. It is for spiritual energy to travel IN. It's something with the spiritual, whereas when you travel it's not necessarily spiritual energy! *(Laughing)* It's more like nosy people moving around! Ophelia works more with the conditions for spiritual energy to descend into certain areas. It's hard to say really, because from my perspective it doesn't really create anything, it just puts a layer around something. But it looks pretty because it glows like a sun. Yes, there is something with the sun that they are also involved with.

D. Does she work with multiple universes?

B. Yes, indeed. As well as your higher masters, those who you report to. They also work together. So, let's say that you create the first model of something *(like a planet)*, then the people from the energetic society, like Ophelia, they come in and they create some sort of energetic layer around the celestial center, so it becomes like a sun. But it's a joined work with those who create the first model. Because you know, if you create, and I'm sure this will be discussed later on, but if you want to create a little solar system, in the beginning you might want to squeeze in all sorts of planets and different things. But, it also has to function so there are no disasters within that little celestial family. That's why there's something with the asteroid belt, actually. I'm sure that will also be discussed later on. Yes, indeed. *(Bob told us there were once three small planets of different sizes following one another in the orbit where the asteroid belt is now found. Some other object came in and caused all of them to explode, sending a cloud of dust and debris throughout the solar system.)*

D. You mentioned once about gravity being adjusted, too.

B. That is also something that is a combined work. I would say seventy percent from your higher society versus thirty percent from Ophelia's higher society. Yours are more of ah, it's been referred to as engineers in this group, but it's actually above that. To say you are an engineer almost makes it smaller than it really is. So, a master designer, I call you, and also one of those who can travel.

D. So tell me about your lab. Where is it located?

B. Oh, it's more like underground, cave like.

D. Is it on Earth?

B. No, it is not. It's another reality in the wheel. It's a realm that cannot be accessed physically from this realm, but you can mentally visit if you are allowed. So, I will describe it for you. It is a lab on a different level, it is a reality within another reality. The lab contains many workers that work on different places in different realities, like galaxies and little solar families. I've always been fascinated with this realm, the Earth.

D. Are you in charge?

B. No. No.

D. What do you do, specifically?

B. Up till now I have been working with plenty of plants and trees in order for them to adapt properly to where they are placed. Because I want the soil to be fresh and clean, and in many ways, it is not. The water that flows underneath the ground can contain poison, and that's when some of my projects actually dies. I don't like it when you cut down trees.

D. Yes, I don't either.

B. I did have a lot of projects in the area which is known as South America. There were several nature groups there that did not stumble and take my projects away, they actually honored them. They're gone now, this was in the past. The soil is actually very good in this region, if they only knew. The waters, the seas, there are groups working more in my lab on the seas, which has not changed much over time. They have different assignments really, those who work with water, putting things which manifest in water.

D. Do you work on other planets besides the Earth?

B. I did, I did, but it was a long time ago. I prefer here at the moment, because it's like creating a garden. If people just knew it was made to grow and to create harmony on the land. Because we actually put in substances, –I'm making it easy for you again–, into the trees and the plants and the things we manifest, which we then put in different places, because it creates balance and harmony in that region. So when it's cut down, all sorts of things occur on the surface. If it remained there, it has the potential to be a more balanced setting in that place, if you like.

D. Yes, I understand.

B. So, you know how things just seem to emerge over time? *(Laughs loudly)* HUH HUH HUH. People went like, "Oooaahhh! A BANANA!" But, who placed a banana there? You know, all these things that man finds, and they're like, "Ohhh, look! A potato!" and then it goes viral and everyone goes, "OHHH." But, where did the potato come from? It is from those who work like me, to create some goodies on this plane. The banana is extremely popular, as well as the coffee bean. I can take, actually, some credit for the coffee bean.

D. Well, thank you. I like coffee!

B. Indeed, you do! That was a project we worked with. I was actually in charge, a little bit, of that group with the coffee bean. SO, then the spices came. Where did those come from? It's all sorts of different friends of mine that create different things. *(Gets quite loud again)* Sometimes it's almost like a race! When I was doing the coffee bean, there was another group working with spices, yellow-orange spices, that also became really popular at the same time. Some sort of curry spice, I assume. It was launched in the Asian region. *(Laughing)* It was like a race between my group with the coffee beans and those with the spices!

D. Did you win?

B. Just by a little bit, I think it was almost like a tie! This is how we work at best, you know. We're triggered by little competitions in the group.

D. Do you have anything you are working on now?

B. Oh, indeed, oh, let's see. Because we did talk about how factories are using plastic in food, and we do not approve. So we are facing this problem by creating something in nature that will grow regardless of rain. And it is a long-term project to fight this factory of plastic. So indeed, I am working on something that is not dependent on rain. It is more of a...it is similar to what people can use to make bread, but it's a seed that can be used and it's very adaptable. *(Bob gets quite excited)* The, the, the, the ultimate goal is that it would even be able to grow in the desert, I'm not there yet, I'm not there yet. But this is what I am working on, because we want to meet this desire (of humns) to create plastic food. So if this (his plant) is spread all over, like a cockroach, *(he was exited and laughing)* HUH HUH HUH then, you know, people will still be able to make their own dish. But this is what we are working on. We're working to meet certain...because events take place and we adapt after that. But the coffee plant was actually mine.

D. So grateful for that!

B. Yes, indeed, indeed. And it's very unique for this place, you should know. Other things exist on other places, but the coffee plant is a little bit unique.

D. Congratulations! Well done, my friend.

*Earth, the 2nd and 3rd Dimensions* 181

B. Indeed, thank you. This is what we do, we meet certain demands and events that occur after the regular things like the bush and stuff are in place. So, this is just to make the job a little more intriguing. Because, you can't elaborate that much with the tree! It has to sort of fit in, you can't really put a palm tree if it's on the ice! So, you know, we are sort of limited by the manuals from the cloud when it comes to those kinds of things. However, the other things we are allowed to explore a little bit more, and then we get competitions, you know, it's like, what are you doing over there? It's like little master minds under the Master Mind! So there is a group within my group, working with the waters. And there's a lot to do for them, because there are areas that are not actually alive, but you can't see it from above. Men do not really pay attention to it. When they see a tree or a forest not alive, then, ohhh, they see this and they react, environmental people react. But because the problem in the water is somewhat hidden, people miss that, and it's a huge undertaking from my friends who work with the seas. I work more on land. It's a preference, simply.

D. Where are the problems in the oceans?

B. There's a group who works on increasing light. Light is oxygen, actually. So when oxygen is in its original form, it actually is a light. I have a group here that work on providing light to certain areas in the sea. There are like three spots I see, that they work on. Well, first we have the West Indies *(Caribbean)*, but there's also an area around the Philippines, and something with Japan. Another one is where it's cold. It's between Russia and you *(North America)*, up north there is a part where it needs a little bit more oxygen in the water, it needs to be cleaned. You know, when water gets dirty, when there's poison in it, it starts to lack the natural oxygen and light. So we provide that in certain ways, and that is what is going on.

D. What about the radiation that is coming from Japan?

B. Yes, in the water south of Japan, it almost looks like oil. It looks like a thickness in the water, in some way.

D. Can that be cleaned up?

B. That's what they do. I see three spots they point out on a map. So, we have this one south of Japan, down, not close to Australia, but down. That's a region where it's dirty. Then from Russia over to Alaska, it's not dirty in the same way, but it's like it's not breathing. The other one is suffocating, whereas in Alaska it's not breathing. And then there is the third area in the West Indies. It's very different, these three, and what they do. In the West Indies, they are not suffocating, necessarily, it looks like it's alive, but life forms here, that are naturally supposed to be here because of the warmth in the water, they are not there. So they are working with life forms here, like coral and fish, and as they put light and oxygen and nutrition into the living life forms, their habitat will improve. So, the light, they work differently on these three. Big problems, all three, but the one in Japan and south of Japan, down, downwards to Australia, it looks dark and dirty, like it's heavy, almost looking like mercury. And Alaska doesn't breathe.

D. That's probably from the nuclear plant in Japan.

B. I know they are working on this. It's a big project with the waters. I don't work on that at all. I just know this because I have friends that work with this.

D. What about the fish in the oceans? Are they safe to eat?

B. Oh, I don't know…you should not eat from that Japanese zone, and maybe not from the West Indies. Those two, not. But the one up, from these three, the one up north is probably the best, but it's still not good. I would suggest a little bit closer to the Scandinavian area, there are fish from there that, if you want to eat fish, are better. Outside Norway, that coast, it is better from that area. As this is still an ongoing environmental project, you should probably avoid anything from those three areas I have mentioned. There is some mercury present, also. The shrimp that comes from outside of the USA, they are somewhat manipulated, and it's not really that well, so you might not eat them. Until waters are clean, it's a little bit of a risk I would say, to find something that is clean and really good. Just make sure to know exactly where it's coming from.

D. It might take a while to clean the waters up, from a human standpoint.

B. From everyone's standpoint, I would say! It's been going on for a while. It actually started in the beginning of the 1900s, because that's when it started to go downhill. Well, so now you know. I visit my friends and they are working on certain things to help the environment and everyone in it.

When Ophelia comes through to deliver messages, the energy is usually quite gentle. But when I brought up the subject of electromagnetic energy, her tone changed and became much harder. We feel that this issue is very concerning to the spirit world. They talk about how the misuse of this energy has damaged the atmosphere and it also damages cells within the human body. Although they did not say it explicitly, it can be assumed that all other life forms suffer cell damage from the microwave signals constantly bombarding everything on Earth. According to Ophelia, microwaves signals from towers and satellites punch holes in the protective web around the Earth, allowing certain energies to come through that are not supposed to reach the planet.

D. I was just trying to get my mind around these different types of energy. The electromagnetic waves are not a form of spiritual energy, are they?

O. No, they are not. However, they travel similar to a spiritual wave. There are different waves that carry different intentions. The spiritual wave moves as a thought, carrying only the good. Those vibrations that are manmade, in some way created in labs with no intention for the result, can actually cause harm to the energetic field that is all surrounding this plane. There are some electric labs that, due to their ignorance of their project, actually creates disharmony within the Earth field in total, yet this is not visible for the naked eye. From the spiritual level, it looks like the web is dissolving. This is not what we wish for. It is not caused by pollution, it is caused by overusing the energetic field that is accessible to this level. Electric devices, disturbances in the general field, creates disharmony within the natural field that needs to be encased on this level, and intact, if you like. To overuse, which is the phenomena of this age and time, creates rips in the spiritual field surrounding this plane. In order for it to not create too much harm, there will be a blackout or black moment, so the grid can rejuvenate.

D. Is that coming up soon?

O. Within the 20-year timeframe, if the speed continues in this pace, with increasing the number of activators doing harm to the field surrounding this plane, which is not necessarily the same as the dimensions we talked about earlier. This is a protective layer around this planet, this celestial body, which is unique for this plane.

D. What is the primary source of this disturbance?

O. The electric use of cellphones, cell towers, satellites. They try to create something similar as the connection from the first dimension to the tenth. Meaning the individual, resembling the first dimension, communicates with a satellite. As more are tuning in on outside sources that is not placed from a spiritual perspective, it disturbs the energetic field surrounding this body. It's a manmade connection, instead of a pure, from a first to the tenth dimension, connection. The layers are not in place for it to function. Satellites will be removed, –shut down, if you like.

D. That might cause things to change.

O. This will be discussed from other councils as you proceed on your journey. This is important for man, the average man, to understand the overuse of technology can only occur if it's done with the right intention and the right substance. As of now it creates, simply, an outburst of undirected energy connecting to satellites that are not fully equipped to handle all the influences they are receiving as well as transmitting.

D. That's a very serious issue, I'm sure.

O. The result is what you see that is referred to as global warming. It is a way for us to make you aware to not over-consume the resources in general on this plane. However, not all create the disturbances within the Earth mass and under the seas. The most negative are the electric waves, as they are not fully operating in an optimal way. Incoming souls will work on creating an awareness in that field. Scientists will change the way they transmit their devices in the future. In order for it to occur, the shift, there might be the blackout, briefly, to understand your vulnerability within those waves. New waves will be adapted, working similar, without causing harm to the environment. You see also results in the weather phenomena and clouds. There are results of overusing energetic frequencies that are not operating completely as they should. So, my friend, this is a concern, and it's something for you to carry and to deliver in the future.

I originally was not going to include Ophelia's warning about the electromagnetic destruction of the protective layer around Earth, but she talked about it in one of our public channeling demonstrations. So we know it is an important issue to the spirit world, and they want us to recognize the problem. I would assume they will have more to say about this in the future.

O. The spirit realm is moving closer at this time. We have an electric field that surrounds the planet that is in need of repair. This is what some scientists refer to as global warming. That is not necessarily correct. What is correct though, is the fact of overusing powers, meaning the satellites that surrounds this plane and in your atmosphere, are overused with electromagnetic waves. This creates disturbances in the field that surrounds this planet. Underneath you see the effect on certain different climate changes as well as in eruptions in the surface as well as in waters. It is an effect of what is going on in the atmosphere. Global warming, in many ways, are caused by the overuse of electricity as well as magnetic fields being overexposed. It has been mentioned that we might need to adjust. As you do this, man might appear in darkness. It's a manufactured darkness, of course, yet you have been too dependent on electricity and technology. Not necessarily in your favor. What can be done? What can be done is to use less power when not needed. Some cities in this country *(the USA)* actually are aware and try to use less power. Smaller cities in the middle of the country. Don't neglect the smaller cities in the middle of the country. A lot of focus is merely on the coasts. Enlightened beings operate in the middle of this country, fully aware, natives as well. Hmm. As we move into a new age, which is not necessarily around the corner, in human terms, it will be of importance that you use powers in a more efficient manner. Those who are aware of prior civilizations misusing powers will be surprised that it happened again. Cycles of karma that has not been, necessarily, cleared. Karma relates to this plane, both in locations, as well as what you yourself collect as you incarnate. There is a karmic event that relates to misuse of power in a prior past, or prior civilization that existed. We do see that it has a tendency to occur again. This is also something that some of you will have the ability to help this plane with. Not everything has to do with working with individuals, but it's also the part of science to progress into a new age, where you don't misuse the resources on this plane.

## The Spiritual Design

Bob has told us about many of the projects he works on, the things he thinks about, and the way he perceives the different realities around him. We are fortunate to have his stream-of-consciousness talks, and are presenting them with only the slightest of editing, usually when he struggles to find a word that matches his idea.

D. You've mentioned that you work with plants and trees a lot, but do you also work with animals?

B. Yes. It's more fun, though. It's like creating something that you see doing really well. You get sad if it doesn't adapt into the environment and the elements. So, you know, several did not work here, and it's a disappointment, but you learn and you create something that endures the elements better. But we never really know if the environment will change. So we create something that looks really good and we put it there, and then something changes, and it's sad. It's not like you get a call saying, "Remove your furry little creatures because we're gonna move and shift things and it's going to rain, and they can't swim!" So sometimes things just happen. But, indeed I do work with animals. You know, some never want to leave just working on plants and trees, but I feel a need to expand my horizons.

D. Yes, you are very curious!

B. I am! Indeed! I really want to learn, and I want to see how you can create energetic life forms that are as much alive as if it's a solid animal.

D. So are you working with us in the sixth dimension?

B. Yes, indeed. I listen. I pay attention. But, I learn about the geometric forms there. I learn about how to blend certain colors and tones in order for it to resonate in a physical vibration, in order for it to create a form. The most ultimate form that can be seen here, that is not moving, that is the pyramid. Because they carry a multiple vibrating colored map, if you like. It is the ultimate form.

D. When were those constructed?

B. Hmm, it was way back. Those who were here, it's not a secret really, but it was before man had a bigger brain. It is not from...when they say slaves, it is somewhat true, since man was helpful and they were considered slaves. But they were not the master worker, because a lot of these blocks were moved by vibrating tones. It's a big geometric mystery to solve it, and to solve it...

D. Do you know how to move objects with vibrating tones?

B. Indeed! *(He smiles proudly)*

D. Can you teach me?

B. Hmm, OH, Ooohhh *(Bob suddenly starts laughing quite loudly)* OH, NO NO NO NO NO!! Ophelia smiled and showed her finger like this *(Wags index finger towards me)* Ohhh, she laughs so, THE FINGER IS FOR YOU, not for me!! Hehehe, Oh, can I say something, what can I say? *(Bob is addressing Ophelia, who controls the information. He often talks to her during the sessions. In this case, discussions about that type of technology is clearly off-limits).* She said you talked about the seventh and eighth levels and that they carry the tones. It was a combined work between the seventh and the sixth dimensions as the pyramids took place. Period. That was it.

D. That's funny.

B. It is the seventh and sixth dimension, it is a work from them. Ophelia says we should talk about my work instead.

D. Well, we can talk about the work you are doing on the sixth then.

B. Oh, yes, yes. I am visiting you on the sixth dimension. I am learning about shapes and forms. The form with six, six points, that is somewhat of a key thing for all lifeforms. It's a six-pointed star kind of thing. Six points, six corners, six points and corners.

D. Can you explain what you mean by that?

B. It is, oh...I can draw it for you.

D. Are there six attributes?

B. It looks like a diamond, six, six..it's...

D. Like two pyramids pointing in opposite directions, overlaid?

B. It's like that. And when it rotates, it creates the engine that makes the solid form move. It is the mathematical form of six. *(Bob showed the form to Christine. A three– dimensional hexagon, maybe like a cuboctahedron, that holds a cross with four points. I guess this is the energetic form that creates and holds what we see as DNA.)*

D. Is that inside celestial bodies?

B. Yes, indeed. In the bigger form, found in the first dimension, it is actually one of those.

D. Is it like a rotating crystal of some sort?

B. Some sort, yes, indeed. But it is the same form, ohhh, can I say this? *(To Ophelia).* Yes, I can, yes I can. This little model, the six points, it is the same structure that is found within the core of a celestial body, like a planet, it is also the same shape that is, is, when a soul comes into a body, it is that connecting point. It is placed in the solar plexus area, and it is where the soul sort of blends in with the physical. So it is a vibrating center, you can say, and it is found within each and all, even in plants, it has that little transmitter or sender. RECIEVER. Receiver.

D. I have a question relating to that.

B. *(Sighs)* Oh, let's see if she approves of these questions. So yes, indeed. *(Ophelia must have sent her approval)*

D. I think you can answer this.

B. Okay.

D. Is the soul, the incarnating soul, in communication with every cell within the body that it is in?

B. All cells, is that what you are wondering? So, if you think of the cells, a healthy cell is white and it's sparkling like a star. However, due to the intake of food, for one thing, as well as the environment with electric waves, it causes some of these cells to no longer be white, and the soul pushes itself away from those cells. So if the cells were white, as they should be, then the soul would be fully connected to their physical being. But, because the body is contained with dirt, creating those cells that are somewhat gray, the soul rejects and almost pushes itself away from them. So you can see that it's a problem because they can't really connect to their soul either. It is that gap between the soul and the physical. As more of the cells become white and cleansed and clear, eating organic food is one thing, but you need to do some changes in the atmosphere, as well. Those clouds above you that effect the human, it creates those gray cells the soul rejects. *(He could be referring to the chemtrails being sprayed in the atmosphere, or the electromagnetic pollution)*

D. Very interesting. Thank you.

B. There is much dirt inside that needs to be changed. And the thing is, you might think, oh, when it's a baby, it's all white. And, you know, it is, it is more white. But because of the influence from the mother, a baby can be born with gray cells, even when it's brand new and it's supposed to be having a fresh start. Because it's not only alcohol and things that are contained in the surroundings, but if the mother eats bad food the baby in the belly also gets gray cells. It's not fair.

D. Well, cells always have a life-span. They live and die.

B. Yes, they generate, they live and die. It's like popcorn or like little grapes. A grape become a raisin, it dies. Hehe, but it's not like they come out the back entrance, they sort of dissolve within. It's a very unique engineering that goes into the physical body, actually, because there are a lot of layers that work together, clearly. But it is highly affected from the surrounding, you know, the elements and the food. In other places, the living lifeforms are not as sensitive.

D. The human body is pretty durable, considering.

B. No, no. Not considering other places.

D. Considering all the bad things in the environment?

B. You think? I don't think. Just because you live longer now than 500 years ago, it doesn't mean, oh, that you're doing well. It's not as good as it's supposed to be. There were actually times way in the past, another cycle here, where the physical people, the individuals, did not get affected by, they could live their lives more in peace because the surroundings were clear. They didn't eat meat. They ate a lot of leaves and some vegetables, of sorts, and there was a liquid that existed that contained more of a food. This liquid looked almost like water, but it was more of a thicker water. So it functioned as a water, liquid, but also as a food. So people were not exposed...oh, okay ay, that will probably be it. *(Ophelia must have cut him off, so he wouldn't elaborate on the subject)*

Bob regularly gives advice about how to take care of the human body. The digestive system, or as he calls it, the engine, is one of the most important parts of the body. He does not like the additives and fillers that are put into food, which apparently have no nutritional value, and only do harm to our digestive systems. Additionally, he had a concern about red meat. The prions that cause Alzheimer's may be much more common in cattle and other animals than the corrupt USDA will publicly admit, as they prohibit any other lab from testing for "mad cow" disease, for obvious reasons. I couldn't help but add this observation he made regarding diet, as it seems a little strange from a western perspective. Bob has talked about many bugs and insects as being light-bearers from the second dimension, so it may be that some of those are quite beneficial to eat.

B. You must take care of your engine. Just like you take care of the engine on your motorcycle. When it is not running smoothly, you have to make adjustments. Your engine has to be taken care of to run smoothly as well. I have been taking notes on what people eat in different areas, different cultures. In Asia, they eat strange things from a Western standpoint, but it's something they have been eating for centuries and it has been working well. The Asians, the way they eat, the things they eat, actually makes them live longer. The Western society, with so much that is not really from the earth—it's like made food. Unfortunately, it seems like that will increase, a substitute for real food. That's going to mess up a lot of engines. Be aware of that. There are enlightened beings here that work against the forces where more of the natural ingredients are exchanged for man-made, or factory-made ingredients, which looks like plastic balls.

D. What are some of the things they eat which are most beneficial?

B. Actually, the bugs. Crickets bear a lot of nutrition and protein, which has made them maintain their physical vehicles better over numerous centuries. The bugs and insects are an asset, actually, to the body. This will never fly! Hahuhuh, huh huh, so to speak. A bug is flying. I made a little joke there, didn't I? It's not what the Western society wants to have on its plate. Which you know, is understandable. It looks a little odd. But then again, do you want to eat plastic balls? What is more gross, really? It's something you need to think of. I do compare notes. There are also tribes in Australia whose food has never been touched over so many ages and centuries. They are sort of isolated, of course, and not influenced by the so-called progressive cultures, which they are not, necessarily. So, I make notes, I make notes of the engines.

D. What about meat?

B. Hmmm. Meat. If the meat is treated well when it was in an animal form, it will not cause harm if you eat meat. Don't feel judged if you eat meat. But the animal has to be treated well, otherwise the body will absorb the fear and the chemicals given to the animal. If you do not have to eat meat, then that is good. But, I don't have a judgement about eating meat, just that it has to be…I don't want to come with pointers of what to do and not to do. But I want people to pay attention to what they put in the belly.

D. Does meat help my engine or hurt my engine?

B. There is something with red meat. The white meat is not necessarily doing either or. Red meat…I would stop for a little while with the red meat and then you can take that on again. There is something that you need to tend to with the engine first before you continue. But red meat, there is something here. Hmm, beef, what is it with the beef? I'm not sure about the beef. It's not necessarily a choice I would give you. *(While we don't know exactly what the problem is, Bob has, on several occasions, expressed concerns about the blood of cattle containing something that may be harmful to humans)*

D. So, what percent of your time are you away from your lab, at Ophelia's or at our lab?

B. I do take a lot of classes, I do. I do not spend as much time in my lab anymore. Now, it's more a time where I learn other things. That's why I said I like to travel, but I do come back to mostly visit friends.

D. Who takes care of your students when you're gone?

B. Well, I teach still, but it's not inside the lab. It's in a little classroom we have. But a lot of time I go back to the lab to meet friends, because it's a joyful environment.

D. Does your teacher, Gergen, come to the lab very often?

B. No, no. Sometimes, but he's busy, he works with other council members from other places, so he's busy. I don't have a lot of time with him either, anymore. I guess that is somewhat of the process, you know. Because I have moved in my own evolution and progress, I'm at the point where I'm not supposed to be that much with my own kind. I'm supposed to be more by myself and others, now. And that's what I do. Primarily when I go back to the lab, it's just to say hello and to tell about my travels. So I'm more by myself. In the beginning, as little souls, you're kind of dependent on your friends and groups. When I go to that classroom where Ophelia exists, I actually bring my students.

D. Ah, okay, they probably like that.

B. They do! I have a group that is more interested in things that I'm doing, so I have a group of six.

In this next set of questions, Bob was trying to get across to me the concept of the core that exists in everything, from stars and planets to the smallest bacteria. I still don't quite understand the idea, but maybe someone else will, so it is being presented as he gave it to us. It seems this core is the initial DNA structure, and then the organism or planet forms itself around that central point. Within humans, it is slightly above the solar plexus, and eventually becomes the location where the incarnating soul will attach to the body. Because it is a universal component, it may very well come up in future discussions, as it really is a bit too complex to understand, at least for me. The closest we could come to the image was either the icosahedron or the cuboctahedron. He counted the corners as he was rotating the object, so it appeared as a hexagon presenting six points, no matter which way it is turned. It is within this mathematical structure, apparently, that DNA is held.

D. I have a question for you, as I always do.

B. *(Bob laughs)* That's how you learn.

D. You had talked about something I wanted to follow up on. The six-pointed form, that's the basis of creation, in some way?

B. Even exists in snowflakes.

D. It's three dimensional, isn't it?

B. I think it's going to be better if I try to describe it for you. It is six points, if you flip it, it's still six points. The top is flat, the bottom is flat, but the center point, if you see as three dimensional, points go out. It's flat, flat, one, two, three, four, five, six. Turn, one, two, three, four, five, six. One thing with this is also, this is the foundation of the engine, to make things move. This is the basic actually, where you can come in and out, it's more like a little machine, like a heart, like something that is the engine in all solid forms.

D. What about at the molecular level?

B. Oh, oh, there's something else here with that. Okay, I'm giving her another picture she can draw for you. It looks like a star, one, two, three, four, it looks like a cross and on the outside there's little circles. Oh, looks like a DNA, one, two, three, four. They exist inside the six.

D. Is it too complex to picture?

B. I think it's better we draw this and you can do the research. I just want to transmit this image. Well, let's just say it like this, inside this little crystal thing we talk about with the six points, there is this similar like a DNA string, but it has a structure of a cross of four. It will be drawn, but it is the foundation within the six-point model.

D. Is this how matter comes into existence, using this specific model?

B. Well, the little thing we talked about with six points, that is actually the engines and that will be considered inside the planet by itself, to make it at all function, and to be also placed in its core to radiate some sort of gravity for those who are on the surface. Every little core in, let's say a planetary system, or even in celestial stars or other things, carries this little engine inside. So it is the same thing here, you know. Let's say we want to create a Ferrari, we have to have the right engine inside for it to move like a Ferrari, and so it's the same thing here. When the Earth was made, the engine inside, which looks like this model with six points, it's actually adapted for those who walk on it to not bounce, for one thing, but it's also to make things like trees be still where they are. So it is that whole chain that needs to function, and it is regulated from this center core.

D. Does this form generate what we call gravity?

B. Uhmm. It creates the foundation of what sort of gravity and settings on the surface that will occur. So, let's say a star, for instance. You're not supposed to walk on it, but it has the same little model inside, however it acts differently. So in that case it's only generated and made to radiate light. So, you see the difference. Within each form, it exists. So, in a human form, it is implemented in the physical body as some sort of foundation of how it will appear and adapt. When changes have been made over time, –which is what they talked about, evolution in some way, and how some people came in and just kick started evolution–, it's actually that little crystal that was changed. When you want to do adjustments and changes to a form, it's all done in the little creature, this model, this six-pointed model.

D. Do you work with this, in your lab?

B. Mmmm. In a miniature version, of course. I'm studying this, in some way, with other layers. On the higher levels there's no solid form, so I don't know about that crystal, how that operates. I'm going to pay attention to that later on, I assume.

D. I guess if you're going to be helping Gergen decide where the recipes are going to go, you'll have to know that.

B. And he works a lot on those spaghetti strings, those DNA strings. BECAUSE, you know, from the cloud comes a manual how you create a new organ. There's also manuals for Gergen, how to create new dots, that's how it looks, in like DNA strings, molecules. So he has different recipes that he works with. So someone gives him manuals as well. Everyone has a manual, but you can't take someone else's manual! *(Laughs)* It's like going to the post office; you can't collect someone else's mail if it's not addressed to you. I can't pick up Gergen's mail, and say, "Oh, Gergen and I will meet later this afternoon, so I'm going to deliver it." It doesn't work like that, at ALL.

D. Well, you'll be able to help him though, in the future, after some more self-study?

B. Ah. He works more on a teeny, tiny level, on things. I like to work more on things that are immediately showing. But Gergen's work and the DNA strings are the foundations for any organ to function, at all. I should tell you that it also exists, some sort of similar strings, within the core of what you're doing *(the planets)*. I can see that, so it looks similar. Looks similar. You're doing something with the cores, you're changing cores. I can see there are strings inside the cores that look similar to the DNA strings that Gergen works with. *(There is a little museum in our lab on the sixth dimension that contains models of different planetary cores, which he has studied.)*

D. It is a living being.

B. It is, indeed. So that is the foundation of everything; light and sound. The strings, the foundation for them to function properly, actually comes from light, even though they are sort of contained, or encased, with sound vibration. The inside, now we go down into really small particles here, but the inside of the string is a light. And then it is held in its place by sound. Light and sound, in different modalities and different structures.

D. Is there any gravity put within humans and other lifeforms?

B. It is a part where there is a vacuum energy within. It's sort of encasing all organs, actually. It is a layer that is holding things in position, like everything we talked about gravity, how it's holding planets in their cores, how they should travel and where they're supposed to go. So it is actually holding everything in its position on the inside as well, in a different modality, or a different structure, but it is the same principle in everything. Because, you don't want the engine to suddenly be up in your throat, or the liver to accidentally, when you sneeze, fall down into your leg! That's no good! *(Laughs at his observation)*. So it's designed to hold the form, within a certain other form, in this case.

D. Is all that kind of programmed within the DNA structure? The light and sound patterns?

B. I don't know, I don't work with that. Maybe Gergen knows more about that. I just know the gravity field holds the form, regardless of whether it's outside in a solar system, or holding the organs within. It holds all forms in their destined position. It's designed to work properly, of course.

D. With you training on the sixth and seventh, are you eventually going to change the type of work you do?

B. *(Nodding rapidly)* That is the thing, that is the thing. What I've been TOLD is that I'm being trained for something that will come in the future. But, in order for that to BECOME the new car *(human body)*, from my factory, I have to understand the engineering behind it. It is the upgrade of the human body, so that is why I'm learning more about form and light, and the engine. Okay, so you know we talked about the center in the human body?

D. Yes, the six-pointed star?

B. Yes, indeed, in the solar plexus area. This is going to be changed. Every time there is a shift in evolution, a change occurs in this center, this crystal, the six-pointed model in the center area, and that is what Ophelia's group is actually working on, to do the shifts in there. But, when the shift takes place in that area, the FORM itself will change. So you may or may not look different, who knows, but it is the form that contains this new vehicle. I'm going to be working later on this completely brand new car.

D. What about the other life forms on Earth, are they going to be upgraded at the same time?

B. No, I don't know that, because this is about the human, because of some sort of adjustment. It's what we talked about before, about upgrading from Windows 10 to Windows 12. So, in order to do that, certain adjustments need to take place within the physical body. There's also something with the brain, I think this is from the ninth dimension, combined with the sixth. There's something with the brain.

D. Humans could use an upgrade.

B. It's something in the brain, you know, the light and sound vibration will be different. Changes in the brain.

D. The new model of a human that's being worked on, are individual babies specifically formed by people in your group, each one patterned, or are they sort of a by-product of...*(Bob interrupts)*

B. We don't create the pattern, the original pattern. The pattern is the container. The physical pattern, I should say, is the container of the spiritual pattern, which is the thing in the solar plexus area. So the physical pattern needs to change, and as that has changed, all our conditions changed with it.

D. I guess my question was, do you have a hand, or any involvement with the patterns or specific design of individual babies?

B. No. No. But that is what I'm in some way learning, the combination of form and light. Sound and light, because it is combined and connected to the new vehicle that will come. Because we don't necessarily create the new human form, but we create the final touch, if you like, on it.

D. But that's not individually specific, it's just a general model?

B. Indeed. So, who created the big form? I have no idea, but it is downloaded into the cloud and we will do the final touches on it. Let's see if I can explain it better. So, let's say, the shift took place from ape, to slightly less than of an ape. We got sort of a call, to make it easy for you, that changes will be made. We had created the ape form. The conditions that were going to come with a bigger brain and a higher understanding demanded shifts on the surface of this particular individual, this ape person. So, groups in my group, teachers if you like, they were involved with how this new being would operate best on the surface. So we did adjustments in the fur, let's say, we took away some, the nose changed, because, the breathing apparatus is connected to how big of a brain you have. You didn't know that, did you?

D. I did not.

B. You did not. You might think, oh, you have a big nose and can inhale all sorts of oxygen with it, and feed the brain. It's not really working that way. It's another thing, it's a part of the whole connecting physique, really. The nose size and the brain size have changed together over time. So, let's say we have a new individual coming in. Adjustment takes place in skin, organs, inside the vehicle, the engine, and what this individual should eat, or in this case, not eat, so that is what we do. We get this container, if you like, and we add the details, the organs inside. You should know, that during human evolution, the organs have changed as well. Not only that the brain became more of a bigger computer, but inside, the kidney, the liver, the engine changed, because of the different things they were going to eat. So we work a lot on the final touch, the details.

D. I have another question about the six-sided star that's in all living beings. Does the soul come with that star, is that how the soul attaches to the body? Or is it part of the body where the soul uses it to connect?

B. It's a connection, and it is an entrance and an exit. It is also where you always feel connected to home. They teach young souls when they are going to travel the first time and feel scared about the exit point, they're shown on big screens, that you come in and you leave through this place in the solar center area. This is similar to when my students feel uncertain to merge with solid objects, because they don't really see how they can exit. Even flowers have these entrances and exits.

D. And once a soul is inside, does it spread out through the entire being?

B. That's when you connect with the part of you that you planned on, at the time. Like in your case, you have a lot of your soul energy divided in your physical and mental realities. So you sort of portion yourself out, within the container, matching certain lessons that you came here to fulfill. It's not as complex as it sounds. But it is sometimes easier to see a picture than it is to describe it in words. But the physical is merely the container, but you can choose a life where you fully want to engage and understand this physical reality. Those souls normally take on different diseases, in order for them to report back how that was experienced.

D. That's interesting.

B. Those souls who came to learn a lot of the mental realm primarily can develop a hyperactive mind, which can sometimes border to mental problems, which is not a funny thing. But it's all part of reporting, and also the fact of experiencing it. So you have all experienced the different physical realities available within the container, the vehicle; this physical reality, the mental experience, as well as the emotional. The emotional being was more spread out when it was an enlightened age, I should say. Then it wasn't that much of physical problems. But as it progressed, the Master Mind wanted the experience of the physique to take place. This laid the foundation for the changes in the physical vehicles over time. So in order for anything to evolve or change, the experience needs to take place from within. So, in this time, for instance, we want to change the engines gradually and make the physical vehicle different. That's why a lot of souls take on certain diseases and experiences within the engine and the physical layers, in order for it to be reported back what adjustments have to be made. The engine will be smaller over time, I assume. It's too big, too clumsy and complex, for the intake of food that you do. Hmm. It will be smaller.

D. When you take a pattern from the cloud, you modify it a little bit, don't you?

B. Well, first we are strictly following the procedures, but not the whole solution comes in from the cloud. So first we follow it and we look into our bowl where we created it and then we say, no, and then we add this and that. It's like getting the framework, if you like, and then we add the little details. Those from the higher dimensions, when they put new designs in the cloud, they do not know the end result. If they want to create a car, it would probably come without wheels, and then we will add the wheels. We get the form, the idea comes through several different destinations, I would say, from some sort of origin of where it is first created as, POOF, an idea, and then it travels through different realities and everyone has a look-see to have sort of an input, I would assume, before it arrives into the cloud, to us. Then my people, our guiding council, would say there are new recipes that have come. And then we look and it's divided, depending on what we're assigned to do on our level.

D. Would it go to different destinations at the same time, like Earth and also other places?

B. Indeed. Some will, but you know, we have different qualities within my group. Some work on other realities, some work on Earth. My lab is Earth related, but some manuals that come, or recipes that come through the cloud, belongs in other places. But in order for it to not get confusing on this level that I work, you sort of remain within your chosen box, if you like. Gergen, he can supervise and he can move between and look, and he knows EXACTLY where the recipes should go. He's a sort of, like a MAILMAN! Mail is here! Then he takes it and he says, "This is not for you, Bob, this is for someone else."

D. Do you think over time you'll kind of take on some of his duties?

B. I am, I am most eager to accompany him into the boardroom where my elders are residing and blending new ideas. Because this is a huge undertaking to know and understand what form goes where. And that is why I am learning about form and higher realities and energetic conditions with you and Ophelia. Then my hope, and my final exam, is to apply it within my reality, so I, as well as Gergen, can know where to put certain things. I am also interested in understanding how to create stars, because you know, they are shining and it's somewhat intriguing because you know it carries some sort of life form within it or around it, and it's somewhat intriguing to see. You know, I study that.

D. Did Gergen study the same type of things you're studying?

B. No, he didn't study the stars. He's been really focusing on, and he's like a real master, when it comes to plants and DNA within plants. He can manipulate and create new DNA strings. He's a master within the lab of form, because he knows exactly how to adjust plants to match certain atmospheric conditions. And it's a quality, his highest skill, I would say. But he has all sorts of DNA in his bank, in his library.

D. So when you modify organisms, like a human, for example, are you changing the DNA as well...is that part of the pattern?

B. Uhmmm, Yes, because you can add or delete. Within that comes certain conditions that will appear on the surface. It's the engineering, the DNA engineering within living life forms, that is Gergen's main skill, even though he primarily works with plants. I actually try to modify it into the mobile living life forms, like a human, but I can't take credit for the human when it comes to that, really, I was only operating the engine. But Gergen and his people worked on constructing the DNA strings. It began with only a few strings, then more were added. But over time, because there was some sort of revolt that occurred, it became too much. The combination with the human brain did not match. So Gergen and his friends, they adjusted things over time. He's like a DNA researcher, almost. I'm not as fascinated by that because it only looks like spaghetti to me. I'm more interested to learn different ways to create form based on the conditions that exists, and how to move them! And how it becomes from the beginning. I kind of know because Ophelia showed the star, and then I know you put things in motion around it. So, I KINDA know because I'm having my model in your lab and we're working on it. So I know, but I just don't KNOW what is the foundations within each physical celestial body that operates around the stars, and why they are put in a certain order. So what is it with the order, how do you know? That is FASCINATING to me.

D. I was curious, too, this one had mentioned that there was a little female that looked similar to you in the vault. *(Bob started smiling and looked very happy.)*

B. Hmmm

D. Do you like her pretty well?

B. Um

D. Is she a friend?

B. Um

D. What do you call her, what's her name?

B. Ia. *(Christine saw the letters, which Bob pronounced as EE-ya)*

D. Where does she come from? Is she also from the second dimension?

B. Ah.

D. Is she in the lab there too?

B. I meet her in the lab. She's very tender, you know, very caring. She is almost like Ophelia, but in my reality. She helps a lot of the little ones, so she is like a kindergarten teacher. She is very caring, and she has a lot of students that listen to her, and she pays attention to all of them and she helps them individually, and she works a lot with healing and energies. So she provides light a lot, like oxygen and light. And she teaches them the importance of always providing and operating in light. So as you blend with a certain object, you have to move into a capsule of light. It's similar to how your soul energy, which is somewhat in a light form, moved into your body. When we, on the second, learn how to merge with things, we sort of encase ourselves with a light capsule, if you like. And she tells about that, so the little ones are not so scared to blend and merge with certain objects. So she teaches about this capsule of light and the importance to constantly update and tend to it. It's like your capsule. As you blend and merge, you need to move into this...it's not like something you step into, like a vehicle, but it's a way you shift your awareness in order for you to become the capsule, if you like. And that is what she is teaching, how you can become your capsule, and how it's not to be found in a store or in a closet. So, she teaches about that.

D. How long do the little ones stay inside things when they merge?

B. Well, first they just go in and out, in-out, really fast, because they don't want to be trapped. But after a while they remain longer. There are actually classes down here you can attend, to help you decide where to go when you merge. Some stay longer, some stay in trees, you know, like hundreds of human years. Sometimes when you see those big trees, like a really big, old oak, for instance, then there could be several in that one, who have just parked themselves.

D. Does it matter in what age of the trees development they go in?

B. Oh, they don't go in when it is only a little bush, so they wait a while. They normally go in when the tree is like a young teenager. Because, first it goes through its own growth progress, and you don't want to interfere with anyone's progress, at all. So the tree also needs to, like, evolve. Ia is very good to talk about where the best places are to merge, and you can take classes with other teachers as well. Most of the students want to be with trees, because the trees have the leaves going up, so it gets more oxygen than a rock. *(They use the oxygen to maintain their light capsule)* But Ia sometimes says, "We can put moss on the rock, if you like, and that will make you feel similar like you are in a tree." So she talks about that. And then, certain classes can be like, "Okay, I want to be in an oak." And then Ia says, "Okay, oaks exist here," and the little ones can see on a map and they can say, "Oh, this looks interesting!" Normally, they go in a group. So that's what they do.

D. They'll be together in a forest somewhere?

B. Yes, indeed. And in those big oaks you can sometimes see, like those who are hundreds of years and really big, and really old, then there are several in there. So, it's like a soul family from the second dimension, if you like. And if you move around it you can see different objects, which is, you know, the encased little ones, sometimes. Normally, when a group goes in an object like that, there is normally one that is some sort of an elder. Ia doesn't go. They do want for her to come, because they like her.

D. Can they communicate with one another when they're merged like that?

B. Inside, yes, they can. And they can communicate with the collective cloud, if you like. So they can somewhat communicate, yes, indeed, they can. They're not just left inside a trunk in a tree. So they can move around a little bit. For instance, when you see a big oak, or a big rock, and when you come back, let's say, a week later, you see something completely different. That's because they have moved. When a group goes together into a big object like that, they normally have an elder with them, because they want to be able to continue their training, but from within. And the collective cloud, the collective mind, communicates normally with the elder, because the little ones don't always hear. The elder is always with them. It's like a big brother of the group, someone who's been merging for a while. See it like the ten-year-olds are going, and they bring someone who is like seventeen, – and that is the elder in the group. Now, you have a picture of what's going on. Ia doesn't go.

D. I guess you've done that before, so you don't go anymore?

B. I have, there's no need to do that again.

D. Did you get your students from her? The six you have?

B. Gergen gave them to me. He said, "These are little scientists, they want to go with you." I told them about what you do, and they are really intrigued about that. And I say, they have to wait until I tell them everything, because it can only be confusing if you are not prepared for the greater mysteries. And then Gergen said, "Well, provide it little by little, provide it in cups." So I do. I kind of like to just sit and talk to them and tell stories about what I do and about the giants and what can be expected as they grow up.

D. I'm sure that's fascinating for them. It's fascinating for me!

B. Indeed! I do visit her and the students. Ia and Gergen, in some way their work is similar. Because of the light she provides in the capsules, she works really closely with those spaghetti strings that Gergen works with. Gergen is actually like a father to us both. SO, we have been with Gergen for a long time. But because I sort of moved into a different expertise, they communicate more frequently. I communicate with you, Ophelia, and Zachariah. So, Gergen and Ia are more from the original group. And she works similar like him, so I guess that makes sense.

**GMO's and Commercial Agriculture**

On another occasion, I was curious how the spirit world felt about the mutilation of the DNA by the multinational corporations who are ruining our food crops. I was quite surprised that he connected the problem to fiat money, which is the cause of much misery in the world. The international banking families bribed enough congressmen back in the early 1900s to establish the Federal Reserve Bank, which is neither part of the Federal government, nor does it have any reserves. It is a privately held corporation, along with the IMF, BIS, and the World Bank, that enriches its owners at the expense of all other humans in the societies they have enslaved. It used to be that one dollar was one ounce of silver, and one ounce of gold was 20 dollars. Within a few decades, they managed to confiscate all the gold and replace the money with credit. By the 1960s the silver was removed from circulation. Now almost all the "money" that exists is debt loaned out at an interest, created digitally with a few keystrokes. The entire Western banking system is like a child's tea party, where everyone pretends to have something of value, but it is completely worthless. It would take more than a few pages to discuss how the fractional reserve banking system and corporations have taken over what was once a free society, and replaced it with modern form of kleptocratic rule.

The money issue aside, the spirit world is very dismayed by the way our clever scientists have employed their new-found knowledge to ruin their carefully designed plants. There is a huge difference between cross-pollinating, and the GMO practice of splicing in foreign pieces of non-related DNA. GMOs released into nature can bring devastation to other life forms.

D. That brings up a question. As you are probably aware, we were discussing genetically modified plants, what's your advice?

B. It's like spraying inside the greenhouse. Oh, let's see. It is because of the fact of high interest, and in some way interest is combined with money that we already understand and know, but it's also in some way to radiate that you are doing something good, that you are feeding the public, so to speak. So it's actually more of that problem. Money would still be made, even if you didn't spray things, so it's stupid really to say that if you don't spray things, if you don't make it into plastic, that you would not make a living, or make a business, or make money. We don't really understand that, because in the old days you exchanged things. So this paper thing that moves back and forth, why would you want that, really? That can't keep you warm, if you put it on a fire it might make you warm.

D. Is that system destined to collapse?

B. It's very unique for this place, I should say. It was implemented to cause a certain disruption, within this group of beings, to see whether it attached in the system, or if it would, oh, you should see it as a test. Way back, when the paper form came in, it was merely to fool those that early on got something, like a shiny thing, and then someone said, oh, this is the same, but it's not, really. It was a test to see how man would react, and interests were involved. From my perspective, I did not understand who put it there, because you already had a good system where you exchanged copper, and gold, and silver, molded into like dots, and balls and coins. There was no need really to change it into paper. Also, paper comes from trees, so I don't understand why that had to happen. It's very unique for this place, for all sorts of trade, in that regard. The way you trade here is very different than on other places, somewhat confusing I must say. It's better if you have something I want, and I have some you want, so we just exchange it. And things that people are charging for here, on this plane, are actually free. So I don't understand this really, why there is charge for things that were given to this plane as a gift.

D. That comes to the greed and selfish interests.

B. Yes, and that together with the paper money. A lot of it was established when the paper money came.

Bob goes on to elaborate on how the food industry exploits the visual senses to create a desire for things that are actually harmful to the human body. People have the choice to select the most natural, organic and healthy food, but are drawn to the colorful foods that often are full of chemicals and may be genetically modified and very toxic. If everyone chose to educate themselves, and to seriously think about what they are eating, they could significantly improve the way their engine operates. Even though I have eaten organic foods for the past 25 years, Bob has advised me to completely avoid anything containing wheat, red meat, alcohol, sugar, certain spices, and all bovine milk products, including yogurt, cheese, and kefir. I was instructed to drink at least 2 liters of water a day, with crushed lemons and mineral salt added. He also gave a recipe for a lemon, kale, carrot and vinegar concoction that I am supposed to drink in the morning. I have to admit that my engine is functioning much better, and my body has begun to detox from years of being somewhat neglected. Jeshua also warned both of us that our bodies need to be very clean in order to reach the vibration necessary to connect with the spiritual beings who are coming in during later waves of knowledge. He emphasized a complete abstinence from alcohol or sugar in any form. I do have a bit of a sweet tooth, so that will be the last to go, I guess.

The main problem with the modern farming seems to be the mass killing of the worms, microbes, bugs, bees, butterflies and other creatures that are necessary to maintain healthy soil and plants. Almost all commercial seed corn and most soybeans are coated with neonicotinoid pesticides and other poisons by the money-hungry agribusinesses. The FDA and the governments refuse to regulate these toxins, but the damage they do to all the little creatures that keep nature in balance is devastating. The introduction of GMOs has allowed farmers to plant the seed and after a month or so, come back to the field and spray glyphosate and other poison directly onto the growing crop. The crop survives, but everything else dies, including all the little creatures that make the soil fertile and balanced. Farmers also spray this poison on many non-GMO crops a few weeks before harvesting, as a desiccant. Glyphosate kills the crop, and as the plant dies, it puts out additional grain, which increases yield. As the plant withers, it also dries out, which speeds up harvesting. All kind of plants get the desiccant treatment, including wheat, oats, peas, lentils, etc. As a result, much of the commercial food we eat, especially anything with wheat, is full of glyphosate and various toxins, which kill off the microbes in your intestines, or your engine, as Bob would say. Many serious illnesses and diseases, such as celiac, originate from problems in the engine. You would be well advised to research these topics and change your diet to one that is more organic and contains less poison.

All life forms have cycles. Even the solar systems and galaxies are born with a purpose and cycle of experience they will go through. Because of the incessant lust for greater profits, corporations dedicate research efforts towards producing animals and crops that grow much faster and have a greater mass or yield than our friends on the second dimension intended or designed. As these clever manipulators of nature push chickens, cattle, wheat, corn, tomatoes, or any other grain or vegetable to give them more and more, something must be lost in the process. As abundant research proves, it is the mineral and vitamin content of the gifts the animals or plants offer their human captors. Our modern vegetables, for example, which are grown in a chemical soup, have but a tiny fraction of the nutritional value of heritage vegetables grown in humus soil, rich in organic matter, microbes, and earthworms.

  B. Greed is a part of the human consciousness, in some way, because when you enter this reality, you are given a choice to act either this way, or that way. To make it easy, let's say that you are sitting at a table and can choose between two meals. There is one dish, which has only peas. The other one has all sorts of goodies in it, and all sorts of colors. So, here you have a choice. You can take the one that makes you happier on several levels, the one that is more colorful and maybe has all these disguised treats or is sweet. It is for people to make a choice where less is more, like we talked about. So the bowl with only green peas in it could actually be more fulfilling for you than if you have a lot of different colors that triggers several senses. It is to understand the balance. I'm not saying that a lot of color is bad, it's just that you can relate to it in a way that you see one color, ohh, there is brown, and on the other side, ohh, all sorts of colors. What will you pick? That is it.

D. Well, I like green and brown.

B. I know you do. But most people follow their first sensation and sense, instead of understanding that their soul might say something different. It's like everything on this plane, the images of success and happiness are pushed on your subconscious mind, in order for you to act in a way that diverts you from your true feeling and the true path. That is why, on this level, we have implemented the drama of choice. It's so you learn how to pick, and also to be a little bit inquisitive. Why don't people investigate? They just swallow all these colors, with no hesitation whatsoever. Which is kind of strange, you know, to put something in front of a human, and if it is very colorful, they just eat it. But what did you just eat? Why don't you investigate and ask yourself, why is that so colorful? And then we come back to the GMO thing. Because it tends to be more pleasing for the eyes, a lot of time. Colors are modified to trigger happiness, and that is something where we might need to engage the brain a little bit. Humans are so triggered with colors, but do not question why it is so colorful. Why is a tomato extra red, why is it so shiny, why doesn't it shrink, and how come it looks exactly the same after three weeks? But it's red, it's shining, so this must be good. If you understand the process of CYCLES, then you know that something is born and it's shiny, and then it shrinks, like a raisin. For some reason, it has come to the point where it's, oh, much better that it endures over time, it stays the same. But why is it like that? That's not how it is naturally made. Things are not supposed to look like that for two, three weeks, it's not supposed to! That should raise a flag, one might think! And then investigate it, but NO! Again, we are back to the fact it triggers the sensation of happiness. And also, the individual perceives that they don't have to buy another tomato, because the one they bought three weeks ago looks exactly the same. So in their mind, they think they are saving, but to the expense of what, one might wonder. I don't understand why people don't investigate this. That is the first thing that people should be alarmed about, that an apple looks exactly the same after a month. It's the same thing, if you go into a store and see the fruits, they put shining *(wax)* on it, and, ohh, you are triggered and think it looks really delicious because it's shiny. Also, they are placed in a way, in stores, so that it will trigger a sense of happiness and need. So, green and red, you normally see together because that is something the human mind responds to as some sort of happiness. Joyful, similar to the experience of when people go on vacation, really. Green and red and yellow trigger that. So, if you HAD PAID ATTENTION, then you will see more things that are red and yellow now, than it was before. That's actually true. Even grapes have started to turn more yellow. If you had paid attention to how a grape looked before, it was actually more green. Now you can find grapes that are more yellowish, really, and who knows what this is going to proceed to. Maybe it looks like a lemon! BUT STILL, no one reacts, no one responds. It's like, ohh, this must be some brand-new outcast from the original green grape. You should really wonder why it's so yellow. People who intake these GMO things should know it's not good in the system. It causes disorders within the engines in particular, and also diseases in the veins. It clogs up the circulation within, so it's not necessarily only the engine, but it is the vascular and the mobility within the joints. Engines are one thing, but it's harmful for the mobility. People are less mobile, and they get hurt more easily. Like arms and knees. They get stiff, that's what it is. People are more stiff now, and they try to compensate by going to the gym. It may give some sort of muscle tone, but it does not improve the mobility in the physique.

Bob occasionally sounds despondent regarding human actions, but he was especially sad when talking about how spraying poison on fields kills the earthworms and beneficial insects. The second dimension cares deeply about this planet, while we, who are supposed to be somewhat enlightened, are blindly ruining so many of the life forms they spent eons developing.

D. And that's caused by the food?

B. Indeed. So one aspect is, of course, the signals that you will receive within the physical vehicle caused by the GMO things. Also, as they spray the fields, that goes down into the tunnels where worms exist, and worms are necessary. They're OUR LITTLE HELPERS, really, to keep the soil healthy. When they spray, it goes down into the earth and into the tunnels, and to the worms. Worms are divine creatures.

D. Ah, yes, the earthworms are an amazing benefit to soil.

B. Yes, how do you think they got there? I can't take credit for the worm myself, really, it was a group effort. But worms are a sign for people that it is a healthy environment they reside in, the earth is healthy. If there are no worms, it is somewhat rotten, and the roots of those vegetables, even though they might look shiny on the surface, on the bottom, it's not. When a plant and a vegetation isn't feeling well, it doesn't exhale or radiate free oxygen, and it does not resonate as well with the atmosphere. It would be better if you did not disturb, because it's a chain reaction, really. And don't only think about the problems within the physical, the mobility in the joints and with the engine and circulation. It's also the circulation outside in nature, because it's a combined chain reaction, really, from the worms, to the plants, to the atmospheric shifts. No one wants to be around that spray. My bugs don't want to sit on those plants, really. That's one thing people should pay attention to. They're like, ohh, I don't have any bugs on it, but the bugs are actually sometimes light bearers. It's not always a bad thing to have bugs.

D. We can only hope these big corporations are held accountable for their destructive actions.

B. Mmmm. They should just leave it alone. It's like going into someone's greenhouse and just killing things in there. We do not approve. And the worms, our helpers in the tunnels, they leave. And we say, you don't have to be there, because you will not feel well. So they communicate and they say, do we have to be here? And we say, no, not at this point, so they leave and we take them away. And as we take the worms away, and the insects away, what will remain is some sort of created, manufactured watermelon, that on the surface will look exactly the same, but on the inside, it's not. So we take away our friends, the worms, as well. *(Bob gives a long sigh)*

D. Well, I don't know what to do about that.

B. One way is to start growing your own things, so that you don't support stores. Create your own vegetables.

D. Thank you for the advice. So what have your friends on the second dimension been working on, lately?

B. Oh, I know that some of my friends are working on some fruits. It's like a peach, but it's a blend of a peach and an apple, so it endures better than a regular peach. Because a regular peach, it has a shorter life span than an apple. So, I know that they are in the process of making a blend of a peach and an apple. It will taste similar like a peach; however, it will endure like an apple. It's going to be launched in, oh, I know they would like to have it in the south of Europe, and also somewhere in South America, north, northern part of South America.

D. Are they working with humans to do this?

B. Mmmm. They are working with individuals in the northern part of South America. Organic inclined people.

D. It's not genetically modified?

B. No, no. My friends are giving ideas to people in the northern part of South America. Venezuela, Brazil. There's a combined team from two countries working on some sort of progress with that.

Later, Bob was giving advice about how people need proof of certain things before they accept it as a truth, but will completely overlook things that should raise questions. He said that people will question the wisdom the spirit world is giving us, but not even notice questionable things they eat.

B. You will be tested, as you go, on a lot of what we have talked about here, because man is so inclined to have proof of all they have around them. Yet, the tomato which stays the same is just ACCEPTED! That's something you could think about a little bit! Ohh, you question beings of higher wisdom in the second dimension, "Ohh, I don't know what THAT is, BUT I fully embrace the manufactured food that has been looking exactly the same for weeks." So where is the logic in it, you can wonder. I'm not one to be judgmental, but it's still the fact some things are just swallowed without any questions whatsoever, yet other things are like, "Ohh, I need proof of it, I need to see it." Here we are back to the fact of choice, really.

If you question the spirit realm and spirit guides and the higher beings and that awareness, yet you accept things that look very unnatural, it should raise a question in your mind, one might think. The whole point, really, is to start questioning what you see in front of you. If you pay attention, then your own conscious or logic mind says to you, "This must be something odd." Sometimes there is more truth in the things you can't see, than in what is right in front of you. What is unseen can be more real.

D. That's a really good point.

B. There should be a PLING, somewhere in your awareness. All sorts of plings, really, come from that.

The next dialogue was from a session in January 2017. Jeshua had just finished talking and Bob observed him exiting. At this point, Bob didn't know him very well, but he was impressed by Jeshua's appearance. Since Bob is always generous with health advice, we will pass along his observations regarding blueberries and lemons. One of the fascinating statements is regarding the enzymes in blueberries and lemons. He specifically says the healing component is C2, C3. Even though I have a chemical engineering background, neither Christine or I knew what he meant. After a bit of research, I am certain he was describing the active compounds in fruit and vegetables known as flavonoids. Flavonoids contain a flavan core with a 15-carbon skeleton. There are two benzene rings (A and C rings), connected by a heterocyclic pyran ring (B ring). The antioxidant potency of flavonoids is primarily derived from the double bond between C2 and C3 in the B ring. When it metabolizes, it donates two electrons, which bind with free radicals. Mixing blueberries and lemons provides a powerful combination to combat many diseases. Bob once again displayed a depth of knowledge that neither Christine nor I have.

D. Hello, Bob.

B. (*He then began to suck his bottom lip and make a smacking sound.*) Huh, ohh, ohhhhhhhh, it was like watching a superstar pass by! He just passed by me! Ohh, grand! Ohh. I don't know him, but he glances at me sometimes when he passes by. But I don't approach, I do not. I do not indeed, not at all! Because I don't know him, and I don't want to appear nosey, and so I'm waiting much eagerly to be escorted to this council! I'm SURE it's on my agenda somewhere in my notes, on a wish–list! You know, I have a bucket list! One is to accompany you to the council, but you laugh about that, but you know, you still humor me, so you haven't said no. So it's STILL on my bucket list.

D. That was Jeshua, my mentor.

B. I'm not in the family tree, but I'm DEFINITELY like a friend to the family.

D. We'll invite you to the extended family reunions. (laughing)

B. Yes, if I come, I like to have my apple. It somewhat of a connection—I have an apple because it sort of reminds me of home, and because it doesn't really exist on so many other places. So, you know, it's a symbol of a garden, and it's a symbol of my reality and a little bit of home. I DO like fruit and berries. And one of my favorite are the blueberries. Blueberries have a healing component, as it actually has the quality to heal several diseases. Those diseases that attack cells can actually be helped by certain ways to prepare and manage the blueberry, as well as lemon. Blueberry and lemon, sometimes separate and sometime together in a dish.

D. Raw blueberries?

B. Huh?

D. Raw, like just picked?

B. Yes. Well, yes, not from the freezer, that's not where they grow! They grow in the wild, normally, because that's where they're supposed to be, that's where we put them from the beginning. We didn't put them on fields, or something, we put them on places strategically, so they would be left alone.

D. Yes, they're kind of sensitive, you can't grow them everywhere.

B. It's sensitive, for sure! But, it's very strong within its structure, within each enzyme, and it has the ability and it carries certain ingredients, that is C2 C3. And it will kill bacteria. But if you put it in a jam with other things, the mystery is lost. That only tastes well, but the mystery is lost. So, it's not like, oh, I eat pancakes with blueberry jam, healthy! It's not like that at all. It has to be prepared in a certain way, as well as together with the juice of lemon. Blueberry and lemon, STRONG components indeed, if used properly.

D. Do you mix them together?

B. Mix them together, and you use different, it's like a potion, so it becomes like a liquid. It's really good for you. IT BURNS inside the belly, but it heals dirt, DIRT that you put in the belly here. DIRT! *(Looks like he's spitting)* Don't like it at all, mess up the engines! You know how long it took to make the engine? It's not like something that was just made overnight. At this time and age, it seems all sorts of things are disturbing the engine. It's like having a car that runs on fuel, and then, thinking, "Ohh, maybe if I put juice in it, it will run the same." It will not run that well, will it? So, tend to the engine. Learn about the different things that already exist in nature. It is a gift to you, and it's free. It's not for someone to take and make into something new. That is what a lot of people do, you know, they take the good things that we create and put it into something that is brand new, when they have no idea how to do it. They are just adding sugar and other things that make it a clegg. *(He uses "clegg" a lot, and implies something that clogs up the system)* The whole purpose and whole quality it carries is lost. Phuuttt. Phuutt. Makes me sneeze, almost. Sneeze, indeed. You know, a big group of my friends worked with the blueberries, and delivered something really good for you, so please try to keep all these things clean. Otherwise, it's just wasted.

D. Could either one of us benefit from the blueberry and lemon?

B. Both, both of you, actually, because you are moving into a phase where you need to clean out a little bit within your own physique. Ah, little things, differently, within you, but it still needs cleaned. It's something that you could put in water, to drink, also. If you put a little bit of the blueberry in water, like you do with lemons, but you have to open it a little bit.

D. Do you crush it or grind it?

B. Crush it a little so it gets soft, otherwise it's just a little bit of blue floating around and it doesn't make sense. Blueberry water, no one really drinks that anymore, but it was a big hit when it was launched, you know, with the civilizations at that time.

D. When was that?

B. The first time was actually in what is known as the Lemurian. They were more inclined to use that kind of knowledge than prior civilizations. They used a lot of fruit qualities and berries, making potions for them to drink daily. Blueberries actually existed a long time before the coffee bean came. Major project, that one. Fond memories of how you create things. I created the coffee bean. Many memories of how, you know, late nights! *(Laughs at his joke, since there is no night in his dimension)* Hahahaha! Different people doing different things, of course, designing, working together. Picking things down from the cloud. "Oh, this is incoming, this is what they want us to create." Always fascinating when you hear that "pling" in the cloud and you know that something brand new is incoming. You know, you get some signal from the little council, you would probably not call it a council, but it is in my reality. My guide, Gergen, is on that council, and he tells me when new recipes have come, so to speak, so that's what we see.

# Dimensions in Detail

By now, I'm sure you have realized we cannot really understand, except in a general way, how the dimensions function and operate together to create what we think of as reality. Our spirit friends have done their best to provide us with descriptive words that point towards what goes on. The reason the transcripts on dimensions are only now being presented was to give you an opportunity to think about some of the other topics first. This section will be more about how the dimensions work with light and sound to create objects and lifeforms in our Universe, our fish tank. The principles, naturally, also apply to other fish tanks where the same energy is used to create structures that are not solid like they are in our Universe. Above all the fish tanks are the higher dimensions. They are like a big umbrella, under whose guidance all the different manifestations occur, regardless of how solid they may or may not appear, from our perspective.

Listening to our spirits talk about their work for the past six years (as of 2021 update), it is clear that everything is created with both a purpose and a destiny. A flower and a distant galaxy are manufactured, to make it mundane, using a common process. The star carries a structure that is a complex version of the flower DNA. The spirits refer to the planet or star DNA as the core. On a living planet, the core contains energy patterns that resonate with every element and creature that is found on the planet. Just like our DNA is a specific pattern that builds our body out of the elements, the energetic pattern in the planet establishes what elements and life forms the planet is destined to manifest in the third dimension. The cores of planets are designed to manifest or materialize certain elements, and to hold the planet within a specific position in the solar system. Of course, these are not principles we can prove, but anyone who seriously studies the mysteries of life, or of the Universe, knows that order exists. If order exists, there is an organizer, and if we begin with that mindset, then nothing in this book is beyond belief.

The fish tanks contain the first through fourth dimensions, or vibrational fields. In Let's say an Earth-like planet has been created out in some distant solar system by the sixth and seventh dimensions. All the material in the planet is part of the vibration within the first dimension. This would include the elements, gravity, electromagnetism, and the atmosphere, if it had any. If the spiritual councils intend for the planet to carry life forms, then other groups get involved. The basic elements can be organized into something that lives by creating an energetic pattern, which is seen on the third dimension as DNA. The DNA is created by the specialists who work within the second dimension, but they are, in turn, assisted by scientists who work on the seventh and eighth.

You can think of it like this; the third dimension is a movie screen. The first and second dimensions are movie projectors that cast images upon the screen of the third dimension. No matter how closely you stand to the wall studying the pictures, it will not reveal anything about the projector, or the electricity that is powering the projector. That is the dilemma faced by quantum physicists, as they are metaphorically staring at the wall, pondering how things pop into our reality. The energetic force and the patterns that cause quarks, protons, and neutrons to become visible and combine into elements will always remain a mystery. We can see the patterns in everything around us, and know they contain an undeniable mathematical complexity, but how it came to be is completely hidden. To return to our imaginary planet, the individual elements are still aware of themselves, but they are also aware they are functioning within an organization. The DNA is the blueprint they follow, and there is a certain joy and happiness each element feels at being part of the group project, as it joins to become part of a molecule or cell. You might think it odd that an element feels anything, but please remember that the primary attribute of the Creator is consciousness. Nothing anywhere, in any dimension, within any universe, on any world, exists without a component of consciousness. There are no dead objects floating in space, because the elements from which they are made are part of the Creator. Within all spiritual realms, this consciousness carries a component that manifests as a vibrational energy we sense and feel, which is a pure form of what we call love. It is a property of everything that exists, woven into the fabric of creation, if you like. So yes, even the basic pieces of matter are alive and aware, just not in a way we can understand.

Most people will acknowledge a human has a soul, but may be reluctant to acknowledge other living things also contain spiritual energy. When something with DNA begins to grow, be it an acorn that sprouts, a tadpole in a pond, or an unborn puppy, at some point in its early development there is a little bit of spiritual energy inserted into the growing form. What gives these patterns life is an infusion of a higher form of spiritual consciousness. There is a cloud of spirit that exists throughout all of nature, vibrating within the second dimension. A little bit of this consciousness is put into each living pattern, without which it will not come to term. You can think of it as a little camera in everything that lives. This cloud of spirit connects directly up into dimensions above the ninth, which is very close to the Creator. Every living thing on Earth, from a blade of grass to a donkey, is animated by various amounts of divine spirit. What is the purpose, you might ask, for the Master Mind to put consciousness in a living creature? It is simply the pure joy of experiencing all the interactions among the creations that we, its children, have made. It is a divine play of vast proportions. While in spirit, we know the Master Mind is the writer and director, but when we incarnate, we forget it is just a play, while we "strut and fret our hour upon the stage," as Shakespeare once proclaimed.

Solid objects are only mixtures of light and sound frequencies, which are invisible to the physical senses. People who have an OBE, when their soul temporarily separates from their body, sometimes observe this matrix of energy holding everything together. The walls in your house, for example, might look like a dark green, bluish fog or haze in the form of the room, and what was once solid, now looks like bundles of light filaments. The spirit body can see in all directions at once, move as fast as thought, and communicate telepathically with other spiritual beings. This mental reality is the fourth dimension. Your soul sends thoughts and receives information within this energy matrix, even though you are normally unaware of its existence. The world appears solid and familiar to our conscious mind only while your spirit is peering out through human eyes. THAT is the great illusion. The core of your being is nothing other than consciousness, if you like. Your physical body, which is of the Earth, is on the third dimension, but your mind is receiving and sending information on a slightly higher vibration within the fourth dimension. The brain is only the electrical-to-spiritual interface between the soul energy and the corpulent body.

In the next series of dialogues, Ophelia and Zachariah give us an idea of how the different dimensions function.

D. I have a question. You had talked about levels of energy earlier. Is this dimension fully vibrating within a certain spiritual band of energy, such that we can't see other dimensions from this perspective?

O. The human eye, the cellular structure of a human eye, is not capable to see all vibrations. Those who are in tune with their own spirit can sense them. However, there is no way for the human eye to detect the vibrations from the higher levels, from the level five and up. Four can manifest. Level four is somewhat like a bridge between the physical versus into the spiritual vibrations. In this plane, which encircles different celestial bodies where evolution and lifeforms are located, layers or frequencies are carried where physical manifestations are visible for individuals located on that specific celestial body.

D. Is this the fourth dimension you are talking about?

O. This is the fourth dimension that carries a mixture of physical manifestation as well as a mixture for the spiritual levels to descend. This means that some can actually manifest and be seen by the naked eye. Those who physically see spirits, or even past life occurrences as they move through different grids on this plane, actually tune in on the fourth. This is where karma is stored. Native Indians are aware of this level, they can tune in on the fourth quite easily. Native Americans, Indians, those in Peru.

D. So within all spiritual levels of creation, is the third dimension what we can see, as a human?

O. Indeed.

D. And the fourth dimension is the...?

O. Is the bridge to the spiritual, the vibration of non-form. In the fourth dimension, it's a mixture of form versus the non-form.

D. And the fifth dimension?

O. In the fifth dimension you are moving through the higher emotional vibrations. The fourth actually carries all vibrations, in some way, and some can be manifested. The higher vibrations from the fifth, the higher emotions, can be manifested and understood by those who are in tune with their emotional vibrations on the third level. So the third dimension is where form is locked. In the fourth, form dissolves, yet it can sometimes be seen. In the fifth, we are moving into the heart center, the higher senses, the higher vibration of the emotional capacity.

D. In this dimension *(the fifth)* the emotional aspects of Earth are not present, are they?

O. Fear never leaves the fourth dimension. When you move into the fifth, the energies, the emotions, are pure.

D. Within the fourth dimension, does that encompass the mental realm around the Earth?

O. Indeed.

D. Is that part of it?

O. Indeed.

D. And then there are higher aspects that are more spiritually oriented?

O. Indeed. This is similar as those layers around other celestial bodies that is a bridge between one reality into the other. Somewhat in that bridge there is confusion and there is a blend of several impulses.

D. So the fifth dimension wouldn't encase the Earth, would it?

O. Not necessarily. In this case, several layers actually encase this planet.

D. Could you describe them?

O. The first is the core, the central point that exists in all creation. It is the still point that will be discussed later on in different books that will come. The still point carries different vibrations. Where one holds an object in its place, whereas another carries a vibration that makes portals for you to travel or navigate through. The still point exists in all living beings *(The Earth and other celestial bodies are considered living beings)*. Depending on its density and mass, it creates different scenarios. That is the first dimension, the base of all. The second are moving into the layer of particles, as well as being the first level of creation. This is where different minerals and particles can be combined and be structured into a physical form that will manifest on the third level. The fourth, as mentioned, is a bridge between the physical reality into the spiritual, a celestial reality surrounding this specific planet. The fourth is the bridge. The fifth carries memories from eras on this plane where the emotional reality was more, it emphasized more on the fifth dimension for a brief period of time. And the sixth dimension, which carries a higher form, where the geometric teaching originates, also had its influence on this plane. *(Ophelia is referring to the fifth and sixth dimensions as being somewhat inactive, now. There was a time in the past when the higher vibrations were operating on Earth, perhaps in Lemurian or Atlantean eras, in vehicles designed to carry those vibrations.)* All these layers have the ability to descend into this plane and manifest within the third and the fourth reality. However, without the second creating its form, there is no way for the fifth and the sixth to manifest on the third. The seventh carries the vibration of tone. This is where frequencies, like music and those individuals who were on this plane, created by the second dimension as potential carriers of the seventh vibration, manifested in some individuals that are known in history. So the seventh vibration is the sound vibration, sound that carries thoughts throughout this Universe. The eighth is the connection to other galaxies. This is where you will find your next level of communicators coming in from the eighth and the ninth. They carry...hmmm, let us leave that, as of yet. This is your future prospects that will communicate from the eighth and ninth.

D. What level do you reside on?

O. I belong in the seventh. We work with tones, as tones carry a vibration that is unstoppable, and have the ability to move like a particle through waves through the Universe without changing its structure. It will always manifest as it was originally sent. That is the difference. *(Based on other conversations with Ophelia, my understanding is that light and sound are combined into a color map for each specific creation, and this color map also has a corresponding vibrational tone that spirits understand. Each spirit also has a unique color map and tone, which is one way we identify each other while in spirit.)*

D. Very interesting.

O. Birds are in tune to with this level. They carry vibrations from the seventh and eighth. Whereas the ninth belongs with the galactic structure of all. The sixth and the ninth operate together. The tenth is the structure that connects them all, communicating directly to the first, if you like. This picture has been given.

D. Does the Earth carry those vibrations?

O. It is encased by them. However, not all can manifest on the third. To leave you with this model, the highest vibration that you can see with your naked eye resonates with the seventh dimension, which are the birds. That is the highest that will manifest for the naked eye to see. Your eye is not fully equipped to detect the reality that you are surrounded by. If you had a different setting in your eyes, a different structure, you would be able to see all the layers. That would be confusing, as your mind is not as equipped.

D. Ah, understood.

*(Ophelia left and Zachariah stepped in to finish the ideas.)*

Z. So the wisdom from the sixth dimension, it is about shapes and forms creating realities. It is about understanding the concept of mathematics and physics. The sixth dimension is about how all levels and realms are interacted into one reality that combines them all. This is known as the sacred geometry where keys to how to maneuver and move between are found.

D. Is that knowledge available to man, or is that beyond human abilities?

Z. Some can tap into it parts of it, remembering work that is done on this level. There is a council that works on connecting other realms. You have both operated in this council...*(long pause)* Let's see what we can expose from this...The sixth and the third dimension is actually not very different, as they both hold physical matter. The sixth dimension contains the reality on other planets and the structures on them where life forms can take place. So those who operate on the sixth dimension feel very familiar on the Earth, because the sixth holds a certain level of physical material as well.

D. Physical, as in physical on Earth?

Z. Yes, this is where you both operate as physical incarnations on a different plane. The sixth dimension teaches where physical matter exists and what sort of structures and forms are needed to create a physical form on certain planes. That's why certain worlds are only mental or energetic forms. The sixth dimension is about that solid form, and the knowledge of how to create the solid form, combined with celestial bodies.

D. When we look out into the Universe and see the stars, is everything on the third dimension?

Z. With the bare eye, you can only see this fish tank, your Universe.

The dimensions should not be pictured as a ladder, where fifth ascends to the sixth, and then to the seventh. The dimensions represent specialties within the orders of creation. The ladder concept does apply within dimensions and in council work. To give an example; there are many professions needed to fabricate a car. Someone draws the design. The frame, body, engine, drivetrain, etc., are each crafted by separate groups. Other specialists construct roads on which to drive the car. In the spiritual realities, the second, fifth, sixth, seventh and eighth dimensions have a similar division of labor. The second oversee living forms. The sixth dimension does celestial engineering of the planets, solar systems, and galaxies. The seventh work with suns and light energy. The elements, electromagnetism, and atmosphere falls within the purview of the eighth. The ninth and above are the councils who do most of the planning. When a soul is born, or created, it carries a blueprint to become a specialist with a certain trade or skill set. Young spirits on the seventh, for example, will attend large lectures on general subjects. As they progress, they will be assigned to smaller groups that are more specialized. They will watch, learn, and do, gradually becoming an expert. Souls will often cross–train on other dimensions, since the dimensions are a united whole. Some souls will be asked to join councils. Others will lead teams or manage projects. Every spirit and every part of creation is equally important. The Creator specifically patterned your spirit to serve a role within one of these dimensions. As part of your education, you were asked to journey to Earth and learn about a few things first-hand. It is really, almost, that simple.

D. Could you answer a question?

O. Yes, my friend.

D. Are the increasing numbers related to an increasing spiritual vibration? Like, is the fifth dimension a higher vibration than the fourth?

O. Indeed, yet the fourth is a bridge, so the fourth operates in a somewhat unique manner. However, it is a fact that the higher levels that we are referring to, each carry a higher spiritual vibration than the one below, yet only some carry the possibilities of form. As I work in the seventh, there is a lack of form. Form, by that I mean, what is considered form from the sixth dimensions. You can see it as a cone and how all energies and levels are moving into the cone, down to the solid form on Earth. First, it is a sparkle moving in from the tenth dimension, the creation. The creation of what something should be, the idea, if you like. The idea comes from the source, that we can refer to as the Master Mind. It is passing through the ninth, the council of form, where your friend Jeshua and other high beings, creators, masters of design are found. The level eight carries a vibration that is a foundation for all form to take shape. It is also an emotional realm, closer to the seventh. There is no logic between the levels, don't get confused by the numbers. Eighth and seventh are actually working together.

D. Are they different types of energy?

O. Yes. If you want to refer to them in, let's say female and male, then seven and eight are actually a blend, more of a female-male energy level.

D. Would seven be the female?

O. Indeed. The sixth is where the form takes shape.

D. From the seventh and eighth?

O. Indeed. The idea first lands in the ninth where the designers, if you like, in order for you to see this as a picture, get the idea on their table, moving it forward to the eighth. The eighth is involved in DNA, the structure and molecules, also where this form should be placed. Everything carries a tone, you all vibrate, and that is the key from the seventh dimension. As all of these levels are done with their work, the sixth dimension takes over. It is a combined project, and this is not only related to this plane. It carries the same similar structure from the Creator through various levels of understanding. However, it can vary depending on the end result. The end result from this level is the Earth.

D. Is the tenth and above closer to the Creator?

O. Indeed. This is the spot she *(Christine)* has seen in visions that she refers to as the star. It has no form, it simply radiates light.

D. That's very interesting. I have another question, if you don't mind. Our friend, Bob, on the second dimension, is he also a soul like us?

O. Indeed. We are all souls, we only take the form, some easier *(less dense)*, on the levels we are vibrating within. That is why you see me as floating, because from the level of seven there is a lack of form, yet the lifeform is as high as if you vibrate physically. It is simply a transition between lifeforms as you leave the physical moving into the spiritual realms. It is the same between the levels, it is simply a difference within the vibration if it manifests physically. However, you cannot move freely between them. Some do, yet it is not from the beginning. *(Ophelia means that the spirit cannot move around between dimensions after it is first created as a sparkle, but may be able to later, after certain development.)*

D. So you, as a soul, progressed to the seventh level from where?

O. From the Source. I never went into…it is not like going into the second and moving up to the third, it's not a ladder. So, from the Source, you are created and placed where you are supposed to resonate and vibrate. Who decides? That lies in the big mystery in the Creator. We are each created in order to operate and vibrate within certain dimensions and realities. However, it's easier for those not vibrating in solid form to transmit or even descend into a physical form. Those, like our friend Bob, who is somewhat in the physical reality, will not be able in the same way to dissolve into the seventh, or even the fifth.

Ophelia, as my guide, knows me quite well, and is aware that I have always struggled a little bit with different issues that are rooted in fear. She advises me to focus on tuning in on the fifth dimension, the spiritual reality where higher emotions are found. From a higher perspective, fears associated with this plane will disappear.

D. Did you have anything else you would like to share with us today?

O. At this point, we feel you are working individually, and together, in the pace we set up for you. Even though, from a human standpoint, you might encounter fears in your process. However, know there is nothing to fear when embarking on the new possibilities that are put in your lap. Possibilities go hand-in-hand with fear. Those who are fearless open their windows. If they choose the path to settle, or to follow their fears, their windows will be locked. That defines an old soul versus a younger soul. However, the human mind can play tricks. Those in tune with their physical vibrations sometimes follow the more primitive signals, which is related to the physical being. There is no fear as you vibrate on a soul capacity. Tune in to the fifth dimension, and you will see from above, not only this plane, but your part within that plane. You do not need to go further than the fifth. But in order for you to reach the fifth, you have to navigate through the fourth, where all sorts of different experiences have the possibility to manifest. This is where you lock down, my friend. In some way, between the third and the fifth, lies your fears. Who created them? You created your own fourth dimension reality. Tune in on the fifth and clarity will be given.

D. I will try to do that.

O. *(Voice softens)* We know you will. Just know that when you are in the part of full understanding of who you are, you have left both the third and fourth reality, and you navigate in the higher spiritual vibrations. You can still manifest them all on the third. The fourth plays a trick with your mind.

Here is a good place to describe the two aspects found in all the spiritual dimensions. The fifth, sixth, seventh, and eighth each have a spiritual side that is energetic and without form, and another side that contains form. Spirits born into the seventh dimension, such as Ophelia, can access the spiritual side of the seventh dimension because that is their home frequency. This is where spirits appear like balls of light energy, and where the soul groups and teachers are located and study. Each dimension has this side, and access is restricted to those who resonate with that vibration. The seventh also has another aspect that contains form, where the labs and other working areas are manifested. If Christine or Bob, whose homes are in other dimensions *(sixth and second)* go to visit the seventh, they will only be able to access the form side of this reality. Bob is permitted to travel, which he describes as projecting part of his energy, to the fifth, sixth, and seventh dimensions. But he only can see the form side of those levels. His method of travel is different than how Ophelia or Zachariah travel. They shift their inner vibration and then reconstruct their form with a density that matches the vibration.

This next conversation occurred early during the revelations about the different dimensions, so I was a little unsure about some of the topics.

D. You had said the fifth and the seventh go together. Is the second related to any of the other dimensions?

O. The second is always connected to the third, regardless of the reality we are referring to. The manifestation take place on the third. The idea comes from the tenth and moves, like we said, in through that cone, and it is somewhat transmitted into the second in order for it to create a result on the third. I understand that it is a struggle to understand, but this is not necessarily something that man, at this point, will understand fully. So don't get lost, don't create more confusion. That is not why you are here.

D. It was a personal curiosity about the progress of souls.

O. In order for the form to finally take shape on the third dimension, the second is always involved. The creations, regardless of whether it is plants or humans, have to resonate geographically with where it is placed. Let's say we wish to create a palm tree. Those on the second dimensions are involved with understanding where this palm tree even has the possibility to grow. That is why they are connected. The first dimension simply operates as an engine. It is the core and the heart within each celestial body. It is like a heater as well as an engine; it is a living life form.

D. And the ideas for new forms all come from the Master Mind, the Creator?

O. Yes. Yes. What you would call the working groups begin with the individuals in the ninth dimension. The ninth is the council where new designs are decided, if you like. To make it plain. So from the ninth, the idea lands, it's engineered in order for it to move on into the sixth dimension. However, nothing can pass without going through eight and seven, who carries the tones and vibrations *(color maps)* for it even to become a solid form.

D. Do those in some way put patterns to the idea, converting it into a design or form?

O. Yes. The eight and seven.

D. And from there, it descends into the sixth?

O. Yes. Let's call the six to be the factory. So, yes.

D. And it's ultimately projected into the third, if it is to become a solid form?

O. Indeed.

D. Thank you for all that information.

O. Because colors also carry a tone, and this is what our friend, Bob, is learning, the combination of colors and tones in order for a new life form to even become. Colors resonate with tones. The picture looks like a kaleidoscope.

D. Within what dimension are these colors and tones?

O. All levels resonate to different colors.

D. So is Bob working with these colors and tones?

O. Indeed. He is eager to learn. He is operating as a student on the sixth as well as seventh dimension. On the fifth, this is where the Library is, where he studies and helps in the vaults.

D. Which library?

O. The vault, and the Library. That can be found on the fifth.

D. Okay, I think I understand. Thank you.

Bob often entertains us with stories about things he does in different places where he travels. He was in a class on the seventh dimension, learning how to combine light and sound vibrations to form a tiny little star, and gave us a first-hand view of the way he is taught. Our spirit family never gives us information accidentally, so even though it was offered humorously, the underlying process he describes points to how all the visible stars are made.

D. Ophelia mentioned that you do occasionally go to the seventh to learn.

B. I learn about energy and the vibrations, how you mix them together in order to make a new recipe, a new dish. *(Bob laughs about the comparison of stars to food)*

D. Do you work with Ophelia on the seventh dimension, or someone else?

B. Oh, there are little helpers, you know, she's busy, I assume. There are younger, like little assistants in that lab. It's very bright in there, so let me see if I can explain it to you...maybe she doesn't want me to. *(He listens as Ophelia sends him a thought bubble)*

D. Are there other beings from the second dimension in there, or are you kind of doing this on your own?

B. Well, we advance within our own group, like you do. But some people *(meaning spirits in his lab)* remain with functioning and operating within elements of water, or with plants and animals. I'm more into understanding how to create new life forms, and also those life forms that are not fully manifested. So that is a long-term project that I work on with Ophelia and those in her school. She has a school, you know?

D. Ah, I did not know that.

B. No, you did not, because you didn't go!

D. Do you go to that school?

B. I do, I do. There are classes that you can attend.

D. How many beings are there in your class?

B. Oh, there are many in that class. It's like a big…it's like an arena almost, there are many, many listening. After the class, you can go with your teacher into a separate room and then practice what you learned. So first you listen, and then you practice. It is like lectures really, classes you can attend, to understand light.

D. Is this when you are working with this light and sound?

B. Oooh, once you learn how to master the waves of light and the waves of sound, you mix them together so they spin! Then, a star becomes! Of sorts.

D. When does the six-pointed structure get put in?

B. This is the first, it's first because in order for anything to move around, it has to have that core. This is to create the center core in anything and everything.

D. Is Ophelia kind of like the headmistress of the whole school, or just runs this class?

B. Oh, there is this board of teachers, in some way, but she comes around and she supervises a bit, but there are assistants that are equally qualified, I would assume, because you're not left by yourself. You're not supposed to just *(makes a puffing sound)* pffft, pffftt, put in all sorts of light and sound vibration into the fish tank, because you don't want this to explode, at all! You have to be very careful about the amount you put in. *(In this case, the fish tank he refers to is a piece of lab equipment where they mix light and sound energies together and create little balls of light, similar to a tiny star. It is like a glass tank, so they can see what is going on inside.)* They look the same as her, but I prefer to talk with her, because she is familiar with my progress and my work up to this point. I DO have a lot of questions, but she smiles and nods and sometimes she says, "Everything comes in due time." So, I don't know what that really means. What time is that, if time doesn't exist? When is that going to happen? *(Bob laughs loudly at his unanswerable question)*

B. But this lab where Ophelia is, I am very grateful I was allowed to talk about it, because I did not really know. But the whole thing, the whole foundation of all, is the blend of light versus sound. And when those two mix together, all sorts of things seem to appear. If you see it as a factory, again, with the car, I'm more at the final step where you put the painting on it and roll it out from the factory. I put the tires on, so it can move! But the whole design, the whole engineering of the car, is done way before it even comes to me. It is that same thing.

D. You make it mobile.

B. But in order for it to even become something to move, someone has the idea of creating all the tubes and pipes for it to even become something. Then your group comes in and creates the form of the car, then I put on the tires, so to speak, so it actually moves somewhere. Otherwise it's sort of confusing why you'd even make it in the first place, if it doesn't go anywhere, one might think. So now you have a picture of how creation works, in some way. *(Bob is comparing the creation of solar systems and life forms to a factory, and making the point that without some expression of life, there is no reason for the spirit world to create anything.)*

D. Very interesting! Thanks for the description.

B. I do, I do like the class, I do like to go to school. You meet all sorts of new creatures coming in, –because it's not just my group that goes–, you meet all sorts of new, different, interesting, and kind of fascinating individuals that you never even knew existed, in this place.

D. Is this strictly the seventh dimension, or are there students from other dimensions in the class?

B. The teachers are from the seventh dimension, I would say, but the eighth and ninth are also participating. It's a combined work, because elements are involved and they belong in the eighth, and the ninth is also a part of this. But, to make it easy, let's say it is the seventh dimension teachers, but the students can come from all sorts of different places. Some are little creatures, little baby seventh dimension sparkles, and some are from other places. Then there is my group, we come together, but I wouldn't say we are overloaded in this crowd. *(Bob also brings his six little students to the lectures.)* You might think that everyone who comes here look like souls, like energies, but we are here in our bodies. Some here look kind of odd! I don't know where they are from, but they look kind of odd! They sit way over to the side.

D. You don't make friends with them, huh?

B. I don't know if I'm supposed to! It's not like we're sitting there like souls, because we're not, we're actually in the way we are! And those who are on the sides, I'm not sure where they are from, but they are fascinating! Fascinating individuals, indeed! They don't talk much, though.

D. What do they look like?

B. One group looks like a small...the ears look like little cones, I don't know why they are looking like that! I guess they have good hearing, but they don't talk well. *(Laughs loudly)* Oh, Ophelia says, you're not supposed to stare! You know, I try to be discreet, but all sorts of different entities, from all sorts of realities and worlds and planets, can come here and they have a listen. Not all who attend the classrooms go to the lab and work with this afterwards, but they can have a listen! So that's what they do, because they have big ears, so I guess they understand and they can hear it. There are all sorts of individuals, and these must be from some far-away galaxy. I wish I could make you understand it. In some way, it is a spiritual level, of course, but it is also a meeting place where all types of entities can meet to learn.

D. Do you also learn on the sixth dimension?

B. I do, I do. It's a different classroom.

D. Is it a similar type of structure, lectures and labs?

B. It's big, it's not like an arena, like this, it's a little bit smaller. I can draw it for you, this place, if you like. It is similar when I go to the sixth dimension, I go to a class.

D. Do you ask a lot of questions?

B. I do, because I take notes. And it's also because some in my group are not very verbal, they're more inclined to work silently in our lab. So sometimes they send me notes to ask questions, and then we talk about it afterwards. It's also a little bit because, you know, my personality is different.

D. Pleasantly unique, I would say!

B. I'm fascinated by the students here, because they're all sorts of different individuals, it's like going to what would be considered the union, all different groups come in from all different countries *(like the EU)*. Then you're like, "Ohh, I wonder what they're going to say? I wonder what they will add? Who are they?" You know? It's similar, but it's just that they look different. A big hearing, one can say. *(Bob got really loud and excited while he was describing the strange creatures he saw in the lectures on the seventh dimension.)*

## Fourth Dimension

When someone dies, their soul leaves the body and their awareness shifts fully into the mental realm, the fourth dimension. Within this dimension, the beliefs of people become reflected in the surroundings. In all spiritual dimensions, thoughts become a reality. Spirits can essentially think objects or surroundings into existence. On the Earth, because of its density, thoughts do not immediately produce physical manifestations. Within the mental realm, however, thoughts do create quickly. Religious beliefs and other ideas can become transient realities for souls after physical death. People having a near-death experience only travel around in the fourth dimension, which explains why their accounts are so varied. The mental realm is full of random creations that linger like space debris. Departing souls are drawn towards energies resonating with what they believe. Above the fourth dimension are the spiritual realities, which are more static and have permanent structures, meeting areas, and labs. Common areas, such as the Library and the gardens on the fifth dimension, have been created and locked into a form by groups of higher beings. When we are in our spirit body, these locations seem as solid and real as any place we might visit on Earth. However, the fourth dimension is not a spiritual reality. Zachariah describes how the mental realm can be confused as a spiritual reality by some souls, which may cause them to linger within this vibration.

D. Can you describe what someone encounters after death, but before they enter into the fifth dimension?

Z. Oh, it can be anything. This is just a level before you reach your destination. It's where you can stop and contemplate about what you've done, either alone or with a guide. It's not really existing, but it's a level before you depart from this energetic field. It is, like I said, not an existing place. It's a realm you would probably consider as a spiritual field, yet it's not. It can look anyway the conscious mind chooses it to be. This one *(Christine)* created a marble bench overlooking the ocean from a cliff. We all have different views, and we can create a place within this realm according to our preference. It's not an existing realm, it's more like a contemplating base before departure. You can choose to communicate with Earth guides at this level. I want you to understand that this level exists, and it can be created in the conscious mind. Some see this as a spiritual realm, be aware of that, and don't judge how people perceive this field. Let them feel and see it as heaven, if they choose to. Some remain here for a while, because it feels safe, as the conscious mind has created it according to preference. This is where religious icons can appear, because it is created from the conscious mind. It's really not a big field, but younger souls see it as such. Let them do that. Not all need to know about departure from this place. It's not their time to explore what is beyond.

D. So are you saying that some younger souls may stop here, before returning to join their spirit?

Z. It's just that they might decide to stay here for a while, considering this to be the spiritual realm. Let them believe so. This is the field where the connection to the Christ energy occurs. Whether they choose to see it as individuals from the Christianity religion, or others, this is where those images appear. So let people believe in this field. Not everyone needs to explore beyond. This is where the conscious mind creates; this is not a true reality, but for many it is.

D. I understand. If a soul comes here, thinking this is the highest realm, can it reincarnate back to Earth from here, or do they move on?

Z. Yes. Oh, this is a level where some can remain, –not all leave this realm–, so in some respect it is a spiritual realm. But it is the closest one to this planet, it almost embodies the Earth plane, which makes it really easy to access. Higher beings can descend into this field and that's when people on Earth can connect up. *(From Christine's work with between lives soul regression, a few clients do report jumping quickly into a new incarnation. There seem to be two categories of souls who may bounce from one body, up into the fourth dimension, and then back into a new body. The first are very advanced souls who don't feel the need to report back home. The second are less developed souls who may be stuck in the mental realm from destructive actions, or strongly held beliefs, in the prior life.)*

D. So, is the connection made by shifting the awareness, or by raising of vibration?

Z. It's about the vibration, it's a tone. Everything is related to a tone. As you increase or decrease, your vibration comes with a tone which makes it receptacle for higher realms to know which one to communicate with. You all resonate in a tone.

D. How is the best way for a person to raise their tone so they can connect with these spirits? Is it a constant effort, or is it a by-product of a certain procedure?

Z. It is a complex question, yet a good one. It is outside influence merging with the soul vibration, the unique vibration of the soul.

D. Is it a matter of intent from the incarnated person?

Z. It has to know to receive the signal. And some are programmed to receive it early, and some are actually not meant to receive it at all. It's a complex picture. To best explain it, if you see the Earth surrounded by a field where signals pass through. Yet on the inside where the receivers are, meaning the incarnations, they have to be programmed for that influence and signal to come into their field. On Earth, as I see it, they radiate light. Those who are receptive, meaning that the outer realms more easily know where to send their frequency, it's like a signal of sound. But if you consider the population as a whole, around twelve to fifteen percent are receptive. Twenty-five percent would be the goal at this particular time.

**Cloud of New Designs**
Bob told us how he, and everyone else in the second dimension, gets information and instructions on what to work on and build. He also understands the process, generally, of how each dimension is involved with creation. The spirit world is quite organized and it seems everyone is given assignments, which filter down from the Master Mind or higher councils. Gergen is Bob's mentor and usually gives him assignments, but Bob also receives design plans directly from a cloud. Every spirit has a role, which changes over

time, so the level of complexity and responsibility increases as spirits become more advanced. We are presenting Bob's description of how he sees creation, from his perspective on the second dimension. The sixth through the ninth dimensions prepares the template and the intention for some new life form, or a modification to an existing plant or animal. This manual is then put into what Bob calls the "cloud", and sent down to the councils on the second dimension. Those manuals are allocated to groups based on their area of expertise. He describes it like a post office where he goes to pick up projects that he has been assigned to work on.

D. Maybe you can talk Isaac into taking you on a tour of the eighth, to study gravity.

B. Oh, I'm sure there's going to be all sorts of openings for me to have other questions during these sessions as well, you know. So if an opportunity comes, I'm going to ask. Because, you know, I do want to learn more about the elements, because I understand they are the foundations of all things, even down to the light particles within the strings, like Gergen is working with. Everything origins from different elements from the eighth, so you are somewhat bound to understand the eighth in order for you to create anything in the other layers, anyway, or other dimensions. So, that is why the eighth, even though, based on its location, you might think, oh, it should be closer to the core, which might be up in the twelfth dimension or something, BUT, it is that filter from the intention and idea that comes from nine and ten. So it filters down, like a rain, through a filter, through eight, and eight makes sure what elements are proper for this specific idea to take place, moving down to seven and six where the light and sound patterns become different manuals. Then from seven and six, and even eight in some way, these manuals are diverted into the cloud, where everything comes down for us in the second dimension, to create the specific form. The second dimension, where I belong to at this specific point, relates to Earth. So, I access the Earth cloud. *(Laughing)* See how easy I make it for you, so you can make a picture in the head?

D. That is very clear. I like that description.

B. Each place has a different cloud. As I'm operating from the second dimension relating to Earth, I don't get access to clouds that operate within other realities, or other planes, or even other planets. The second dimension can only access manuals from the cloud that are connected to that specific reality they are working on, and I can only access manuals for things I am working on.

D. Avoids some confusion.

B. Kind of makes sense, don't you think? Otherwise everyone would be saying, "Which is my cloud, excuse me, coming through, coming through, is that my cloud?" "NO, this is mine." So, you know, you want to make sure you only focus on what is in your dish, so the manual is almost parked over where you are at. There are other second dimensional realities operating in other solar systems as well, if it's created, and if it has an atmosphere.

D. Well, Gergen, he has access to that, doesn't he?

B. Oh, Gergen, he has access to something like the cloud library. Cloud library. He can say, this cloud belongs here, and those manuals go here. It is somewhat of a vault, where he is, where he studies, and he can access all sorts of clouds. I saw it once, and he showed me some of these different clouds.

D. I would think he would take you on little tours of what he is doing?

B. Ia goes more, because she works more with the clouds. I did work with another cloud that was related to that greenhouse planet I once talked about, –that was a different cloud. It was more passive because it was not to be interfered. But I haven't worked with multiple clouds. So Gergen has more access to all that knowledge, similar to Zachariah in the Library, he sees reports that come in. Gergen has all the clouds in his possession, or access, if you like. He can choose to look in all different clouds, relating to other areas and life forms.

D. Sounds like a lot of responsibility.

B. He's like a keeper of knowledge, just as Zachariah is. They can get information from the clouds, the Master Mind that is sort of hovering over different physical realities. But also, I do know that there are clouds, because he did tell me, that not all clouds are connected to a physical manifestation. There are also energetic manifestations, and even those that are half and half. That's sort of tricky, I guess. You don't want to have legs and then something on top that is mysteriously floating! I don't know how that is operating, really. But he said, "No need to worry about that, Bob." But he shows me that it exists. Half and half, interesting.

D. Is that within the Universe that we are aware of?

B. Nay.

D. Different fish tank?

B. *(Popping lips)* Different fish tank. Different fish tank. But similar like Zachariah having more of the written word, reports, stored memories, in from all corners of different universes. Gergen has the same, but he has access to the different manuals, all the different clouds that operates within, hovering in different fish tanks.

D. He's a good guy to know, then, if you want to learn something.

B. Yes, but, it's not like a library. You can't just go, "Oh, can I borrow the manual from the half and half cloud?" And they say, "No, because you don't work with the half and half." It's not like a library that you go and borrow a book, and then return it. That's not how it works AT ALL. Once you have collected your manual from the cloud, it doesn't return UP into the cloud.

D. It's yours?

B. It is yours to keep, and it is yours to operate from, and to create what its predestined evolution is that you are supposed to create.

D. So, it's like your personal responsibility?

B. It is your personal responsibility and you can't just put it back. So everything comes out of the cloud, but it doesn't return into the cloud. However, you can get additional information again from the cloud that is connected to the one you are operating and creating. So yes, indeed. There are those who operate as somewhat of a librarian, if you like, underneath the cloud, so you can ask them for additional information. Oh, this is tricky for you, but it is like this; you receive your manual and you start to create, and you don't question that manual, but it is only a frame that comes in the manual, it doesn't come with all the different details, that is what you are supposed to do with it. You get the frame from the Master Mind in the cloud, and based on your knowledge and your teachings, you create the picture of the creation that you are supposed to do. But, if you need additional information you can actually somewhat return, and through different guardians, keepers, in some way similar to librarians, you can say, "Oh, I have an atlas here over Europe, but I would like more information about Italy." And they go and collect another book simply about Italy. You see what I mean? Similar like that.

D. Well, does the manual get put in there through the eighth, seventh, and sixth?

B. Yes. The idea comes from nine. I don't know about ten, but I do see that the idea comes in from above, into nine, but I don't know who they are. But nine creates the idea of what is to become a new project, let's say, and they send this new project down to eight, for them to encase it in what elements are needed for that specific project even to become something. Moving down to seven and six, they are somewhat light and sound related in order for it to become something. And when all this is done, there is somewhat of diversion that goes, not down, but to the clouds.

D. And there are some other people that distribute the work?

B. Oh, I can't see them because the cloud is somewhat locked.

D. The elements themselves are comprised of light and sound energy, aren't they? It's part of what makes up the color map?

B. They create the color map. That is correct. In order for a color map to even become something, you have to master certain elements and its combined resonance with each other. Primarily they use the components of three and five, in different ways.

D. Can you give me the components in the three and five?

B. Three and five. I did look at this with Ophelia, and there is something on this plane, on Earth, with the components in different varieties of three and five, and they are somewhat moving into the light reality in order for them to become the sparkle within the DNA. You can add more combinations than three and five, but on this specific plane...but, when I say three and five, I want to show you the picture of it, because it's like it rotates in different ways, and it blends in certain different modalities, so even if I say three and five, it comes in MILLIONS of different varieties of solutions, even if they are only three and five in their structure. (*He shows Christine that these bundles of three and five elements are stacked in a chain, in different orders, to make DNA structures.*) This is the secrets of eighth. I don't really know, but I do know that Ophelia said the color maps on this plane do not carry more than three and five components from the eighth. However, they are matched into several millions of different options, before it moves into the light forms of everything that is created. Then comes sound and it holds it in place. This is how DNA is made. It is confusing; indeed, it is, but it somewhat describes a picture I saw when Ophelia talked about it. But it also resonates with some sort of sound.

D. I'm sure that will be covered more in later waves, I hope. But, let's say you are working on an engine in a human, is that an entire manual, or a piece of a manual?

B. Ahh, Ohhh, because first comes a big manual, let's say, number 1, and that is like the whole frame; we're going to create an engine, and this is how it's going to operate. You receive the information of why you are creating this, and what is the function, the primary function, of this specific organ, what is it supposed to do. And you receive this manual, the framework of how this specific organ is going to operate, and also, the location is normally mentioned in this number 1. So you take that down and you start working with it, based on your expertise. Normally, you work with a group, and somewhat discuss how you can create this to function. But then, you might need additional information, especially when it comes to kick-start it. Because the first part is somewhat of a dead object, so it's in hibernation. So then you need additional information that comes from additional manuals, in order for it to become something. The color map comes in, after, and how you kick-start it comes in after. So, you work on this in a certain order. It takes a little while.

D. I see that.

B. The circulation group is involved, and they have their manuals. So, I get the manuals, "OK, this is the form, and this is the primary function of the engine," and then the circulation groups says, "OK, we have received information about the location of this specific organ and how our circulation is going through it, or surrounding it, as well," and then you sort of combine it. And you have to be somewhat clear before you receive information, so that's why you don't get the whole picture at once, because you're building something. *(This again shows the group effort of creation, and how we are all in some way co-creators)*.

D. Ah. So, when it's eventually done, you possess the manual, are you responsible for maintaining it?

B. Well, it is stored, similar like in a vault. As long as we are building it, it is my possession, yes.

D. And if they decide to discontinue a model, then you take all your notes and put it in a vault?

B. Yes. And I also, if something really doesn't work, I also store that for future projects, so I don't do the same mistake again.

D. Must have a lot of reference material in there.

B. I do, indeed.

D. How do you categorize it? Fur, no fur?

B. Hehehehe! Oh, I kind of like to create things with fur. Organs are fine, but it's not as funny to observe them, because it doesn't go anywhere, it doesn't experience much, in that way.

D. When you're making fur, do you get to design the color patterns? Is that all up to you?

B. Ah, you know, if it was up to each and every one, there could be all sorts of different colors that don't blend in well with nature, really. So you don't get a variety of choices here, you know, it has to blend in. You don't want it to be exposed; you don't want to have a pink one, because it's really hard for it to survive. Even white, you don't want too much white when there is no snow. You want it to be disguised.

D. So, how do animals perceive their environment? Most of them are color blind, aren't they?

B. Nay, it's not really true.

D. Can they see energetic fields?

B. Yes, they can. And they see like waves, so they can detect colors, because there is information that actually comes through different colors, as well. So they actually see vibrational layers in colors, and they are programmed to understand certain colors which are triggering certain emotions within them. The Master Mind communicates with them through vibrational waves that are carrying color codes, so I don't know why they say animals only perceive black and white, because they do communicate with colors. There is a different group on my level that works with this, but, let's say that red is danger. So if they sniff up a plant they are not supposed to eat, then that specific plant will radiate the color red to the animal, so it doesn't eat it, because it's programmed to understand and to avoid that specific vibration. But it doesn't mean necessary they see a color, but they understand. It is sent to them in colors.

D. I see, that makes a lot of sense. Can animals read each other's mind?

B. In a similar way.

D. Like a thought bubble?

B. Not a bubble, it's more like waves. It's like waves between them. But, if they're not programmed to understand... let's say they have an access to, say, 10 different varieties of color that would resonate with certain information. If one has access to ten, and the other individual only has to five, then they don't understand each other. So it's based on what the Master Mind has programmed that specific individual to possess within its awareness.

D. It's all very complicated.

B. Not really. It's like, you know, you only have one language activated in you! *(He is laughing loudly at this)* and you know, you only talk in that one. So you, in this case, it would be like you only understand the one color blue, but another who understands and speaks several languages, they maybe have five colors programed in them! So, you know, it's the same thing. Your animal *(refers to me)* only has one, and the others have five, so you can see it's the same thing.

D. Well, humans, can they sense vibrational energy like that?

B. No, not those humans who are alive at this point, no. Prior civilizations, those who lived in caves, way, way, way back, in fur, they could somewhat. Because they were designed just after animals, in some way, so they still carried the awareness to understand, –this is what you call telepathy–, but it is understanding certain frequencies that exist as an awareness within the individual. Man was evolved to only move up into a stored computer. By that, it somewhat lost the other frequencies to communicate with the trees and animals and plants in its surroundings. So, in some ways it has more capacity in the computer than an animal, but it has been cut off from the collective Master Mind that exists in animals and trees. Man has become color blind, one might say.

D. That's a really good explanation.

B. So, now you know.

D. I read about a species of bird on an island where the flowers they used to eat all disappeared.
B. Then they were on snooze, they took them away.
D. Well, they changed the length of their bills so they could eat other flower nectar. It was done in a very short period of time, like in a generation or so. Is that something the second dimension will work on?
B. It will come through the clouds. All these changes like putting something to sleep, like we talked about, where Ia can take away the capsule *(They said all living beings are encased in a light capsule)*. But, if you want to take something away, you sort of make the capsule go to sleep and then it disappears. But if you wish, in this case, for the bird to continue its evolution, then you will instantly bring in something else.
D. And then all the new birds that are born, would change?
B. Different color map. If that is the decision, if that is the choice, on this specific island, then yes, that would be the case where that would happen, indeed. It can happen somewhat quickly or it can have somewhat of an evolution. So you will see where it appears to be an evolution, because man see, oh, it's been a timeline here. And then you have these specific places where this occurred, for instance, then it is an instant evolution, it's a kick start, it's a reboot. And that is somewhat tricky to scientists, because in their mind, evolution has the same timeline. But it doesn't, really.
D. That's good to know. I assumed that's the way it worked.
B. It's just different, and it is designed. It is not from the general individual in the second dimension. It is designed the same way *(from the higher dimensions)*. It origins from an idea and it goes through the dimensions to us, it just goes faster in order for it to become. But then again, there is no time on those levels, so it carries the same timespan for an idea to become something, but from this plane it will appear to be like a rebooting, and not following the general timeline of evolution.
D. So, because the Master Mind exists in all these little birds, it's aware its food supply is disappearing, and it just adjusts itself?
B. Because the Master Mind was the one that shut it down, and make the capsule to go to sleep *(the flowers the birds fed on)*,

but if they wish the birds to continue its existence, they will immediately transform either the bird itself, or bring in a new plant for it to feed on. In this case, it seems like they changed the bird itself.

D. That's amazing.

B. It's just a different way of evolution. Not everything follows like, 10 years, 20 years, 500 years, so, you know, everything has a predestined evolution planned. BUT, the Master Mind can change it when it comes to plants and animals, if you like, because it doesn't carry a soul. It's a little bit more tricky when there is an incarnation in it. So you tap into it almost, like molding.

D. So, I guess with almost all creation, the Master Mind doesn't really do it himself, it's sent through all different levels of soul energies?

B. Indeed! It operates as a conductor from what has been decided in nine, eight, seven, and six.

D. And all these spiritual beings are created by the Creator, so they are they like vice presidents?

B. I would say, or maybe the director, because they are the ones that execute the orders. *(Laughs at his analogy)*. You can't see them, you can't go to the cloud, you can't go to the Master Mind, you can't go. I asked about that, because I did want to talk about why my favorite creature was taken away. *(Bob had created, all by himself, a little bearlike animal that carried a lot of spiritual awareness. He has talked about this gentle creature in numerous sessions, and how it was removed from the Earth plane before the introduction of the first humanoids).* I wanted to go there and discuss, but no one goes. I asked you. I asked everyone. I asked Ophelia, I asked Gergen, and said, "Do you go?" I tried to sniff around the subject and tried to see if I could sort of join and go to the Master Mind. You know, maybe there's like Master Mind meetings that occurs, and maybe we can go. But it doesn't seem like anyone goes, really, to that place.

D. It must know what you're thinking, though, sometimes?

B. Yah, I'm sure it does, because it sort of hovers over everything. Well, anyway, I think that will be it for today. And I do feel like you're getting a bigger picture here of how things are operating. But animals actually read levels of colors, because each color from the Master Mind is carrying a different kind of information or awareness. So it could be, for instance, "don't eat me." It could also be, "move away." It could also be, "get closer." So it carries different instructions. That's why sometimes you can see, let's say, an animal that would normally attack another one, but it doesn't, because that specific other individual is sending off a frequency that the predator interprets as, "Don't eat this, care for it instead." So either it stays and protects it, or it leaves. You see these nature movies and you see a bear, and you see like a little sheep or something, and suddenly you think, oh, it's going to eat it, and then it doesn't. It's because the sheep sends off a frequency that the bear interprets as, "This is not to eat."

D. And that comes from the Master Mind?

B. Ah.

D. That's fascinating.

B. So, if you observe these little things in nature, you can see where the Master Mind interferes. You know, you have eyes. Have a look-see! Look around, see things! Man tends to just see other man.

D. Pretty blind.

B. Very selective, indeed. Because we *(on the second dimension)* are working with the Master Mind in animals and so forth, we are trained to put a lot of effort into creating pictures that are somewhat universal as a language, you know, the galactic language, I would probably assume.

D. So, when animals see things, they kind of see a picture in their mind?

B. Yes, they can see a picture in their mind. And some pictures are resonating and it could be simply, –it doesn't have to be like, "Oh, I'm sending you a flower picture." It's normally not sent like that at all. It's sent like a pattern, so it looks like, –it doesn't really look like something you would think, "Oh, this is a flower, this is a car." It's merely like a pattern which resonates with information.

D. Oh, like we talked about last week?

B. Yes. So, normally we use those patterns that are known for the bees. We patch it up for different modalities and different colors, and that is how we communicate. Because if we were supposed to sketch all sorts of stuff, like a flower means, you know, "eat", and an ocean means, "go take a swim". So that would take longer. It's better to have a universal language that is perceived on all different realities, really. So that is somewhat of a trick that the second dimension has. If you are on a place where there are no flowers, let's say, and you send a flower, then those that operate on that plane will not understand a flower, but they do understand the universal language of those patterns we send.

D. I was wondering, if there is an animal that is really hungry, can you tell it where food is? Or how does it know?

B. In some ways it's the same with you! We somewhat send a sniff-sniff signal to it. They do have a higher ability in their nose region, that apparatus is actually more developed than yours. So sometimes it can be sent to those animals that have a highly evolved breathing apparatus, it can be sent to that region. Some signals are sent to the mental, and some are sent to the nose for animals. It's not necessarily working like that with humans. So don't expect there to be sniffing signals sent to you, because we operate more with the brain here, and the soul particle. But with animals, for instance, we resonate with both the mental signals as well as the sniffing, because the sniffing signals can somewhat say what to look FOR. However, when you send to know WHERE to go, that is sent into the mental within the animal itself.

D. So, they get the urge to go in a certain direction?

B. Indeed. First, we might send a sniffing signal, making it aware. If an animal is old and laying down, near the end of its cycle, if you send a sniffing signal, the food might need to be just around the corner, so to speak. So you send a sniffing signal and that makes it come alive a little bit, and then you send to the mental realm where to head. So it's a dual signal.

D. It's always been sort of a mystery to me how the animals know where to find food.

B. Well, it's because it's communicated, mainly, to the mental capacity within it.

D. So if there is an abundance of food, you don't really interfere with it?

B. There's no need. There's no need to send sniffing signals to it. Then you can work on other communications that need to take place.

D. That's really interesting, thank you for the explanation.

B. Oh, it's not that tricky, really. Sometimes the Master Mind, if there is, let's say, too many of a certain species, then the Master Mind might not actually interfere, and not send sniffing signals or mental signals at all. It has to be balanced in nature.

D. So, does the second dimension help animals because they are instructed to by the Master Mind, or do you do it of your own accord?

B. The Master Mind is mainly operating the signals. The second dimension can assist, especially to care for the individuals that are placed here. However, if there is a blend sometimes, like when we merge with an animal or a tree, let's say, then there is a combined effort from us as well as the Master Mind. But normally it's like we simply take care of it, like if it is hurting, because they don't go to doctors. So if they have an injury, it's not the Master Mind fixing it, that's us. The Master Mind somewhat hovers and directs them on where to go and also when to not go to certain places, because it's been overly populated. Sometimes you wish they could do that here with humans as well.

D. I wonder why they don't?

B. Well, because you're not connected in that way to the Master Mind, it's on the other levels. It's another source, really. But, let's say that in nature there is a place that needs to somewhat come alive again, that there's been like an overeating of sorts, then the Master Mind interferes so that animals, in some way, either disappear naturally, or are diverted. If there are too many elk or deer, what they can do is put predators in the region, so they instantly start feeling like they need to go away. That is done by the Master Mind, that's not done by us.

D. Are you aware of what the Master Mind intends for certain things?

B. Oh, sometimes, on a smaller scale.

D. If you are supposed to help an animal, how do know to do that?

B. Well, it's only those times when one of us is inside the animal, in some way, we can detect that. Otherwise we detect it a little bit after, and we respond. But if we are inside, somewhat blended, then we have the ability to get a little bit of a preview, if you like, and we can act earlier. If elks are overproduced in certain places, and they want them to move—because they eat up all the grass and it doesn't have time to come back into full blossom, and the Master Mind wants them to leave for a little while—so they put in predators in that region. Then, if that group collective soul interferes, –and there is normally a lot of us present–, then we help them to understand that it is time to move a little bit. It's tricky for you, don't get stuck in the details, but it's a combined work. Mainly it is the Master Mind that operates on this level and makes sure certain things are flowing and in harmony in nature, and between animal species as well. We tend to care for what takes place afterwards, if you like, to make it simple for you.

D. That's a very good explanation.

B. Because when animals are hurt and stuff, we tend to that.

D. There is something else I was curious about. Do groups of animals have like a group soul?

B. It can have it if it's like a big flock, for instance, then it can be the same group soul, as you refer to it.

D. When the animals die, does it go back into the cloud?

B. Somewhat like that.

D. But a pet, someone's personal pet, does it also have the same type of soul energy?

B. Well, some pets actually have the presence of a being from the second dimensions. But, to not get confused, when animals or plants die, they carry the collective soul, if you like, and that resigns to that source, collectively. Even though, let's say, a flock of ten individuals, and they don't die at the same time, but they all resign to the same particle.

D. And that particle is somewhat separate then from the Master Mind?

B. Oh, it's somewhat looks like a cloud, but it's not where the manuals come from. It's somewhat of a collective soul. But it appears to me as a cloud as well, but it's not where you go to collect manuals. Your soul is a little particle that goes back to its source. This is more like a big ball of light, and a piece of it detaches when it merges with something on this surface, but then it just goes back, up into this big ball, when it dies. You don't go back into the light ball, whereas the collective soul resigns into a bigger ball. So it's somewhat more of a concentrated spiritual awareness, because it is compact, but it detaches in a different way than when a soul goes. It's not on the same mission to report back, it's simply to experience. The difference being, as an animal dies, the little snowflake returns back into that source, it doesn't report anything because the Master Mind hovering over the collective soul, let's say, they already know and they already experienced firsthand. They don't need to wait for the sparkle to return home to report.

D. Huh, I understand that. I was only asking because I've heard some people say some animal souls can progress up to higher and higher levels of being.

B. I don't know about that. I don't think it needs to be too complex for people, it's complex enough as it is! It's complex for me too!

Creation was not a one-time occurrence. It is a continuous process, orchestrated by elaborate coordination between the various dimensions. Each of us are actively involved and serve a special role in creation. Your soul is a piece of your spirit, which is a piece of the Creator. Even though you are out here in a remote part of the galaxy, in a distant area of the Universe, floating on a rock through space, you are experiencing and creating, along with all your spiritual relations, the majestic Universe that surrounds us. As one of our guides said, the spiritual world is like a chain and we are all connected. We all rely on and help each other.

# *The Art of Living*

What the spiritual entities were teaching, and what finally became apparent to me, is the magnificent organizational structure that runs through all of Creation. The main purpose of the spiritual dimensions is to create form–based objects or living creatures in the first through fourth dimensions. For something to become in our Universe, the Master Mind passes an idea into the higher councils on the tenth or eleventh, who make it into a project. Depending on the specialties required, the work is assigned to the proper councils on the ninth, where the initial engineering and planning is done in coordination with seventh and eighth. Launching a new galaxy or a new species is done by spirits who inhabit the second, or sixth through ninth dimensions. All spirits do the best they can with the knowledge that is available. But even if designs are nearly perfect at inception, nothing is static. The Wheel of Creation is always rotating, forcing the fish tanks to evolve. As conditions shift, new designs are needed to restore balance. Learning is continuous, and this leads to improvements over time, not only in plants and animals, but in stars and planets. New spirits are born, and they grow and learn, following the blueprint given to them by the Creator. Even the spirits from the higher dimensions do not really know where all this is going, or the greater purpose envisioned by the Master Mind. Alfred Lord Tennyson said it well in his poem, *Ulysses*.

"I am a part of all that I have met;
Yet all experience is an arch wherethrough
Gleams that untraveled world whose margin fades
For ever and forever when I move."

We are made to follow a certain path, but the end of the road is never visible, only what lies beneath our feet. Our soul came from somewhere, and when this life is over, will return home. Taking this larger view that we have each been gifted a body for the journey, some consideration should be given to how it is maintained.

The difficulty always lies with the doing. I, for one, am very much a creature of habit, so embracing change does not come naturally. However, the goal of these teachings is to focus on what is achievable for us, and once again, we come back to the fundamentals of thoughts and actions. While it is very important that we understand the big framework of the spirit world, what is most valuable is being able to exit this life with fewer regrets. So, in this section, we will try to summarize a few of their teachings, as they relate to our daily life and the inner dimensions of the physical, emotional, and mental layers.

## The Third Layer, the Physical Body

The physical vehicle is our connection between this plane and our spirit. The body was designed and built so the soul could interact with the third dimension. Since it is both a tool and a gift, we have an obligation to use and treat the body well. And this always involves choices and decisions in We can go for a walk, work on a project, lay on the couch, eat a salad, drink a bottle of wine, complain about the neighbor, or any other thing you can think of. Those are all actions that occur after you decide to do something. Even if you have to go to work and sit at a desk, you can choose to sit up straight, or to slouch. Many of the decisions made during the day actually result in mistreatment of our own body. For example, a person may have a craving for greasy fast food, along with a drink made with carbonic and phosphoric acids, and a lot of fructose. Repeatedly giving in to the urge may result in obesity, diabetes, and other illnesses stemming from acidic conditions in the body. Giving in or not giving in to a signal from either the mental, emotional, or physical layer is a choice. If eating a pint of ice cream gives you indigestion for five hours, it's the body's way of telling you it doesn't want a bucket of ice cream. If drinking half a bottle of vodka makes you sick, perhaps the body is suggesting it prefers not to be poisoned. These are obvious signals, but there are many subtle ones that, if listened to, would help us avoid all sorts of health issues. Being aware of the physical layer makes it easier to choose actions that are beneficial to the body.

Our modern society has advanced technologically much, much faster than it has spiritually. The evidence of this imbalance is all around us, in the food, the water, the atmosphere, and the land. Fortunately, people are becoming more educated about how the residual toxins in food grown on commercial farms can cause neurological, hormonal, and digestive diseases, and are choosing to buy organic products instead. The water in most cities is deliberately laced with poisonous industrial chemicals such as chloramine (mixture of chlorine and ammonia) and hydrofluorosilicic acid, which is a byproduct of synthetic fertilizer production. Water is also indirectly contaminated with pesticides, herbicides, and toxic industrial pollution. On average, there are dozens of carcinogenic chemicals in the tap water of most cities. If you labor under the assumption that the EPA is protecting you, consider that they are the ones who demand that chloramine and HFS acid are administered to the population. They also set ridiculously high acceptable levels for all toxins. You should research the ill effects that municipal water can have on your body. If you live in the USA, UK or Australia and don't have your own water source, you may want to consider drinking water that has been processed through activated charcoal and reverse osmosis membranes, which removes most of the toxins. If you do drink RO water, be aware that it is demineralized, so adding back calcium, magnesium, potassium, selenium, and other trace minerals is a good idea.

The air we breathe circles the globe, carrying all sorts of unknown particles. There is abundant evidence that nano-particles of aluminum, barium, lithium, carbon, and other strange jet fuel additives are continuously being sprayed into the upper atmosphere as a way to manipulate weather conditions. Since governments have gone rogue, the only option for humans is to minimize the toxic effects of the aerosols being sprayed from above. You should know that Alzheimer's is a result of a replicating misfolded protein, called a prion. There is compelling research that points towards aluminum as one of the metals that can provoke proteins to become abnormal. Aluminum combines with fluoride to make aluminum fluoride, which then combines with oxygen in your blood to make aluminum oxide, or alumina. Alumina can pass into the brain and potentially cause Alzheimer's. The fluoride is conveniently delivered to you in the water supply (predominantly in the USA), and aluminum is abundantly available in deodorants, pots and pans, toothpaste, processed foods, and antacids, all of which should be avoided like the plague.

As we mentioned in an earlier chapter, electromagnetic pollution causes a lot of problems in humans and the environment. Your DNA has the structure of a fractal antenna and is highly reactive to electromagnetic fields. DNA damage occurs when the EMF causes the DNA strands to fragment, which can lead to tumors and cancer if the cells cannot replicate properly. Each generation of cell phone, from 2G, 3G, 4G and now 5G, becomes increasingly dangerous as the energy output increases. You should never hold a cell phone against your ear to talk, unless you really want to cook your brain. The cell tower and satellite communications networks create holes in the protective layer around the Earth, allowing radiation and other energies to pour through the atmosphere and damage life on our planet.

Rounding out our discussion of modern technological blunders is the destruction agricultural chemicals cause in nature. This largely goes unnoticed, because most people live packed into cities, far, far away from the corn silos and GPS guided tractors. Bob is very saddened by the killing of earthworms, insects, butterflies, honeybees, frogs, toads, birds, ladybugs, and microbial creatures that are absolutely essential to a stable environment. As various bacteria and fungi die, the soil dies. The vitamin and mineral content of organic fruits and vegetables is much higher than in commercial products. The deficiency is directly related to the chemical destruction of the microbial action in the soil. Microbes are responsible for making carbon, nitrogen and other elements available to plants. Soybeans, almost all of which are genetically modified in the USA, are high in phytic acid, which blocks the uptake of zinc, magnesium, calcium, and iron. If you are a vegetarian eating tofu, odds are quite high you suffer from mineral deficiency. If enough people reject the genetically manipulated and toxic food, it will encourage independent farmers to grow organically. The real problem, as usual, is the federal government and their corrupt agencies colluding with the chemical manufacturers and agribusinesses to destroy small farms. The vested interests of this syndicate prohibit any research that will prove how harmful their farming methods and GMO seeds are to the natural balances in nature. You should take it upon yourself to learn about these topics, and then use that knowledge to reduce the amount of poison you ingest.

There had not been a lot of discussion about the physical layer within the inner dimensions, so I asked Ophelia to add a few of her ideas to help flesh it out, so to speak.

    D. The physical layer, I'm a little confused about what to say about that. Is that regarding actions the body can do?

O. It's also the neglect of the physical. You see that all the time. The physical experience can be about, let's say, eating too much. A soul can come in to experience physical dilemmas. Meaning, some will be illnesses, others will be like overeating.

D. Are those pre-programmed dispositions?

O. In some way. I would say that the physical experience plays tricks, and hinders the emotional and mental realities to come fully into blossom. A soul normally chooses a mental or emotional journey. However, it becomes more tricky, as the physical experiences cause some people to get stuck. So a Coat *(of Karma)* for someone can be attached to the physical. Meaning, a tendency to be a little bit too aggressive, which is related to the physical. Also, the fact of overeating, as has been mentioned. So the physical can actually play tricks at some point with younger souls, as they choose merely to come into an emotional or mental reality. The physical can be a trap, for some. And some souls choose specific teachings about the physical vehicle, like one of your friends *(in Sweden)*, for instance, she learns about the web inside. Impulses, reporting back, teaching medical industry about certain impulses in the nerves and web, the DNA structures. In that specific case, it's different, it's not a jacket (*Coat*) this soul has been attached to. It is a way to report back, and also to teach the medical establishment about the nerve system and the frequency of light. But at most, the physical relates to actions, which in some way will be confusing to you, as you will see it as an emotional or mental source, whereas the physical simply project that first source. Again, don't make it too complex.

D. Thank you for that.

O. Do you wish me to clarify?

D. That's always helpful.

O. What do you need for clarification?

D. It seems most physical actions come after the thought, so it seems the thought or emotion would precede.

O. Indeed. If you have a Coat that is inclined to physical activity, meaning, it takes over control from the emotional or mental source, that becomes a karma for that specific soul, for instance. So it's merely, ah, what can I tell you? It's a vehicle that will prolong the intention set in the emotional or mental realm. For instance, overeating, as I will return to, it is created within the mental or emotional layer as well. But if you have a Coat of Karma related to physical dilemmas, then the physical reality will channel that impulse in a different way. You will all have the same origin of, let's say, overdoing certain things, but if you are too much in your physical reality, you will channel it in a way that will not necessarily be to your highest good. You can see it as a chain reaction, the emotional and mental working side-by-side, or hand-in-hand, but the physical, that is where you get lost. A mental action of, let's say, anger, it could be channeled differently. For someone who does not necessarily have a past, or a karma, with the physical realities, that will never be channeled, but if you are more primal, then you will channel EVERY impulse that comes, not reflect before action. If the physical is too much induced in the souls' capacity as well as exploration, then it will never reflect or dissect any sort of impulses.

D. That would suggest the mind, your consciousness, is ultimately how you would control these impulses?

O. It's a filter, if you like. Again, they are working hand-in-hand. To make it easy for you, let's say an idea originates from the mental, like a thought, then that takes upper hand. The emotional sort of rests. The mental will send off an impulse through the physical, or into the physical. Know that there are several beings *(layers)* operating the three realities. The human body is an experiment to see if the filter will work, the physical, that is. I know this confuses you.

D. The filter is within the physical layer, or is it between them?

O. Between, in this case, the mental into the physical, lies a filter, a vibration, where choices can be made. If you look back when man had no filter, as soon as an impulse arose, a thought or an emotion, it simply was channeled directly, instantly, instincts. Animals operate like this. The filter is thinner between the source of an intent to the actions.

D. What develops the filter?

O. Oh, that is way beyond what we are going to talk about. But the filter is increasing, if you like. That is the awareness. If a filter is too thin, primal, then it will be similar to ancient man. As we are creating a new humanoid, the filter between thought and emotion, into action related to the physical, will be expanded.

D. I see. I actually understand what you mean.

O. Very good. We will leave it before we create more confusion on the matter.

Bob regularly gives me health advice, as he is one of my guides and has always followed me, communicating by putting images in my mind. Now, since he can speak directly to me, he is making up for lost time. He frequently advises to drink water with crushed lemons and mineral salt, which is interesting to me, because Edgar Cayce, one of the greatest trance healers, often instructed people to eat lemons for various ailments. One of Bob's recipes is to grind up three or four lemons, along with a bunch of kale leaves, one carrot, a handful of blueberries, and mix with a little apple cider vinegar, orange juice, water, a gram or so of potassium chloride, and sea salt. All organic, of course. This is to be drank as a morning tonic. Some might find it to be bitter, but I like the taste. Years ago, I used to get muscle twitches, and that can be a sign of magnesium and potassium deficiency. I replaced iodized table salt with potassium chloride, and by adding magnesium citrate to my diet, the muscle twitches vanished. As a legal disclaimer, we're not giving medical advice, nor are we recommending you, or anyone else, to ingest potassium chloride, apple cider vinegar, lemons, or magnesium. Please consult your physician to get their valuable opinion on these matters. Bob, however, could not care less about the medical establishments' need for credentials, and he freely gives me health advice, which I very much appreciate. They would have a hard time apprehending him anyway, since he can just step into a rock and hide. Here is one of his observations on doing yoga and tending to the skin.

B. If I can suggest, I would like for you to have 15 minutes or so in the morning when you stretch. It is because you are tender, and you are stiff. And when you wake up it's even worse. So to get the day going you can just stretch a little bit. On the floor. And you can bend and move and roll around. You know how you sit like a Buddha and tip from left to right, back and forth. It's like a ship in the ocean. It almost looks like that, and with your head it's like the mast. Tipping and move and roll, roll. It's good for you because it also helps with your lower back. And in the morning, you are a little bit extra stiff. So, I suggest you do 15 minutes in the morning. You could have your coffee next to you, if you like. But it is a morning procedure that will help you.

D. Okay, I will do that.

B. One thing you have not done that you could do is to take baths. Baths with oil will help your skin.

D. What kind of oil?

B. Lavender oil is good, rose oil, also. There are also those oils that are from herbs, especially the roots. Anise roots smoothen the skin. You could even use them afterwards as sort of a lotion. Oils are better than the lotion you buy in the store, which are not really good for you. Neither of you. We wish for you to change them and use real oil, organic, with different flavors of your choosing. You do not need to go around smelling like a bark, or a pine cone. She would not like that. You don't care, but she will not like it. There are rose oils she can use, just to please her a little bit. But, actually, the lotion you are buying doesn't help the dry skin. It only puts a layer for a little while, and contains chemicals that are not good for the body. So we want you to go to that store you like, where you get your coffee. They have a lot of different body oils that you can use. And you can also drip it in a bath. A bath also makes your body warmer, and you will need that during the winter months.

D. Is that a morning or evening routine?

B. Oh, that can be in the evening, please. Afternoon or evening. Morning is for yoga. And for your coffee, we know you like that. If we add more, like baths and all sorts of things, nothing's going to happen. That's why we pick one that is more important, and that is the yoga. Think of the boat. Sit like a boat and feel how you move on, over the waves, rolling, rolling, and so on. If it's boring, you can think of the boat. But it's good for you, my friend. You need to be mindful about your body. As you, or the body, grows older, it tends to stiffen naturally, and you are already a little bit stiff. So, we need you to do the best you can.

## The Fourth (Emotional) and Fifth (Mental) Layers

Bob frequently addresses the evolution of the human vehicle, as he was involved with bringing about some of those modifications. He tells how accountability for actions has increased, as the brain capacity and connection to the soul energy has expanded.

D. Humans are still a lot like their ancient ancestors, aren't they?

B. The first humans were creatures that had more of a capacity to move around and act, but less of a brain. It was more of a physical individual than the emotional and mental. So the way they felt, they only felt like, hunger, and like, need fire, need warm, need cold, thirst. It was more pinpointed, it didn't come as a variety of, or a chain reaction of, emotions or thoughts, it just came like one point. Hungry. Thirsty. If it comes in, not with the option of choice, then the physical will just simply act, because it was more in control.

D. Seems like there's still a lot of those around.

B. Well, the difference is that the emotional and mental is very much activated. It's just that some, they ignore the signals that come. Before, they didn't ignore it because they didn't understand it, because it just came as an impulse. Now everyone has the whole spectra, or the whole information, BUT, they neglect to act upon it from a higher way, or a higher perspective. So they simply act, SIMILAR like the ones that took furs. There is a spectra you can see in the physical. You have the ability to act like you were the caveman, but, it's gonna be JUDGED differently, BECAUSE NOW it doesn't come as an impulse. Those in the past who acted similar were not judged, because they didn't have the same filter. But NOW you DO. Choices demand that you are paying attention and select wisely. Now you are judged more for the choices made in your thoughts and actions, because the soul energy is bigger than it was back then, when it was operating more from a physical standpoint, if you like. Because the physical was more in charge, those impulses only came like a dot from the emotional and mental layers, not a whole spectrum of choices, like it's doing now. So now you're being judged in some way, for all your actions and all your thoughts, because you are actually more in tune with your soul. With that comes also more responsibilities.

D. That's a very good description, Bob

B. Umm, you can get stuck like a bug in glue, if you don't act wisely. If you had the same filter, like the ancient person had, then your actions would not be judged. But, now when a soul comes in with more knowledge and more of a choice, really, then it's also demanded that you are acting in a certain manner.

D. So all humans can control themselves?

B. Oh, there's still some that act like the caveman did. So when you see that, you can actually be a little bit upset, because you know the inside is not as primitive as it was in the past. You now have more soul energy and also more options on how to act. We don't judge the earlier humanoids, because they didn't have a variety of choice. They felt hunger, and they ate. They felt cold, and they took someone's fur. But now, "Okay, I'm hungry," but you can choose to not kill something. You can go to the store and eat a variety of things, you have the choices now. Back then they didn't have the choices, they didn't have like a Whole Foods to go to. Now, you're cold, you don't have to wear someone's skin, you have the option to do something else. That's what I'm saying.

D. Yes, that's understandable.

B. With choices comes responsibilities. That's what I want to say about that.

**The Sixth Layer of Healing Energies**

Within all these readings, certain ideas seem to not stand out as clearly as they deserve. The sixth layer of the inner dimensions, the level of healing energy, perhaps falls into this category. It is a vibration above the mental and emotional, but below the spiritual dimensions, and acts in some way as a bridge between the physical and the spiritual. The spirits have said that those who try to use the energies of the sixth layer, but still retain attachments to the fourth and fifth layers, are not operating as true healers and teachers. To use the energies of pure love and empathy, to heal themselves and others, requires the participants to be disconnected from the physical, emotional, and mental layers. This can best be explained by example. If someone has a holistic healing practice, be it a prayer group, massage, Reiki, psychic healing, crystal therapy, hypnotherapy, acupuncture, or others, the intention becomes a critical component of the ability to connect with the higher energies. If there is a hidden desire to be admired as a great healer, for example, it should be understood that seeking admiration is a vibration from the fourth layer. The presence of this energy will actually dampen or suppresses the abilities of the healer to channel energies from the sixth layer. To be at their best, the most effective and connected, healers need to have no attachments to the patient or the outcome. Even a feeling of pity, which is not the same as empathy, can interfere with the inner state of the healer. In a similar manner, the patient needs to release third, fourth, and fifth layer attachments as well, in order for the sixth layer vibrations to have a strong effect. Someone who goes to a healer carrying fear, anger, lust, self-pity, or related thoughts is not properly tuned-in with the spiritual intentions necessary for healing. When doing this type of work, healers open themselves up to the higher vibrations, but also sometimes to other vibrations that may be present. Both healer and patient should maintain a protective energy bubble around themselves. Healing energy flows in one direction; from the highest, through the healer, to the patient. As a case in point, recently one of Christine's friends in Sweden, who is a healing practitioner, developed a bad headache after working on a client, which lingered for several hours after the treatment. It would seem she had picked up vibrations from the client that did not resonate well with her own energetic body. It's not easy, sometimes, to be detached from those you are trying to help, but the healer should always block these stray energies. One way is to prepare and set the intentions before opening up your energetic field to outside influences.

Christine and I always smudge ourselves and the space we use, before we begin a session. Once when Bob came in, he was kind of coughing. He told us that he doesn't like the smoke, and that spirits actually flee from the energy released when white sage is burned. While Bob doesn't care for the energy released when things burn, he encourages us to have our rituals and set the intentions for them to draw near.

   D. Is it good that we smudge the area before we start?

   B. You should have thought of that before you smudged me! I'm a little bit sensitive to smoke and stuff like that. I do get clogged up in my nose apparatus if it's too much smoke. I avoid, all my people avoid, as much as possible when it comes to smoke. It's not something that actually exists in a spiritual reality, it's something man created here in order for them to communicate with the higher beings. However, not all of us likes to come when those smudge rituals take place. It is more of a signal, really, that someone wants to talk. It's more like that. In some way, it is good, because you set the intention, like Ophelia said before, so in some way you clean the system. Because you are walking around in somewhat of a filthy environment, in that someone could almost be attached to you, so it's actually really good that you do it as a ritual. However, know that beings like myself, on other places, can resonate differently with smoke. All sorts of scents, we're kind of sensitive to different kind of scents, so we avoid certain things, and we are drawn to others. Why do you think the bees and the wasps don't come when there is that smoke device? *(Beekeepers use smoke to get bees out of the hive before opening it, which Christine did not know)* Because they don't like it, they don't like to be burned. So that's what man understood, why they put out that little spiral thing and lit it, and it's a smoke so mosquitoes will not come, for instance. So they don't come, that's a sign for you. Just know that we do approve that you do it, because it sets the intention for the work you're supposed to do, and it's also to protect the room, so you know, smudging this room is a really good idea. It's not like there is a high traffic of other beings, but it's a good way to come into that space where you are allowing spiritual beings to communicate with you. But, I'm a little bit more sensitive than others.

Native American cultures have always ritually purified with sage, cedar and other herbs, so what Bob said makes a lot of sense, knowing that the smoke actually drives spirits away. Christine and I perform the same rituals every time we sit, which is very helpful in getting the mind to become quiet and focused. We set up a circle of quartz crystals we found in the nearby mountains. After the space is cleared, we ring our Tibetan singing bowls and then call on the Great Spirit and our guardian angles and other higher beings to surround and protect us in a golden light of love, and allow only those entities that are there for our highest good to enter within the sacred circle. Ophelia, Zachariah and the others always provide a protective bubble for us to work within. Most healers, I am sure, have their own ritual that set the intentions related to their work.

**The Seventh Layer, Connection to Spirit (by Christine)**
What is a spirit guide? Do I have one, and how can I work with my guides? These are some frequently asked questions, and there are many ways for you to practice the communication with your own team of spirit helpers. From my perspective, I will try to shed some light on the different guides you can come in contact with, what signs to be aware of, and how to work with your own team. Also, what you can do if you wish to improve your connection to spirit and, above all, your higher self.

Working with my spirit guides is a great joy, and a continual source of self-awareness, comfort, and higher learning. Even though my helpers have changed during this journey, their love has been constant, and the wisdom progressively fascinating. It is very humbling to feel the tremendous support and care they offer when we welcome them into our lives.

When I first embarked on my spiritual path, I didn't know that much about these wise helpers we all have around us. Yes, even if you never feel, see, sense, or hear your guides, you can be as sure as the sun sets in the evening that you have at least one spiritual helper. My first contact came during a guided meditation in Stockholm, which was designed to meet a spirit guide. While I didn't know what to expect, during the meditation I had a sense of seeing and hearing "something," but thought it was only in my mind. About six months later, I enrolled in a class for spiritual and intuitive development, which lasted for eight weeks. At this point, I had somewhat forgotten all about the beings I had seen and heard in the meditation. However, it didn't take long for them to once again make themselves known. This time they didn't pass by unnoticed.

I was full of excitement, because not only could I hear them clairaudiently, and see them clairvoyantly, but I could also sense the shift of energy in the room around me as they drew closer. My first guide gave me the name Cicero, showing himself as a Roman soldier, and was quite firm in his presence and teachings. He and I have shared several lives together during the era of the Roman Empire. In one, he showed himself as my trainer in mastering the sword. Our guides will take on the features and personalities they know we will most likely respond to. Needless to say, the soul of Cicero doesn't walk around dressed in full armor as a Roman solider in the spirit realm. He simply showed himself in a way that would trigger a reaction and activate my cell-memories. Cicero remained with me for about a year, after which our work this time around was probably considered done. He moved on, and in my case new spirit guides came in with other teachings.

As a seeker for higher wisdom and purpose, I am extremely grateful for the support and love from my spirit team. They have provided me with profound insights. They guided me to my husband by giving detailed visions about us and our future, making sure I wouldn't miss him when he showed up two years later. They also assisted me to connect with my higher self and showed glimpses of my whereabouts in the spirit realm, providing pieces to my own puzzle of who I am and the reason for being here. Spiritual development is a lifelong process, and I continue to learn and sharpen my skills with an open heart and curious mind. If you are interested to pursue a spiritual path, it is an endless journey filled with opportunities and happiness. It will expand as you go, and will constantly bring surprises your way.

**What is a spirit guide?** A spirit guide is someone who briefly, or for a longer period of time, joins us on our journey through life. These wise beings can come in many different shapes and forms, but they all share one objective, and that is to help us through different life events. Though one thing is for sure, they don't just hang around waiting for us immortals to contact them, but when we need them, they will instantly respond. View these helpers as your best friends, who not only hold your highest good and well-being as a sole priority, but also have the bigger picture at hand. They follow you closely, or from a distance, depending on your personal development or stated agreements before you entered this life. Their affection is limitless, even when you seem to do everything wrong, they will patiently help you back on track without ever saying, "Didn't I tell you?", even though they actually did. Spirit guides are our invisible friends, who care about and love us unconditionally.

**What different spirit guides exists?** There are countless numbers of spiritual helpers, originating from different realities, who are assigned unique missions based on their own stamp of creation. They can assist us personally, tend to Earth and humanity as a whole, or can be caretakers for larger matters beyond our human comprehension. We will focus here on some of the most common guides you will meet when working with the spirit realm.

The first guide you will probably encounter is one that you have shared several lifetimes on Earth with. We can call this helper a personal guide. This is usually not your main guide, but someone well familiar with your skills and challenges as you incarnate.

<u>Personal guide</u>: When you come to Earth, often someone you have frequently incarnated with will act as a guide. This spirit helper will show him/herself in a way that will mirror what they looked like in a prior lifetime. Normally, this helper will assist you in your personal development, pointing out your pros and cons, if you like. This guide will help you to

understand what skills to enhance in order for you to activate your true mission. He/she will also open your eyes to old habits, patterns that might prohibit you from reaching those goals set, and what might be beneficial for you to release. *(Ophelia is Dave's personal guide, who incarnated as his mother in a distant past)*

Loved ones: Just because a dear family member or friend has passed, doesn't mean they have left us. In many ways, our loved ones share the same assignment as a personal guide, even though their main purpose is to provide comfort and loving presence for us to know that they are fine. Both personal guides and loved ones take great interest in our day-to-day life, and will not complain if we call them up for a chat after hours.

The gate-keeper: This helper can actually be your personal guide or a loved one. My guide Cicero acted as a gate-keeper for a while, and I have a close friend whose father in spirit works as hers. The primary function of your gate-keeper is to make sure that the environment around you when practicing spirit communication is safe. View this guide as your personal bodyguard, and if you later choose to work professionally as a medium, the gate-keeper's role will become even more important.

Specialists: These guides assist your personal or main guide with specific matters, such as schooling or work. They are sent to sharpen or awaken certain skills, providing discipline and clarity on the bigger steps in life. *(Zachariah is a specialist of education for both me and Dave)*

Main guide: This is the one who knows you the best, the one assigned to you in the spirit realm, and the one in charge of your soul's progress. This is often the father or mother entity who is in charge of your soul group. This guide is with you through the entire cycle of progress from when you began to incarnate till long after you are finished with Earth. You have probably incarnated at one point together, but as you evolve, your main guide normally takes a step back. View this wise being as a parent, allowing its children to test their own wings, yet always present to make sure you are flying in the right direction. *(Isaac is my main guide, and Jeshua is Dave's)*

Nature spirits and animals: As we have discussed, the Master Mind is present in all living beings, in a greater or lesser degree. Sometimes this energy is joined by entities from the second dimension, who can add another level of intelligence to any living thing. This spirit activity and presence in nature, such as within trees and plants, in the waters and the rocks around us, are well-known phenomena for the natives. Our dear friend, Bob, is one of many from this realm, and has shared numerous insights during the progress of this book. The amount of energy from the Master Mind can be adjusted in animals, so certain pets are often given more loving energy from the Creator, specifically for you. In this way, the Master Mind is directly guiding you with insights about companionship, unconditional love and pure happiness. Your pet can also contain a nature spirit, who brings awareness for the care of Earth and to honor all lifeforms. If a certain animal attracts you, or frequently shows up in your meditations, that is probably your power animal. The characteristic behaviors of animals represent something within ourselves that needs to be studied, and there are many books about how to interpret animal symbols. Spirits from the second dimension often use animals to interact directly with humans.

Healing guides: This is like a personal physician, the one who tends to your physical, mental and emotional well-being. Your healing guide will monitor you throughout life, and can easily be felt as you sit in the power of light. Usually, the healing guides work with us when we sleep. They can appear with familiar features or simply as a pole of light. Coming from several dimensions, those from the second dimension are probably the ones most connected to this kind of work. Other dimensions may help with emotional or mental disharmony. *(Bob has several times told us how he monitors and works with Dave's physical body, which shows that he is a healing guide)*

Guardian Angels: This is somewhat of an imprecise term. All the spirits who work on your behalf could be considered guardians, even loved ones who have passed. There may be a class of spirits who are masters at manipulating physical realities, and they come in to interfere in certain events at the request of other guides. Miraculous experiences, like walking away unharmed from a terrible accident, could be a result of their activity. Spirit guides can appear to us in male or female form, and have very different personalities. Angels, on the other hand, are androgynous beings of light who never walked as mortals upon the Earth. With respect to free will and the cosmic laws, which no spiritual being stands above, guardian angels will assist you to fulfill your mission. However, there are limits to how much they can interfere with your souls' plan of development.

Archangels: These angels are extraordinary beings, the extensions of the Creator itself, and they are all healers. The archangels are essentially everyone's guardians, concerned with almost every advancement of humankind. Ophelia once mentioned these reside in the tenth dimension. They are the protectors of all planets and all lifeforms, and like all angels, these high vibrating spiritual beings have never incarnated on Earth.

Masters of higher orders: These beings belong in the higher dimensions, they are the galactic masters, the co-creators of star systems, galaxies and the cosmic laws. They are the master teachers of all dimensions and universes. Some are involved with Earth and the transmission of knowledge, scientific teachings about sacred geometry and physics, as well as spiritual guidance, such as found in this book. They often seed ideas into certain people's consciousness in order to bring technology or ideas into our reality. *(Jeshua and Zachariah are both considered masters of a higher order)*

The higher self: Doing spiritual and inner work, you will progressively be more in tuned with your own soul and the nature of your spirit, also known as your higher self. This is a process, and depending on your soul's energy, it could first be perceived as a spirit guide. Once the understanding of your true identity is established, you will operate from your own source and get direct guidance from within.

Now when we have covered some of the spiritual beings around us and with whom you might come in contact with as you work with spirit, it is time to learn more about how you can communicate with your guides. But before we do so, know that your spirit team doesn't monitor or investigate your thoughts twenty-four-seven and they never trespass into your private space. It is also worth mentioning, that from the spirit realm nothing is ever viewed as a hierarchy, there is only a difference in vibration and frequency. Therefore, if someone tells you that they only speak with the Archangels, never to the regular ones, or how they only chit chat with the ascended masters, then you should proceed with caution. Know, that the desire to be above, or on a higher level, is merely a human perception and invention, not a spiritual one.

**What are the different ways to practice spirit communication?** Like with everything, we all have different tools in our toolbox, we are better at certain things and less equipped on others. Practicing spirit communication is like learning a new language. It is a two-way-street, where your spirit guide and you both need to figure out which tools are the sharpest and then use those.

For instance, if you are not clairvoyant by nature, your spirit guide will probably not spend a lot time trying to transmit pictures to you. But if you are, let's say, clairaudient, then your spiritual helper will send you information through words. Here are some of the most common ways to connect with the spirit realm and your own intuition.

- <u>Intuitive seeing</u>: The ability to gain visual telepathic information about an object, person, location or physical event through inner rather than physical eyes. This experience is called *clairvoyant*.
- <u>Intuitive hearing</u>: The ability to hear sounds or words from the spirit that are not audible for the normal ear. This experience is called *clairaudient*.
- <u>Intuitive feeling</u>: Some people don't see images or hear voices at all, but are likely to experience strong sensations in their bodies. I tend to believe that these empathic or *clairsentience* skills are the most common psychic gifts in our society.
- <u>Intuitive knowing</u>: The spirit realm makes a direct contact with the mind. This is called *clair-cognizance or clair-knowing*.

Once you have figured out your strongest channel to sense your spirit guide, which can be more than one, then there are numerous choices for you to communicate with your spiritual helpers. When working with the higher realms, it is always advisable to begin your session with an opening prayer, inviting only those sent to assist you in the highest and most loving way. This allows the blessings to come, it sets the intention for your work, and operates as a beacon of light for the spirit realm to respond to. When ending your session, don't forget to thank your guide(s), and most importantly, don't forget to shut down that beacon of light again, so you are grounded and completely back in the earthly vibration.

**What signs should I pay attention to?** Common signals, when your spirit guide approaches, could be a buzzing sound in your ears, or a tingling feeling in your fingertips or around your scalp. You can experience flashes of colors behind your eyes or simply sense the shift of energy in the room. Depending on the guide's purpose, you may tune on that, which can be a sudden sensation of; strength, safety, empathy, love, clarity, goofiness or joy, to mention a few.

**Some tools when working with spirit.** Meditation and dreams are two known channels for the spirit realm to speak to us, and can be deeply powerful messengers. Regression therapy allows you to explore important soul information directly and is another way to gain insight about your soul companions and spirit guides. Some other tools for spiritual practice are; crystals, tarot/angel cards, pendulums, a spiritual journal, candles, and incense.

**Your journey to mediumship.** The first step is probably to enter a workshop, or one of those week-long-classes, focusing on spiritual development and intuition. Here, you will be offered a smorgasbord of creative and spiritual practices in order to enhance your **psychic awareness. You will learn how to work** with **pendulums and tarot. You will** practice psychometry and learn more about the chakras and how **inspiration and creativity are two sacred keys in your spiritual awakening. This will give you the foundation needed before you move into** the different aspects of healing or mediumship, where you will not only improve your gifts further, but also understand the ethics and responsibilities involved if you later wish to practice this publicly or work with clients.

Another reward when entering classes like this is the people you will meet. Normally you gain new lifelong friends, and not uncommonly, these are souls you have met several times before, in other lifetimes. I mention this in almost all lectures and when meeting with clients, the amount of improvement that comes from working in a private psychic circle, and how much joy it offers. I was part of a couple different circles until finally ending up with two other women, both whom I met during my mediumship training in Stockholm. For about three years this private circle met on a regular basis, and it was in this environment that my communication with spirit guides and other light beings increased.

Here I learned and created my platform, especially working with trance, channeling, and transfiguration.

I highly recommend anyone on a spiritual path to join, or start, a private circle with others who share the interest of psychic and spiritual development. Not only for your own progress, but it is free of charge and a good complement to the formal training programs you might wish to attend

Briefly about spiritual channeling and trance mediumship. If you wish to develop trance mediumship, generally you must be prepared for the long haul. It's highly desirable to have someone with you when you sit for trance development, not only for documenting and assisting you with questions, but also to monitor the session and you. I do not recommend working alone. However, as mentioned earlier, we all have different tools in our toolbox, and there are many other ways to practice spirit communication which may suit you better.

All the best on your spiritual journey!

*- Christine*


**Ophelia Talks about Guides**
The world is not ruled by chaos and random chance, like the scientific community would have you believe. The spiritual world has a very high degree of control over what happens on Earth. Since it is a schoolhouse, unfortunately, decisions made by throngs of poorly developed souls are usually allowed to play out, because it teaches the lesson that there is a cause and effect to all thoughts and actions. You are here to learn and experience certain things, and everything about your life is organized for your benefit. Think how improbable it would be to meet your soulmate, for example, if there were not some coordinated effort going on in the background. This knowledge should provide a feeling of hope for everyone, even in the face of the human tragedies that seem ever-present, because our fate is always guided by those who care deeply about each of us and this world.

> O. We are pleased that you are addressing the numerous ways that spiritual beings interfere with those on this plane.
> D. I think that is important for people to understand.

O. What we wish for is an index in the end of the book, what the spirit guide is, and how it can come about. That would be helpful, and this includes loved ones.

D. What would you say about that, if you were to help me write?

O. Simply provide a guidebook of what a spirit guide is, and how they can communicate with their counterpart on this plane. You have been given information from the little friend about nature. Loved ones is another area. Animals a third, pets. Angels, don't forget the angels, a lot of people resonate with that reality because it makes them feel safe.

D. Are you from the angelic realm? Would you be considered an angel?

O. Seventh and eighth are in some way related to what is considered an angelic realm. However, ten is also.

D. Do the angels that people talk about all the time, like Gabriel, reside on your level?

O. They reside in the tenth and eleventh.

D. Are they truly as people describe them and see them?

O. Don't take the image away from them, it is somewhat true. They are perceived as big birds, with wings. There are beings within the angelic realm that resonates with pure love, because of the embrace they provide. That is why they have been mirrored and imaged as birds with wings. It is the fact of the embrace that souls resonate with, yet they are not birds, simply mirrored as such. The energy from the tenth is a pure embrace of love.

D. Do those beings occasionally intervene on people's behalf on Earth?

O. Hmm, those who intervene personally are from seventh or eighth. Tenth resonates with humanity and planets as a whole. Guardian angels can be found in all realities, in some way.

D. Is it true that people have one main guide assigned to them?

O. Normally, yes. One that is assigned for each destination. Yet, understand that a lot of those that you will come in contact with, do not necessarily travel to other destinations. So, yes, they do have a guide when they incarnate on this plane. You are assigned a mentor, if you like, when you travel from your source. Someone who is familiar with your destinations and your progress on each and every one of them.

*The Art of Living* 269

D. Who is my personal guide, when I'm not incarnated?
O. Your personal guide resides in the ninth. His name is Jeshua. He is the one that has known you the longest.
D. And you?
O. I travel with you, my friend, especially when you travel far, to physical realities, as you do tend to not want to come.
D. So, both you and Zachariah do this?
O. Zachariah is in charge of your training.
D. And what do you do, specifically?
O. I make you feel safe. I make you feel loved as you travel. I surround you with a motherly energy that you long for when you are on this plane. Numerous lifetimes as orphans have put a mark within your soul, and I wish that to be erased.
D. Thank you for that.
O. Even though in this lifetime you came to share with siblings, you still operate as an orphan. You still feel within you as that orphan, numerous lifetimes, especially related from the year 800 and ahead, AD. Some were by accident, but it has placed a scar within your emotional being. My presence is to make you aware that you are never an orphan, you are always part of your family.
D. Well, thank you. And what about my friend, Bob?
O. He is a pure joy for you. He is the source when life has been laughter. Look in rewind, those times when you simply burst into laughter, you could feel him. As I am here to surround you in an embrace of motherly energy, he is here to encourage you to continue on, to see it as a little play. That is he. His view of this reality is that it is somewhat of a little play. He's also here to make sure that you remember the importance of nature and animal life. To not take more than you need. He was somewhat concerned of your line of work, as that came about. Did not understand fully why you picked it. He wished for you to work with the oceans.
D. Understood. Do deceased family members act as guides, in some way?
O. They can. Especially grandparents. It has been known, as parents are a little bit too close, yet grandparents do tend to operate as spirit guides as they move on.
D. Can they do that from their home in the fifth and above?

O. They descend into the fourth, in order for them to receive and connect with those on this plane. There is always the meeting that occurs within the fourth. Some have the ability to transmit their awareness up into the fifth. Yet you have the ability to communicate with those from your home. See it as sparkles that rains from the dimensions you are residing in when you are not here. If you pay attention to those signals, as you are programed to do, you still meet them in the fourth reality, but just at the border, if you like, in that reality *(between the fourth and fifth)*. Once you travel and seem to connect to higher realities, know that they have descended themselves down into that layer between the fourth and the fifth. This is why you remember certain realities. Your mental capacity cannot fully connect and leave to visit, if you like, until you depart from this plane.

D. When people sleep, does their soul leave their body to travel to other places?

O. They can leave up to the fifth. The two of you have actually traveled further, no need to address it in the book. Some actually do.

D. When people are asleep, can they have meetings with their guides and others?

O. Normally in the fifth, classrooms, familiar areas of study, meeting places in gardens normally takes place within the fifth. This one traveled in her mind one time to the classrooms of the seventh, fully aware that she was a guest, yet collected the images from this reality. As it was confirmed by her friend, she knew she had the ability to, hmm, similar as your friend (Bob), project herself. This is what she does, she has the ability to project herself to other realities, and that is what is to come.

D. Is that something humans will be able to do?

O. No. Some have been known as being able to project their inner eyes to outer destinations. This is what is to come, no need to explore it further at this time.

D. Very good, thank you.

O. Oh, you are much welcome. End your writing with the fact that each and every one are joined by a spiritual being and how they can appear in a variety of images or features that is familiar to the soul.

D. Is the personal guide normally from the same dimension as the incarnating soul?

O. Hmm, very good question. No, not always. This one travels with Isaac, not from the same reality. Assigned due to dynamics and missions over time, as well as you and I, not from the same. Complimentary energies suitable for missions. This one needed the male fatherly energy projected from Isaac, whereas you needed the motherly energy present. It is provided based on what you need as you travel, not what you need when you are at home. Quite different.

D. Does the main guide, or the guide that travels, change each lifetime?

O. No. It can somewhat change based on certain minor details, missions, detours, if you like. That is when different guides come in, normally those who are in training to become spiritual guides. As this occurs the main guide will normally take a step back, allowing the younger guides to simply be in charge of training and communication. Different being when it is someone addressing from the second.

D. From your perspective, when a person on Earth needs help or guidance, how do you know when that happens?

O. It is sensed simply as a signal, like a pulse. Everything carries a tone. Some see it as colors. We resonate with tones. As you encounter certain events on this plane, you all transmit tones. Some through the chimney. Those are not necessarily always attending to the upper levels, yet when something occurs from the soul particle within you, when signals are sent from that source, we respond and we send (*a guide*), normally. This is cared for (*directed*) by the main guide. That doesn't mean that this guide will come directly, but may send a trainee to operate and communicate, for comfort, education, and protection. So, as you move through life, you all send off energy waves that certain spiritual layers perceive as tones, colors, it doesn't really matter, as they all carry information for the higher levels to perceive, and we respond. At certain times we do not respond, and if that is the case, then it has been pre-arranged that the soul wishes to address events within its own capacity.

D. I think that is important for people to know.

O. Yes.

D. They might see it as abandonment.

O. No one is ever abandoned. Yet the soul can have decided from departure from the spiritual reality to manage certain lessons by itself. If that is the case, then the spirit guides monitoring the tones, vibrations, from the soul on this plane, will monitor how the soul interacts with those lessons and events that takes place. Always present, yet might not interfere.

D. So things that happen to people during their life, things they would consider traumatic, are the majority of them preplanned?

O. This is not for you to deliver. You are not in charge of the souls' missions. Yet understand that they do come down to train themselves in how they react to certain events, so in that respect, yes, they have picked it. Yet, on this plane, because of the tendency of judgement, it is somewhat of a tricky field to move into.

D. I understand.

O. No one wants to feel like they have not succeeded, that they are punished. It has to be handled delicately.

D. I do see and understand.

O. No need to address it fully. You are here to spread light. Understand that light and darkness are perceived differently from this plane than it is on the higher levels.

D. Yes, that was the question I had earlier, that people's lives are guided, there are no mistakes.

O. No mistakes. The big events are no mistakes, and they are monitored always from the highest source available to that specific soul. Yet understand that based on the level of soul development, they can have picked to operate somewhat secluded, as this is more from a higher growth.

D. Thank you.

## Spirit Guides in Animals

The closest companion for a great many people is a beloved pet. Animals have a capacity for unconditional love that many humans lack. And some animals seem to be unusually intelligent or sensitive. Bob describes how the amount of soul energy in animals can be adjusted. Some pets carrying more spiritual energy than others of their species, either from the Master Mind, possibly from a spirit like Bob, from the second dimension. He also said something quite interesting about how spirit guides can actually connect with the link between the Master Mind and any plant, tree, or animal to obtain a view of our reality through the senses of those creatures. Your spirit guide could be watching the data stream being sent from your dog back into the cloud. Bob didn't indicate your spirit guide does that too often, but it is another way for them to collect information they can use to help you during certain times.

D. Are you aware of any other second dimension people that do this? *(I was asking about talking through a human channel)*

B. Nay. Ah, they communicate, indeed they do, but I don't know if anyone talks through their friend, like this, so I don't know that. But I'm sure that there are, from my reality, those who want to come in and talk directly through. Because we do blend with entities that are designed for the Master Mind to interfere with, so we can interfere with that individual as well. It's like a meeting, us with the Master Mind, somewhere in between. We can do that, but it's like I said, if you choose to do that with an animal, it doesn't really communicate and talk out, so you are somewhat limited. But you can certainly write about this because it is a fact that people can see this in their own pets. Some pets are more of a blend from the second dimensional energy and the Master Mind. It is a blend between. But it doesn't talk, clearly, like this.

D. What about other spirit guides?

B. The second dimension operates as a spirit guide, so that is what it is, in an animal.

D. If I had a dog, could Ophelia or Zachariah join with it?

B. NO.

D. Just second dimension?

B. Second dimension, or the Master Mind, which is somewhat of a spirit guide as well. But it's not like a personal spirit guide that follows you from different incarnations, back and forth, in different realities that you travel to. But it is a spirit guide, indeed.

D. So, the Master Mind can...

B. *(Interrupts)* Ophelia is not, she never blends. She can't blend with an animal.

D. That's good to know.

B. However, she can in some way, and this is on a higher level, but like Gergen and Ophelia, I'm sure as well, and some from the council, they can in some way, supervise views through the Master Mind into an individual. So in that regard, they are present, but not in the way you are referring to. So they can have a look-see, but they don't go IN. So, like your dog, it could be an abundance of energy from the Master Mind, or it could be a blend from the second dimension individual and the Master Mind, or it can only be a very personal, let's even say someone you know really, really well from the second dimension, someone like me. If I blended with an animal, that could be also it.

D. Okay, that's wonderful. Good information. I appreciated you coming to our little public session the other day.

B. Where should I be otherwise? *(Laughing)* Huhuhuh! I'm ready!

D. Do you like to talk to other people?

B. I do, I do like to look at them and see where they need a little bit of correction and assistance, so they can sort of blossom. Because some are sad inside and when they go out in public, they put on this little, sort of like a capsule, almost, and some just wants to be seen. So, you know, I do feel like that is some of the things that I want to do, is just to make people seen. Because, you know, it's like you go out somewhere and someone asks you, "How are you doing?" And everyone says, "Oh, I'm doing really, really well," but then they aren't. Because you put out that capsule, because you are supposed to say you are doing really, really well. But sometimes people just want to be seen. And so, you know, when I detect that, I try to provide that.

**The Final Words**

This book was written because our group of spirit friends requested their messages be presented to the public. We have tried to faithfully deliver both the words and the intent of what they said during hundreds of hours of fascinating discussions. It has been an honor and a privilege for both Christine and me to be part of this project. We have been told there are many additional waves of knowledge coming forward during the next few years, so we will continue to do our part in organizing the teachings in other books, as they allow it to become available. Until then, it is only fitting they be allowed, in their own words, to give you their final thoughts and encouragements.

Z. You should draw some sort of ladder, for people to understand how they can move, if they wish to, up and down this ladder. The ladder of individual progress on Earth, and how as you move up one level, you might have problems understanding your past self before taking that step. And how people should be prepared to leave certain things behind. Those things that do not favor them anymore. A lot of people are heavy. As you move up on your own personal ladder, it has to be known that certain things will be left behind. Ideas, events, circumstances created by others. Also, people, this is the tricky part for some. The separation from certain events in people's lives creates some sort of stress, we have seen.

D. Can you give me an example?

Z. The part of, hmm, when someone close passes, it arises I would say, a wall, for the one left behind to continue their walk up their ladder, because of feeling like they would be forgetting what they had.

D. I understand

Z. As they do so, they tend to stop, even though the ladder is just in front of them. It creates some sort of feeling of being a bad individual, cheating, in some way. Why should I be happy? That is a lot of the questions that people carry, you should know. A lot people feel that they have no right for their own happiness. You are only in charge of your own ladder, and we encourage you all to continue, to not get stuck in what you thought someone or something had put a label on you. Mostly this might be found in separation of partners where someone leaves early, but can even be found if someone lost a child. To have another child can sometimes indicate within the individual as forgetting the first one. Hope is something that you are providing, a community of learning, no judgement. Certain scriptures are way ahead of that! And you should know that it is not looked on easily. There is no judgement from our level. Letting go doesn't mean to forget.

D. That's very good, thank you. Ophelia had mentioned one time about ending the first book with do's and don'ts. How would you describe the topics we are supposed to be discussing?

Z. One of the topics should be about the Coat of Karma, and your thoughts being a creative force. Allowing people to believe, how can one say, don't put judgements in the way they think. Encourage them that their thoughts are within their own creation and their own power. Judgement comes from themselves if they misinterpret. That is not up to you to place judgement on their thoughts. The soul will do that, anyway. But, address the fact of choice. The willingness to work on your Coat of Karma, and your thoughts, the process within each area, connected on this plane. Everyone wishes to fold their jacket, to be through with these lessons. Some people have dreadful assignments this time around, and are eager to hear the message that it lies within their own choosing to fold a jacket, even if it's not necessarily happening in this lifetime. Make them aware of the possibilities that lies within their own choice. Empowerment is unique for each individual. Don't act as your neighbor, you have no idea about your neighbor's Coat. It's easy to allow patterns and behaviors to be rubbed off on you, if you are not willing to have your own. It's easier to be a follower than it is to stand unique in your own choice of ideas, thoughts, and activities. We are encouraging social chains, as well, to be released. Misconceptions about how one should act or think in order to be approved. We do NOT approve of how someone states a format of how to behave in order to be approved. There are several chains that needs to be broken. Address the fact that it is easier to follow, because you have been taught that this is how you should act, look, behave, or what you should have! Says who, one might wonder? This is something that can be addressed from a spiritual level, a soul is always approved. Your actions, thoughts, and conducts will be judged by yourself, first, as you depart. That is the Coat of Karma. You can pick and choose the way you act, making sure that the next time you return, your Coat might have a different color. A color perhaps you like better, let's say. So thoughts will be addressed. People only focus on the actions. Thoughts are equally strong as a physical action. Seen from the spirit realm, there is no difference.

D. Thank you very much for that summary, Zachariah.

D. What advantages do souls who graduate from Earth have when it comes to their spiritual work?

Z. Hmm. Your question comes with a variety of answers. *(Long pause)* We don't necessarily see the evolution as graduation, first of all. It is the experience by itself that the soul brings with it to teach others. The folded jacket, which could be related to, "OH, YES, I graduated here, indeed!" In some way, this makes the soul feel like it has understood the boundaries on that level. Many souls can go back without incarnation, simply return mentally, if you like, energetically, to the fourth dimension, simply to remember its path. It's an ongoing process, yet one has mastered, if you like, certain topics on this plane, spiritually related. Not all are spiritually related for you to grow by. But certain things, like empathy, once that has been mastered, then yes, you graduate. Empathy is easy in the spiritual realm. Not here. Certain topics will create what you referred to as a graduation. How can one be empathic if everyone around you acts in harmony and with love? No problem, is there? Empathy lies in understanding and relating from your heart, or solar plexus area, to those who do wrongs. That is one of the greatest teachings on this plane.

D. Some spirits are created, born to come to Earth specifically, are they not?

Z. Yes.

D. Do you have any advice you would like to share, before we close?

Z. You all carry different skill sets, and you are encouraged by your spirit guides to use them wisely and to share your knowledge with others. Some of you might not know this specific tool or skill set that you possess. Know that it is just beneath the surface, ready to embark on this journey together with others. At this time, a great shift is occurring in this nation, as well as globally. This nation needs to be released of chains; religious, social, and political. We are here to encourage you to do your part, in whatever field you feel most engaged in. Some of you here have the gift of speech, yet are, at this point, not aware of the voice within.

Z. The message that we wish you to share with others relates to Earth and the way it has become passive in many ways. Fear can make people passive. At this time, the awakening means to step aside from being passive and act, and you can do so in different manners. The spirit realm will assist in the way we can, individually as well as globally.

O. *(Ophelia comes forward during a group trance with a message for all)* Good evening. This is Ophelia. Hello, everyone. I'm here to send comfort to those who don't necessarily understand what is going on around them. The world is in need, again, as has been mentioned, of comfort. Those of you who are enlightened and who follow your inner voice have the ability to assist this project. Awakening also means to deliver messages to others in small parts, if you like. Your work is not to drown others with the knowledge that you possess, but to invite them to listen and to share, bit by bit, of that knowledge. I am ever so grateful that you are embracing spirit, your own soul and spirit, as well as your guides that constantly follow. We are proud and we follow you through hard times as well as in joyful experiences. You yourself have chosen your life, and your experiences are yours. You designed your path; we merely help you to remain on that path.

D. *(Our dear friend, Bob, now gets the final words)* Do you have anything else you would like to share?

B. Well, I'm happy to make myself known to more people, and to have some of my expertise shared, really. Because, you know, a lot of times, everyone's like, "Ohh, higher up, look up to the angels and all sorts of other beings, way high up!" But they forget to look down at their feet, and we're just sort of below the feet, if you like, we're really close. So, you know, I do like to talk about the fact of things that are a little bit closer to this reality. Because, sometimes, people can have problems with connecting with the idea of, "Ohh, I have to be so divine, I have to do all this good, and I have to reach so high, and all sorts of things." But, you know, the little things count as well.

B. I would also like to say that everyone should understand, and should know, that you carry a different pattern of expertise within you, because that is how you are designed. If you don't find or follow that pattern, it is like you are neglecting who you really are. You are neglecting your potential and where you are supposed to do good and to progress. I do know there are some who try to resist following their design, but they are encouraged by their own peers *(in their soul group)*, to explore the pattern and map they have within. Some call it blueprints, it is that inner map you have within you, that the Creator put in you, and in everything that is created, because everything is created to operate and to do a certain mission, if you like. I'm sure the Creator, who creates the intention for everything, wanted at this specific cycle for all the dimensions to move closer, and to become known on this plane. I'm happy to be included and to be a part of this.

***So are we, dear friends. So are we.***

## About the Authors

Christine Kromm Henrie is a spiritual channel, a certified past life and between lives soul regression therapist, psychic, and karmic astrologer. She was born and lived in Stockholm, Sweden until 2014, when she moved to the USA and married David Henrie, with whom she now shares her work.

She had an intense spiritual awakening in 2009, during a past life regression, which became the starting point for her practice with the higher realms. She began to receive messages and visions from her spirit guides about her soul assignment to develop the skills needed for them to speak through her. Accepting their advice, she studied different modalities of mediumship, psychic development and astrology in Sweden and England during the next five years. This intensive training enabled her to perfect the link and the ability to maintain this altered state for extended periods of time.

After moving to the USA, her formal training continued in soul regression and hypnotherapy, becoming a licensed regression therapist. Christine has two offices in Stockholm, Sweden, where she offers private soul regressions and progressions, assisting people to recall lessons from past lifetimes and memories from their spiritual home. Astrological consultations are also available online.

A near-death experience at age eleven and a transcendental epiphany in his early twenties led David Henrie to lifelong inquiry into the nature of the spirit. His studies focused on NDE's, reincarnation, spiritualism, and the theological beliefs within Buddhism and other pre-Christian religions. After a lengthy career as a petroleum engineer and executive in the U.S., he now lives in Sweden with his wife, where his time is dedicated to writing and research. David conducts the trance sessions and converses with the spirits Christine channels. He transcribes the recorded dialogues and assembles their teachings into the co-authored books.

Christine and David give lectures about the channeled material and the regression work, helping people to remember their soul mission and purpose. Their practice and publishing imprint is through **Access Soul Knowledge**, a Swedish company with U.S. proxy.

For further information, please visit:
www.AccessSoulKnowledge.com.